THE TEXT OF THE OLD TESTAMENT

THE TEXT OF THE OLD TESTAMENT

AN INTRODUCTION TO KITTEL-KAHLE'S BIBLIA HEBRAICA

BY

ERNST WÜRTHWEIN
(Professor of Old Testament in Marburg)

TRANSLATED BY PETER R. ACKROYD

Authorized translation by permission of the Privilegierte Württembergische Bibelanstalt, Stuttgart

THE MACMILLAN COMPANY
NEW YORK
1957

First published in the United States in 1957
by The Macmillan Company

Printed in the Netherlands by E. J. Brill, Leiden

Professor Paul E. Kahle

Hon. D. Th., Hon. D. Litt., Hon. D. D., Hon. D. Litt. Heb.
F.B.A.

in honour and gratitude

CONTENTS

PREFACE

This book has been written to meet a practical need. It becomes clear again and again, when Hebrew texts are being read with students, that many of them do not avail themselves of the wealth of material provided in Kittel's *Biblia Hebraica*. They disregard it, or feel uncertain how to use it, and, as a result, it serves them no useful purpose. This is because they are not sufficiently familiar with the history, the characteristics and the problems of the various witnesses to the text; nor with the methods of textual criticism. The Prefaces to the *Biblia Hebraica*, valuable as they are, cannot provide a complete introduction, nor can it be expected that textbooks on Old Testament Introduction should give an account of all the material which is referred to in *Biblia Hebraica*. It seemed convenient, therefore, to propose to the Privilegierte Württembergische Bibelanstalt the publication of a supplement to *Biblia Hebraica*, which would provide the reader with the necessary information for this purpose. I am greatly indebted to the Bibelanstalt for the readiness with which it has accepted this proposal.

In carrying out the plan, the writer has found it necessary to go considerably beyond the original scope proposed. Even so he has often had to compress the material more than was desirable. In many sections of the book, it would have been easier to write a much larger textbook in which the problems could be fully set out and a detailed account given of the discussions on them. But the attempt has at least been made to give the reader not merely the basic facts, but also, so far as space allowed, some insight into the most important problems. Only by so doing can the right attitude be adopted towards the actual problems of textual criticism. There must be freedom from prejudice, without mere subjectivism.

The addition of the fourth chapter on Textual Criticism seemed particularly desirable in view of the practical purpose of the book. The points raised there, necessarily in mere outline, make no claim to provide the book of rules for textual criticism which P. Volz once said was so desirable. But I hope that they will serve to help the student towards a certain clarity and reliability of method in textual criticism.

I acknowledge with special gratitude the decision of the Bibelanstalt to include 40 Plates which make it possible to present a good selection of illustrative material. In the choice of the Plates I have preferred to use less accessible manuscripts. Some of the points which could only be briefly touched on in the sections on the history of the text have been elaborated in the explanatory notes to the Plates.

Vocalisation has been used sparingly, in view of printing problems. The reader, it is assumed, will refer to his *Biblia Hebraica* as he reads, and can easily supply what is omitted.

Finally, I wish to place on record my gratitude for the assistance I have received. Professor Otto Eissfeldt was good enough to read a proof of pages 1-82 and made many valuable suggestions. I have been advised on individual points by Professors Albrecht Alt, Artur Weiser, and Karl Elliger. In obtaining photographs for the Plates I have been greatly helped by Professors Paul Kahle of Oxford, and H. H. Rowley of Manchester, and by Fathers A. Dold and J. Schildenberger of the Benedictine Abbey of Beuron. Last but not least I am grateful for the encouragement and interest shown by the President of the Bibelanstalt, Dr Schlatter, and its business manager, Dr Diehl. It is a pleasure to me to express my gratitude to all those whom I have named.

FOREWORD TO THE ENGLISH EDITION

The present work has been revised for the English edition with as much reference as was possible to more recent literature.

Since the author's relationship to the *Biblia Hebraica* has sometimes been misrepresented, I should like to make the following comment. When a reviewer of the German edition writes: 'Würthwein furthermore identifies himself so completely with BH^3 that he fails to realize that serious misgivings have been felt about the app. crit. of this edition', there is clearly a misunderstanding. It should be quite obvious to a careful reader of the fourth chapter of my book that the principles of textual criticism there set out are not those of the *apparatus criticus* of BH^3, but include a criticism of it. It was not, however, my purpose to write a polemic against the *apparatus criticus* of BH^3, but rather to encourage its intelligent and at the same time *critical* use.

Dr. Peter R. Ackroyd of Cambridge deserves my particular thanks, not only for undertaking the arduous work of translation, but also for making many valuable suggestions.

Marburg/Lahn, September 1955 E. Würthwein

TRANSLATOR'S NOTE

This translation has been made from the author's revision of his *Der Text des alten Testaments* (1952). It also incorporates references to the literature of more recent date. The translator wishes to acknowledge here the ready assistance which Professor Würthwein himself has given, and to record his gratitude also to others who have helped him in the preparation of the translation, more particularly Professors D. Winton Thomas and B. J. Roberts.

INTRODUCTION

If we take up a book produced in modern times under the supervision of its author, and just as the author himself wrote it, we may assume as we study it that the text we read represents the intention of the author in every word and even in punctuation. We are thus on a sure foundation as regards the text. It is quite a different matter if we have to deal with texts which were first produced hundreds or thousands of years before the invention of printing. Here the originals are generally lost, and the ancient texts are in most cases available to us only in copies which are separated from the original manuscript by several centuries, and by an unknown number of intermediaries. We ourselves know how easily errors occur in copying. A word may be accidentally missed or repeated. The order of a phrase may be inverted. A word of the same or similar meaning may unconsciously be substituted, and so on. We may even read wrongly or be compelled to guess, when the handwriting is difficult.

Carelessness may thus produce many errors, the more so if the copyist happens to be a man who does his copying as a profession, who works rapidly and as a result is casual; or if he is not capable of understanding the text he has to copy. But even the scribe who approaches his text with great interest and devotion may himself introduce corruptions. He may reflect upon what he is writing and think to himself that the author did not really mean to say what stands in the manuscript; he meant to say something else, namely what the copyist was expecting to find. So he puts the text right, as he thinks, just as we may readily correct a printer's error which has escaped the proof-reader. Such a correction may itself be the result of misunderstanding.

Thus not only the thoughtless and hasty copyist, but even the serious one may produce an erroneous copy. One can easily imagine what happened when it was necessary to re-copy a faulty manuscript—and none is quite free from error. The next copyist had to deal with the errors of his predecessor. He did so carefully or by guesswork, and so what was intended to be a correction may have led to a still further departure from the original text.

All writings handed down to us from antiquity have suffered from such accidents as these, and this includes the Old and New Testaments [1]). The interpreter of such material cannot act on the assumptions which are normal in the study of a modern book. The original text is not immediately available, but must itself first be sought out. The traditional witnesses to the text must be examined so as to reconstruct from their evidence a text which may be assumed on scientific grounds to be the nearest possible to the original, or, ideally, to be identical with it. Before interpretation, and bound up with it, there must therefore come the work of textual criticism. At one time this was perhaps over-stressed and today it tends to be neglected; but it is in any case quite essential.

Critical editions of the Bible are meant to serve just this purpose, and ultimately to help in the actual understanding of the text. They bring together conveniently the widely-scattered material, a task which would in any case be too great for each individual student, and so provide the first requirements of methodical textual criticism. But to handle this material and to use it properly, we must understand the peculiarities and value of each piece of evidence. In a difficult passage it is not sufficient to set the various readings side by side, and decide in favour of the one which seems to offer the easiest solution, preferring at one time the Hebrew text, at another the Septuagint, at another the Targum. The witnesses to the text are not all equally reliable; each has its own character and its own separate history. These must be known if inadequate attempts at a solution are to be avoided.

We shall survey first the available witnesses to the text, divided into three chapters:

1. transmission of the text in the original language;
2. translations from the original language;
3. the remaining translations.

In a fourth, concluding chapter, the aims and methods of textual criticism will be outlined.

---

[1]) It is however true, as we shall see, that successful efforts were made to safeguard the Hebrew text of the Old Testament from accidental and deliberate alterations. But this happened only after a certain date, whereas in the preceding centuries the text was entirely at the mercy of the common fate of ancient texts.

CHAPTER I

TRANSMISSION OF THE TEXT IN THE ORIGINAL LANGUAGE

A. SCRIPT AND WRITING MATERIALS

1. Script. Excavations and discoveries in the last 80 years, have shown Palestine and Syria to be unexpectedly rich in literary activity. In the second millennium B.C. several systems of writing were invented there, and foreign scripts, such as the cuneiform, were in use as well. It was presumably here that the alphabet, so important for the intellectual history of mankind was evolved. The change was made from the complicated systems of writing with several hundred signs to the simplest conceivable, the alphabet, with some twenty odd signs. All this was certainly not without significance for the formation of the Old Testament, and must be taken into consideration when we discuss the part played by oral and written tradition among Israelites and Jews. This problem can only be mentioned here. We must limit ourselves to some comments on those systems of writing which were of direct importance for the writing down and transmission of the Old Testament text.

With few exceptions, all the manuscripts and fragments of the Hebrew Old Testament which have come down to us from the Jews, are in the square script (כְּתָב מְרֻבָּע) still used to-day. This is true of the oldest known, the Isaiah Scroll (cf. pp. 23f.) and the Nash Papyrus. This script is also termed כְּתָב אַשּׁוּרִי, the Assyrian script, from its place of origin. It was in general use in the time of Jesus as may be seen from the saying in Matt. v. 18 which presupposes that the letter Yod is the smallest in the alphabet, which is only true of the square script. It was produced by a gradual process of development from the widely used Aramaic script, and one of the earliest witnesses to it is the short inscrip- *Pl. 4*
tion from 'Araq el-Emir in Transjordan, from the third or early second century B.C. The Jews were, however, aware that this script was not their original one. One Jewish tradition relates that Ezra (about 430 B.C.) introduced it [1]). It was thus regarded as an innovation of the post-exilic

[1]) Cf. D. Diringer, Early Hebrew Script *versus* Square Hebrew Script in *Essays and studies presented to S. A. Cook*, ed. D. Winton Thomas (1950), pp. 35-50; W. F. Albright, *Archaeology of Palestine* (1949) pp. 190ff.

age, and this was abhorrent to the later Rabbis. They related therefore how the Law was first given in the square script, but was later changed because of the sin of Israel, and in the time of Ezra the original situation was restored. This is obviously an expedient to which no historical value can be attached, but it clearly shows that it was known that a change of script had taken place in the post-exilic period. Probably the Aramaic script became normal in Judaism with the gradual adoption of the Aramaic language, which was at that time the *lingua franca* of the ancient Near East, so that the sacred writings were also written in it, and hence ultimately in the square script which developed from it [1]).

When the older parts of the Old Testament were first written down in the pre-exilic period, another script was in use in Palestine and Syria, the Phoenician-Old Hebrew script, the mother of all alphabets, past and present. It is known to us in a younger, more developed form from the eleventh or tenth century onwards in a series of texts. The best-known of these are: the Aḥiram sarcophagus from Byblos (about 1000 B.C.), a
Pl. 1 farmer's calendar from Gezer (about 950), the Moabite Stone (about
Pl. 2 840), ostraka from Samaria (c. 778-770), the Siloam inscription
Pl. 3 (about 700) and the Lachish ostraka (about 588). It is also found in an
older form in the Shaphaṭbaal inscription from Byblos (possibly thirteenth century or earlier). A precursor of this script seems to be the Sinai script which is preserved in a series of inscriptions from the Sinai area, dated by Albright at about 1500. Related to it is the script in some finds in Palestine (Gezer, Lachish, Shechem 14th cent.). We need not here go into this pre-history, of which the details are not yet completely clear. Only the Phoenician-Old Hebrew script, and later the square script, are relevant both for the first writing down and for the further written transmission of the Old Testament texts.

The transition from the one to the other took place between the fourth and second centuries B.C.; a more precise date cannot be assigned to it. What is certain is that for a long time the Old Hebrew script remained in use alongside the square script. It is still used, for example, for the lettering of coins from the time of the revolt of Bar Kochba (132-135 A.D.)
Pl. 12 and in fragments of Lev. xix-xxiii which were found in 1949 during a
further search in Qumran Cave I near the Dead Sea [2]). This latter may

---

[1]) Cf. also G. R. Driver, *Semitic Writing* (Schweich Lectures 1944, rev. ed. 1954), p. 231: "The Hebr. כתב אשורי or simply אשורית 'Assyrian script' = כתב מרבע 'square (post-exilic) script' was so called because it was the (originally Aramaean) script which had been coming into use in business in Assyria and Babylonia since the 8th century B.C. and which was brought back by Jews returning from the exile".

[2]) Cf. now Barthélemy-Milik, *Discoveries in the Judaean Desert* I, *Qumran Cave* I (1955), pp. 51 ff. Further fragments in the Old Hebrew script were found in 1952 in Qumran Cave IV, but are not yet published. According to provisional reports, they belong to approximately the same period as the Qumran texts in square

be regarded as evidence of an archaising tendency, rather than as an indication of origin in the period before the square script. From Jewish reports in the Mishna and the Babylonian Talmud, it would appear that in the first two centuries of the Christian era there were still manuscripts in the old script. There was not, however, attributed to them that highest degree of holiness —the Levitical 'defiling of the hands'—which was attributed to scrolls in the square script. Yet even so, the old script must have been treated as specially holy for a time . At least it is on such grounds that one of the peculiar features of the newly-discovered scrolls might be explained, namely that in the Habakkuk commentary and the *Pl. 11*
Hodayoth (Songs of Praise) the square script is normal, but the divine name Yahweh (or אל and אלי) is always written with the old letters. As late as the fifth century A.D., we find the divine name written in Old Hebrew letters in a fragment of Aquila's Greek version [1]) (cf. p. 132).

The Samaritans too, separated finally from the Jews about the end *Pl. 23*
of the fourth century B.C., handed down their sacred book—the Torah—in the old script, perhaps because they claimed to be the preservers of an older and purer tradition, and may have regarded the introduction of a new script as an unwarrantable innovation.

2. Writing Materials. We know of various kinds of material used for writing in Biblical times. Job expresses the wish that his words could be "graven in the rock" (Job xix. 24), and the successful completion of the Siloam tunnel (at the end of the eighth century B.C.), was recorded on the rock face by an inscription which was discovered in 1880. We read *Pl. 2*
in Exod. xxxiv. 1 of tablets of stone on which the divine commandments were inscribed, and in Deut. xxvii. 2ff. of 'plastered' stones, on which presumably the letters were painted. Wooden tablets for brief writings may be meant when the prophets Isaiah and Habakkuk are instructed to write down a prophetic oracle (Isa. xxx 8, Hab. ii. 2 and perhaps also Isa. viii. 1.). The clay tablets so frequently used in the ancient east were not appropriate for the Hebrew script because of its rounded form, as they are only suitable for a straight-line script like cuneiform. On the other hand, it is known from the finds in Palestine that for everyday affairs, there as elsewhere, fragments of baked pottery (ostraka) were *Pl. 3*
used, on which it was usual to write in ink. Thus, for example, in 1935,

---

script, and show that the Old Hebrew script 'was used extensively in Qumran over a long period of time' (Frank M. Cross, Jr. in *The Biblical Archaeologist* (1954), p. 21).

[1]) In August 1952, at an unknown place in the Judaean Desert, Beduin discovered a leather scroll, surviving only in fragments, containing the Minor Prophets in Greek, which was probably written between 50 B.C. and 50 A.D. This also contains the tetragrammaton written in Old Hebrew letters, and thus confirms the information given by Origen that, in the more correct copies of the Greek Old Testament, Old Hebrew letters were used for the tetragrammaton. On this leather scroll, cf. D. Barthélemy, *Revue Biblique* lx (1953), pp. 18ff., and P. Kahle, *T.L.Z.* 79 (1954), cols. 81ff.

in the course of excavations at Tell ed-Duweir, ancient Lachish, ostraka were discovered in a room by the city gate. These proved to be a military correspondence from the last years of Judah (588 B.C. approx.) It has been suggested that isolated prophetic utterances, wisdom sayings, etc., may have been written down on fragments of pottery before they were collected into books. This would well explain the inconsequent arrangement which is found in some Biblical books, but we have no certain information upon the matter.

The materials mentioned so far were, however, only suitable for writings of limited size, and hence at the most for the earlier stages in the formation of our Biblical books. For the books themselves the appropriate materials were papyrus and leather. Both are indicated when the Old Testament speaks of a scroll (מְגִלַּת־סֵפֶר: Jer. xxxvi. 2ff.; Ezek. ii. 9; Ps. xl. 8; מגלה Ezek. iii. 1-3; Zech. v. 1f.) since they are the only materials that can be rolled up.

Papyrus was in use in Egypt as early as the third millennium B.C. We learn from the famous travel tale of the Egyptian Wen Amon (c. 1090 B.C.) that this convenient material was being exported from Egypt to Phoenicia in exchange for wood. The fact that Wen Amon took with him 500 rolls of 'best-quality' papyrus—there were several qualities—makes it clear that it was already being manufactured on a considerable scale. Egypt later supplied the whole Mediterranean area. The papyrus reed was used for its manufacture, the pith being cut into thin strips. A vertical layer of these strips was placed upon a horizontal one, and the two pressed together, the natural gum serving to bind them. They were dried and smoothed, and the sheet was then ready for writing. Several sheets stuck together to the desired length produced a scroll. This was inscribed in columns, from right to left for Hebrew texts. In general only the inner side with the horizontal strips was used for writing, but scrolls with writing on both sides also existed (cf. Ezek. ii. 10). It was presumably a papyrus scroll on which Baruch wrote at Jeremiah's dictation and which was burnt by king Jehoiakim piece by piece in an open brazier (Jer. xxxvi) [1]. In any case papyrus must have been widely used in Palestine. It is unfortunately very perishable, becoming brittle with age and reacting to moisture. It has only survived the centuries where the soil and climate are sufficiently dry, as in the desert sands of Egypt. This explains why in Palestine up to the present only a few papyrus fragments have been found, namely in the caves discovered near the Dead Sea since 1947, where suitable climatic conditions obtain (cf. pp. 10, 23).

Leather no doubt also played an important role as writing material in Palestine as elsewhere in the Near East. It has the advantage over

---

[1]) Others think it was of leather, as a knife was needed to cut it up.

papyrus that it does not wear out so quickly and was thus the most suitable material for writings which had to last for a long period, or were subjected to heavy use. Jewish regulations still require that the copies of the Law used in worship must be written on leather from clean animals, and this no doubt represents ancient usage [1]). The Letter of Aristeas, at the end of the second century B.C., speaks of magnificent Torah scrolls of leather (parchment?), written in gold; and not much later than this literary evidence may be the Isaiah scroll found in 1947 *Pl. 8, 9* which gives us an actual example of such an ancient Bible scroll. It consists of 17 leaves of carefully prepared leather (not parchment as is often stated). These were sewn together to make a roll 7.34 metres long (26 cm. high). In 54 columns, averaging 29 lines of script 12 cms. wide, it contains all 66 chapters of the book of Isaiah. Lines were marked in the leather with a semi-sharp instrument. This also meets Jewish requirements. This scroll and those found with it were wrapped in linen and placed in jars, a method of storage mentioned as early as Jer. xxxii. 14 *Pl. 7* and customary also in Egypt.

By a special treatment of leather (lime mordant was perhaps used from an early date) there became possible from about 200 B.C. the production of parchment, (Gk. πέργαμον) named after the city of Pergamon in Asia Minor. This became the main material for books from the fourth century A.D. onwards, and was the chief writing medium in the Middle Ages, whereas papyrus gradually lost in importance. Parchment is greatly superior to the older writing materials. It is durable, smooth and hence easy to write on; it allows writing on both sides and its light colour sets off the ink clearly. It was also possible to use it several times by scraping, a characteristic which leads to the frequent appearance of palimpsests (= scraped down again). Parchment is the material of the important fragments from the Cairo Geniza, of which an account is given below (cf. pp. 24f.). From the ninth century, paper appears as well. This had been invented in China, and knowledge of its manufacture reached the Near East towards the end of the eighth century, and came thence into Europe.

3. Scrolls and codices. The ancient form of a book was the scroll of papyrus or leather. But such a book-form is inconvenient, since the reader must use both hands to hold it. In the case of Hebrew scrolls, because of the direction of the writing, the left hand holds the scroll while the other slowly draws out the writing before the reader and rolls it up again on the other side. For its next reading the scroll must be rolled right back again to the beginning. We have seen that the 66 chap-

---

[1]) The Jerusalem Talmud states, with regard to the preparation of Torah scrolls: "It was a decision (halakah) given to Moses at Sinai: to be written on leather, written in ink, and lined with a reed." (Meg. I. 9).

ters of the book of Isaiah require a scroll about $7\frac{1}{2}$ metres long. It would scarcely be practicable to make a scroll much longer which would still be convenient for general use [1]). Thus it comes about that a scroll could only very rarely, with a large size of scroll and a very small script, contain the whole Old Testament or even several of the larger books. Most of the Biblical books circulated in separate scrolls and the division into books seems in certain cases—for example in the Pentateuch—to have been made with reference to the normal capacity of a scroll [2]).

Only the invention of the Codex in the first century A.D. — initially of parchment—made it possible to bring together several books or the whole contents of the Bible. Remains of papyrus codices with Old and New Testament texts in Greek go back to the second and third centuries A.D. In the fourth century the codex came to be generally used, and although the scroll did not disappear altogether, it became less and less important. It is of interest to observe the share of the Christian movement in this development. "It was really the victory of the Church which gave the pre-eminence to the codex over the scroll. The codex belonged to the Christian movement from the start. The scroll was restricted to deeds and contracts, while the codex became the normal book-form". (Schubart). Its advantages over the scroll are obvious. It makes for easy turning of pages and finding of the place, and both sides of the material may be used for writing. The Jews also adopted the codex, but kept the leather or parchment scroll for copies of the Torah and of Esther, for use in worship. The fragments from the Cairo Geniza are mainly of codices, and to a lesser extent of scrolls. (cf. pp. 10, 24 f.).

4. Writing implements and ink. The Old Testament mentions as instruments employed the חֶרֶט (Isa. viii. 1) and the עֵט (Jer. viii. 8; xvii. 1; Ps. xlv. 2; Job. xix. 24). The חרט is the stylus with which the letters are cut into a suitable material. The same tool is probably meant by עֵט בַּרְזֶל, the iron pen with diamond point (Jer. xvii. 1) and the stylus (עט) of iron in Job xix. 24 (on this passage cf. now J. J. Stamm, *Z.A.W.* N.F. 24 (1953), p. 302). On the other hand, the עֵט סֹפְרִים in Jer. viii. 8 and the עֵט סֹפֵר in Ps. xlv. 2 are to be taken as the reed-pen of the professional scribe, with which he applied the ink to leather, papyrus or ostraka. In Egypt, and, we may conclude, similarly in Palestine, rushes were used

[1]) The longest surviving scroll in papyrus is the Harris Papyrus in the British Museum, 40 metres long, not, however, intended for practical use. It is far longer than the average, which was about 6 to 10 metres in the case of Greek papyrus scrolls.

[2]) The uniting of the two parts of the book of Isaiah (i-xxxix and xl-lxvi) from completely different periods is, by contrast, best explained on the assumption that two originally independent books—admittedly related in vocabulary and ideas—were put into one scroll and then regarded as one book.

from a very early date, their ends squashed and made fibrous like a small brush, or, later, cut at an acute angle like a goose-quill. The reed-pen (kalamos) can be traced to the third century B.C. This was cut to the shape of a feather and its split tip permitted more continuous, cursive writing. It has remained in use in the East until modern times.

Ink (Hebr. דְּיוֹ) was used for writing on ostraka, leather and papyrus. It is mentioned in the Old Testament only in Jer. xxxvi. 18, in such a way as to suggest that it was well-known. There were two kinds of ink, the non-metallic made from lamp-black (especially from olive oil) in a solution of gum (resin) or oil, and the metallic, usually made from a mixture of gall nuts and acid [1]). The use of metallic ink, which was not very durable and damaged the writing material, was opposed by the Jews in the early Christian centuries, but came into general use in the Middle Ages in spite of Talmudic prohibition. The ink used in the Dead Sea Scrolls is not metallic, but vegetable or carbon [2]). But as such inks were in use side by side with metallic ink for a long period and are still used to-day for Torah scrolls, no clear argument for the dating of the Scrolls can be derived from this. It only suggests an early rather than a mediaeval date of origin. The ink used by the ancient scribes did not penetrate very deep and could be washed off with a sponge or something similar. If it faded the script was restored. Nevertheless the Egyptian papyri and the Dead Sea Scrolls indicate that the ancient world produced an ink which was astonishingly lasting and often superior to the later metallic ink in its durability.

B. THE MASORETIC TEXT

1. General considerations. The Hebrew text of the Old Testament is called the Masoretic Text because in its present form it represents the Masora (Hebr. מָסוֹרֶת), that is, the tradition preserved by the Jewish scholars known as the Masoretes. It is indicated in the Biblia Hebraica edited by R. Kittel (BH) with the letter 𝔐. 𝔐

a) In BH, from the 3rd edition onwards 𝔐 has been printed from the manuscript B 19^A, in the Leningrad public library (= L. Leningradensis), L, *Pl. 20*
written in the year 1008 A.D. The first two editions, like other editions, for example that of Ginsburg (1908ff.), follow the text edited by Jacob ben Chayyim, printed by Daniel Bomberg in Venice in 1524/5 (= 𝔅) 𝔅
which depends upon late mediaeval manuscripts. Thus in BH we have a text which goes back several centuries earlier than all previously

---

[1]) The ink used on the Lachish ostraka appears, on analysis, to have been metallic (cf. p. 88). According to G. R. Driver, *Semitic writing* (rev. ed. 1954), p. 86, non-metallic ink was used for parchment, metallic for papyrus.

[2]) Cf. H. J. Plenderleith, in Barthélemy-Milik, *Qumran Cave* I (1955), p. 39.

printed editions. But even the manuscript on which this edition is based is extremely late when we consider the age of the Old Testament and compare the fourth and fifth century dates of the important manuscripts of the Greek Old and New Testaments. We have indeed no Hebrew manuscript of the *whole* Old Testament written before the tenth century.
Pl. 17 The oldest dated codex, which contains only the Prophets, belongs to the year 895 A.D. Considerable fragments from the sixth to eighth centuries were found in the latter half of the nineteenth century in the Geniza of the Old Cairo Synagogue, which had been the Church of St.Michael up till the year 882. A Geniza is a kind of lumber room in which unusable or incorrect manuscripts were hidden (Aramaic גְּנַז, to hide), until they were eventually destroyed, in order to prevent misuse or profanation of a manuscript which contained the sacred name of God. The treasures of a Geniza would be ceremonially buried from time to time. Chance alone preserved the Cairo manuscripts from this fate, for the Geniza was at one time walled up, and as a result forgotten.

It seems even more a matter of chance that considerably older, perhaps
Pl. 6 ff. even pre-Christian, Hebrew manuscripts which were hidden in a cave near the Dead Sea should have survived two millennia and be discovered by goatherds in 1947. Among these only Isaiah of the Biblical books appears complete. The first two chapters of Habakkuk are also included in the find, but only small fragments of other Biblical books [1]. Thus even after these discoveries, which are so important for scientific study, we are still dependent for the *whole* Old Testament on manuscripts of the tenth century and later.

We should not in fact expect anything else, as Jewish regulations required that unusable or incorrect manuscripts must be destroyed. To those who finally established the text in the tenth century, all older manuscripts represented earlier stages in its development. They would rank as not fully correct and so would disappear in the course of time. It is certain too that in the course of persecutions of the Jews in the Middle Ages, old manuscripts were destroyed, partly by opponents of the Jews and partly by the Jews themselves who did not wish their sacred books to fall into the hands of unbelievers.

Nevertheless if we are rightly to assess the surviving manuscripts, the

---

[1] In 1952, further caves were discovered at Qumran with a great wealth of Biblical and non-Biblical fragments. These have not yet been published. The first information concerning them was given by the excavators, P. de Vaux and L. Harding. Accounts summarising these discoveries may be found in Frank M. Cross, Jr. *The Biblical Archaeologist* (1954), pp. 2ff., H. H. Rowley, *The Dead Sea Scrolls and their Significance* (1955), and elsewhere. In the last few years, interesting Biblical and non-Biblical texts have also been found in caves of the Judaean Desert other than at Qumran. These are not, however, by any means as important as the Qumran texts.

majority of which are thus relatively late, we must recognise that the value of a manuscript does not depend solely or even chiefly upon its age. When papyrus fragments of Greek classical authors were discovered which were of considerably greater age than the mediaeval manuscripts known up till that time, they disappointed the extravagant hopes which they raised especially among laymen. They proved in general to be inferior to the later manuscripts. The fact is that the mediaeval manuscripts went back to the careful studies of the great Alexandrine philologists, whereas the papyri came generally from private manuscripts which circulated in the provincial towns of Egypt and reveal that confused state of the transmission of the text which made the work of the Alexandrine scholars so urgently necessary. Thus more decisive than age is the circle from which a manuscript comes. This applies also to the Hebrew text of the Old Testament, and the history of its transmission must be taken into account in making judgments upon it.

b) Until the period of the Renaissance and the Reformation, the Hebrew text and its transmission were in the main the concern of Judaism. In the first thousand years A.D., in which the determinative work was done, we find both Palestinian Jews and members of the large Jewish colony in Babylonia engaged on it, and we have thus to differentiate
between the Masoretes of the West (Occidentales מַעַרְבָאֵי) and the Maso- **Occ**
retes of the East (Orientales מָדִינְחָאֵי). The chief centre in the West, to **Or**
the end of the third century and again in the eighth to tenth centuries, was Tiberias. The centres in the East were the schools of Sura [1]), and of Nehardea (destroyed in 259 A.D.), and later those of Pumbeditha, which were for centuries the controlling influence especially in matters of Jewish scholarship. Eventually, however, the Babylonian schools lost in importance and came to an end in the tenth or eleventh centuries. The West again took over the intellectual leadership in Judaism, and the Masoretes of the West were concerned to eliminate the recollection of a text-form which deviated from their own. Thus the version of the school of Tiberias alone became determinative for the following period, while the eastern tradition was completely forgotten for a whole millennium.

c) It is well known that the Hebrew text of the Old Testament existed for many centuries as a consonantal text alone. Vowel signs were first added at a late stage when the consonantal text already had a long history behind it, and had reached a completely fixed form. We must therefore discuss separately the history of the consonantal text and that of the vowel-pointing.

---

[1]) The Masoretes of Sura (= Soraei) are indicated in BH by the abbreviation Sor. **Sor**

d) The men who were occupied with the transmission of the Biblical text are in the earlier period called Sopherim, in the later period Masoretes (בַּעֲלֵי הַמָּסוֹרֶת), and also, after the eleventh century, Naqdanim (נַקְדָנִים), punctuators. סֹפֵר was originally a term indicating an office (writer, secretary). It is first used with the meaning of scribe with reference to Ezra in the work of the Chronicler. Down to the time of Jesus, the סֹפֵר is the expert on the Law, the professional theologian [1]). After that time the word indicates the teacher of the Bible and the copyist of the Bible, two professions which naturally have a special responsibility for the preservation of the correct writing and reading of the Biblical text. The traditional picture of the older Sopherim seems to have been based upon such later activities.

2. The consonantal text. Our present consonantal text goes back to about 100 A.D. when an authoritative text of the Old Testament was produced in connection with a great Jewish revival. A fully reliable text became a necessity with the completion of the process of canonisation, and as there became dominant in Judaism, particularly through the work of Rabbi Akiba (c. 55-137 A.D.), a method of exegesis in which even the smallest details and peculiarities of the text are of significance. "Thus there came into existence first an authoritative text of the Torah, which is in all essentials the consonantal text which we have in our Masoretic text. This text was established with the aid of the available ancient manuscript material, and in contrast to the well-established popular texts, of which the Samaritan Pentateuch survives as a good example, it gives the impression of greater antiquity and reliability. The remaining books of the Bible followed. We cannot trace all the stages of the work in detail; only the final result is clearly observable" [2]). The existing manuscripts were brought into line with the text thus declared to be normative. Eventually, in the course of time, correct manuscripts took their place.

This text has passed through a critical revision, as can be seen from several older witnesses to the text which differ from 𝔐: α) the Samaritan Pentateuch (cf. pp. 31 f.); β) the Nash Papyrus (cf. p. 24); γ) the Isaiah manuscript from the cave (cf. pp. 23 f.); δ) the older translations of the Bible, notably the Septuagint (cf. pp. 34 ff.). Also instructive for the history of the Old Testament text is a comparison of duplicate passages (II Sam. xxii = Ps. xviii; II Kings xviii. 13-xx. 19 = Isa. xxxvi-xxxix; II Kings xxiv. 18-xxv. 30 = Jer. lii; Isa. ii. 2-4 = Mic. iv. 1-3; Ps. xiv = Ps. liii; Ps. xl. 14-18 = Ps. lxx) and of the books of Samuel and Kings with the writings of the Chronicler which are dependent upon them.

---

[1]) J. Jeremias, *Th. W.Z.N.T.* I (1933), pp. 740f.

[2]) P. Kahle, *Die hebräischen Handschriften aus der Höhle* (1951), pp. 28f.

From these witnesses to the text, which all go back to a time before the authoritative fixing of the consonantal text, we may see that texts which differed from 𝔐 were then in circulation. They have as a common feature a tendency to popularise the text. (This applies also in some measure to the Chronicler over against the books of Samuel and Kings). They insert the *matres lectionis* more frequently than 𝔐. They assimilate many of the forms to the spoken language of their own time, using Aramaic forms (employing על for אל), preferring the Hiphʿil, substituting the imperative for the infinitive absolute where this is used with imperative sense, and so forth. They also show a tendency to fill out the text with the help of parallels. These popular texts are of great importance since they enable us to assess more accurately the relationship of 𝔐 to the text in circulation before it, and to estimate the nature of the text-revision undertaken in the second century A.D. From this two quite distinct points emerge.

On the one hand, it becomes clear that the fixing of the text was based upon an older form, earlier than that of the popular texts. We are indeed told that the text was established with the assistance of ancient manuscripts. This explains why, in accordance with the older usage, 𝔐 employs the *plene* forms more sparingly than the popular texts. The Aramaic elements are largely excluded, and older readings are restored. Thus 𝔐 gives the impression of greater antiquity and reliability by comparison with all other witnesses. The conservative procedure adopted in the establishing of the text and in its further transmission is revealed by a few peculiarities which have survived in 𝔐 down to the present day:

a) The *puncta extraordinaria*. In fifteen places there are dots over single letters or whole words: Gen. xvi. 5; xviii. 9; xix. 33; xxxiii. 4; xxxvii. 12; Num. iii. 39; ix. 10; xxi. 30; xxix. 15; Deut. xxix. 28; II Sam. xix. 20; Isa. xliv. 9; Ezek. xli. 20; xlvi. 22; Ps. xxvii. 13. These dots indicate textual or doctrinal queries of the Sopherim concerning the traditional text, where they did not however dare to correct it because it was regarded as unalterable.

b) The *inverted Nun* (Nun inversum) is found nine times: before Num. x. 35 and after Num. x. 36, and with Ps. cvii. 21-26, 40. Kahle agrees with Blau in seeing in this an abbreviation for נָקוּד "pointed." The נ is reversed to prevent its being accidentally reckoned as part of the text. The queries here seem to concern the position of the relevant verses.

c) *S*^{e}*bir*. In many places—Ginsburg counted altogether about 350 in Seb
various manuscripts—where a word appears in an unusual form or meaning in the text, the normal form, or the word which would normally be expected, is placed in the margin introduced by סְבִיר (pass. ptcp. of the Aramaic root סְבַר "suppose"). Thus in Gen. xix. 8 האל has the meaning

האלה; in Gen. xlix. 13 על bears the meaning of עד; in Gen. xix. 23 the masculine יצא appears for the expected feminine יצאה, and so on.

K, Q d) *K*[e]*tib* and *Q*[e]*re*. In many cases objection was felt to the traditional text on grammatical, aesthetic, dogmatic or other grounds. In these cases the difficulty was overcome by enjoining that the text should be read differently. A distinction was thus made between the כְּתִיב, the written text, which could not be altered, and the קְרֵי, that which was to be read. In the course of time the number of such passages increased to over 1300. From the observation that many of the Q[e]res in Samuel and Kings stand in the text itself in Chronicles, which has preserved the more popular form, it has rightly been concluded that a number of Q[e]res represent popular variants which were preserved in this form so that they should not be completely forgotten when the text came to be established [1]).

On the other hand, the restoration and preservation of the old traditional text, even where it was open to criticism, is only one mark of this revision. A second points in the exactly opposite direction. We have clear proof that there was no hesitation in making alterations in the text, expecially when this appeared necessary on doctrinal grounds. Thus, for example, proper names compounded with the abhorred name of בעל frequently retain their original form in Chronicles, whereas in the parallel texts in Samuel and Kings they have been altered [2]). This indicates that the second part of the Old Testament, the Prophets, which enjoyed a higher rank in the Canon than the Writings, was subjected to a more thorough-going revision, and dogmatically objectionable passages were consistently removed. Knowledge of these alterations in the text is preserved even by Jewish tradition in what it records concerning the *Tiqqune* and *Itture sopherim*

Tiq soph a) The *Tiqqune sopherim* (תקוני ספרים "corrections of the scribes"). There is no unified tradition concerning their number, for while the Masora enumerates eighteen passages, this is hardly a complete list. These corrections were in the main undertaken to remove objectionable statements about God. Thus the original text of Gen. xviii. 22 read: "Yahweh however remained standing before Abraham", which is the correct reading as can be seen from the context. But since "to stand before someone" can also mean "to stand in service before someone, to serve" (cf. Gen. xli. 46; I Kings i. 2), the original wording in Gen. xviii. 22 was felt to be unsuitable and was altered to the present text. The other Tiqqunin are: Num. xi. 15; xii. 12; I Sam. iii. 13; II Sam. xvi. 12 (בעיני

---

1) Cf. G. Gerleman: *Synoptic Studies in the Old Testament*, (Lund, 1948), pp. 24ff.

2) Cf. I Chron. xiv. 7 בעלישע — II Sam. v. 16 אלידע; I Chron. viii. 33; ix. 39 אשבעל — II Sam. ii. 8ff. איש־בשת; I Chron. viii. 34; ix. 40 מריב בעל — II Sam. iv. 4 + מפיבשת. Cf. also Gerleman, op.cit. p. 23.

for בעינו); xx. 1 (לאהליו for לאלהיו, thus also I Kings xii. 16; II Chron. x. 16); Jer. ii. 11; Ezek. viii. 17; Hos. iv. 7 (כבודם בקלון אמיר for כבודי בקלין המירו); Hab. i. 12; Zech. ii. 12; Mal. i. 12; Ps. cvi. 20; Job vii. 20; xxxii. 3; Lam. iii. 20. (Where no details are supplied, compare the apparatus in BH).

b) The *Itture sopherim* (עטורי ספרים "omissions of the scribes"). In the Babylonian Talmud (Nedarim 37b), it is recorded that four times with the word אחר (Gen. xviii.5; xxiv.55; Num. xxxi.2; Ps. lxviii.26) and once with משפטיך (Ps. xxxvi.7) a ו was omitted by the scribes. Seven passages are also mentioned where certain words are to be read although they do not appear in the text (קרי ולא כתיב : II Sam. viii.3; xvi.23; Jer. xxxi.38; l.29; Ruth ii.11; iii.5, 17), and five passages where words which appear in the text are not to be read (כתיב ולא קרי: II Kings v.18; Jer. xxxii.11; li.3; Ezek. xlviii.16; Ruth iii.12). The majority of these are also indicated in the Masora of BH.

We shall not go far wrong if we regard these traditions as pointers to a small part only of a much more extensive process. (cf. also pp. 74 f.).

The text established by the Jewish authorities, and in some measure critically revised, needed careful transmission. According to Josephus, one mark of the sacred writings of the Jews is that their wording is unalterable. Care had therefore to be taken to ensure that no errors should creep into the sacred writings, and any which did slip in must be discovered and removed. This was the function of the Masora, the tradition, and it is in this sense that Rabbi Akiba says of it: Masora is a (protective) hedge to the Law. The meticulous work of the scribes served this purpose. They counted verses, words, letters of the Law and of other parts of the Bible, in order to facilitate the preparation and control of manuscripts. One passage of the Talmud derives the name scribe from this activity: the ancients, it says, were called Sopherim because they counted (סופרים) all the letters of the Law. Thus they established for example that the ו in גחון in Lev. xi.42 was the middle letter of the Torah, and that דרש in Lev. x.16 was its middle word. The writing of many letters in a special manner goes back to them and their successors. Thus some are "suspended" as for example in מנשה Judg. xviii.30 (read משה cf. the apparatus in BH) and מיער in Ps. lxxx.14 (the middle of the Psalter). More especially we may probably trace to them the beginnings of those studies on the text which later found their expression in the Masora.

They performed their most important service to the history of the text, however, by gaining general recognition for the authoritatively established text, which, in spite of its links with an older text-form, must have appeared as an innovation in its time. The Hebrew manuscripts of the Middle Ages give a remarkably unified picture of the text, even in the form of the specially written letters and other minutiae.

For a long time the most plausible explanation of this appeared to be the one, put forward by Rosenmüller in 1834, taken up by Paul de Lagarde in 1863, and still maintained to-day by some scholars, that the Hebrew manuscripts all went back to one single copy, the archetype produced in the second century A.D. We know to-day, particularly from the material of the Cairo Geniza, that for centuries there were variant texts, though admittedly the variants were not very numerous; and the same fact may be deduced from the Biblical quotations by Jewish scholars as far as the eighth century and beyond, which differ from 𝔐. Similarly also, the fact demonstrated by Hempel[1] for Deuteronomy that a group of mediaeval Masoretic manuscripts agree in many details with the Samaritan text is in my opinion to be explained on the ground that the above-mentioned popular texts continued for a long time to influence he transmission of the text. We must therefore assume that the consonantal text established in about 100 A.D. did not immediately supersede all other text-forms, but rather that manuscripts with a variant text-form, and especially those in private hands, continued to circulate for a long period. The fact that the manuscripts of the tenth century and later give so unified an impression is, as Kahle in particular has demonstrated, the result of the work of the earlier and later Masoretes who gave their support to the authoritative text and helped it to final victory over all variants.

Divisions. BH indicates various divisions of the Old Testament books as they were customary among the Jews, in some measure even at an early date, though they did not at that time have a division into chapters. The first of these is the division of the whole Old Testament (except the Psalter) into open and closed paragraphs. An open paragraph (פְּתוּחָא) starts at the beginning of a line after either a blank line or an incomplete one. A closed paragraph (סְתוּמָא) is always separated from the previous paragraph by a short space within a line. Eventually this distinction was no longer maintained in the actual writing, but was
פ, ס indicated by a פ (= פתוחא) or a ס (= סתומא) prefixed to the paragraph. This is followed in BH. A second division was made into rather larger sections amounting to some 452 Sedarim (סֵדֶר = order, arrangement). This division is Palestinian, and in it the Torah was allowed sufficient Sedarim (weekly sections) for it to be read in worship over a three-year period, as was the original Palestinian custom. In Babylonia, where the Torah was read in one year, it was divided accordingly into 54 (or 53) Parashim (weekly sections). In BH the beginning of a Seder is
ס̄, פרש indicated by ס̄, and that of a Parash by פרש, both in the margin.

1) *Z.A.W.* N.F. 11 (1934), pp. 254ff.

The division into verses — in which the Babylonian and Palestinian traditions differ—was also already known in the Talmudic period, whereas that into chapters was taken over into Hebrew manuscripts from the fourteenth century onwards from the Vulgate (cf. p. 66). Numbering of the verses is only found from the sixteenth century onwards.

3. Pointing. In the matter of the vocalisation of the text the whole position was very different. There was no written tradition on which to work; a new beginning had to be made. This was done by the Masoretes from about the fifth century onwards. The fixing of the consonantal text alone and the indication of pronunciation by the use of vowel-letters, the so-called *matres lectionis*, employed only to a limited extent in 𝔐, were not satisfactory. Nor did this go far enough, since it was still possible to read and interpret many words in more than one way, though allowance must be made for a certain fixity in the traditional pronunciation.

At an early stage there were evidently circles which needed aids to the reading of the sacred text. Before the complete fixing of the consonantal text, when it was still possible to treat it freely, the correct reading could be indicated by a frequent use of the vowel-letters [1]). We have a valuable witness to this stage not only in the Samaritan text but also in the Isaiah Scroll with its aburdance of *plene* forms. The authoritative consonantal text of the second century, following the older pattern, gave much less place to the *plene* forms, and thus brought to an end the practice of inserting vowel-letters at will. It appears that another expedient was then found. For Jewish believers who needed it, a text was produced in a transcription, which reproduced in Greek letters the Hebrew text as it was to be pronounced. Such texts were evidently taken over by Christians; Origen provided one in the second column of his Hexapla. But Jewish sources also seem to refer to this practice. Eventually the Jewish disinclination to use anything Greek made this resort impossible. From the fifth century A.D. onwards, there began the practice, adopted perhaps from the example of Syriac, of indicating the vowels by signs placed above and below the consonants. This is called pointing, from the Jewish technical term for it (Hebr. נִקֵּד). The first stage was to fix by the insertion of occasional vowel signs the pronunciation of the Biblical text which was normal in the contemporary reading of the scriptures in worship (Kahle). This procedure is revealed by many of the Geniza fragments, and the Samaritans never advanced beyond it. Later the text was fully pointed. In the course of time different systems of pointing were developed in the East and the West: the Babylonian, the Palestinian, and ultimately the Tiberian.

---

[1]) The employment of vowel-letters is very ancient. They may already be found in use, though sparingly, in the Siloam inscription and in the Lachish ostraka.

The Babylonian system is supralinear. Originally the consonants א, ע, י and ו were used for the vowels ā, a, i and u respectively, and from them simplified forms developed which later became the normal vowel signs. This system went through two stages, an older, simpler stage represented in fragments from the seventh and eighth centuries
E, *Pl. 14* (E) [1]), and a later, more complex stage which appears in fragments from
K, *Pl. 15* the eighth and ninth centuries (K). The development of the more complex system may well be connected with the emergence of the Karaites, the sect founded about 760 A.D. by ʿAnan ben David. As they rejected the Talmud in favour of the literally interpreted Old Testament, there arose a new interest in the study of the Bible text and a consequent need to fix its pronunciation as far as possible. On pp. XLIV-XLVII of BH, Kahle has compiled a list of the Babylonian fragments known to him, belonging to more than 120 manuscripts [2]), (cf. also the list in *Z.A.W.* N.F. 5 (1928) to which are appended 70 excellent facsimiles). Variants from the manuscripts collected by Kahle, and in part published by him in *Masoreten*
V(ar)^{Ka} *des Ostens* (1913), are cited in BH as V(ar)^{Ka}.

Pl. 16 The Palestinian system, also supralinear, is an imperfect one. The system used in Samaritan manuscripts is clearly dependent on it. The comparatively few Biblical manuscripts (sixth to eighth century), which differ among themselves, were published by Kahle in *Masoreten*
Var^{pal} *des Westens* II (1930), and are cited in BH as Var^{pal}. Their significance lies in the fact that they give us an impression of what vocalised Hebrew manuscripts of the Bible looked like when the Masoretes of Tiberias began their work. Such manuscripts lack above all the consistency in fixing the pronunciation which is characteristic of the Tiberian Masoretes.

The Karaite movement, whose influence on the intellectual life of Judaism seems to have been of great significance, led to a flowering of Masoretic activity in the West in about the years 780 to 930. This brought matters to an essentially definitive position. The location of these studies was Tiberias, and their most important exponents the family of Ben Asher. The pointing of the imperfect Palestinian system no longer sufficed for the demands of the time. But it was not so readily capable of development as the simple Babylonian system. On the basis therefore of the experience of this Palestinian system, a completely new one was created, the Tiberian. With its system of accents, this provided a means of indicating the finer nuances, with the result that the pronunciation and reading of the Biblical text could be fixed down to the smallest

[1]) Manuscripts with this pointing were presumably still available to the editors of the Complutensian Polyglot (1514-17); cf. Plate 41 and the notes on it.

[2]) Kahle concludes from the fragments Eb 4 and Eb 8, which belong to one manuscript, that an older system antedated the Babylonian system here discussed, working only with points and related to the method employed by the Eastern Syrians (*Cairo Geniza* (1947), p. 48).

detail. It was further the aim of the Tiberian scholars to achieve unanimity on all matters still in dispute. The result can be seen in the manuscripts of the Ben Asher family (cf. pp. 25 f.). The final unity thus attained in vocalisation and accentuation gained authoritative status in the period that followed. The manifold preparatory stages which had led up to it were successfully concealed and forgotten. Only in the insertion of Metheg, which was used sparingly by the Ben Asher school, and in other small matters of vocalisation and accentuation was the work continued, until in the fourteenth century a kind of *textus receptus* was formed, used, for example, in the edition of Jacob ben Chayyim (cf. pp. 27 f.).

For the formation of this late mediaeval *textus receptus* the influence of the text of another Masoretic authority, Ben Naphtali, proved of importance. The differences between the text of Ben Asher and that of Ben Naphtali are recorded in a tractate by the Masorete Mishael ben ʿUzziel (tenth to eleventh century), and Kahle has succeeded in showing that a number of manuscripts represent this Ben Naphtali text, among them the famous Codex Reuchlinianus in Karlsruhe. From this material it appears that in the Ben Naphtali text we are dealing "with a system of pointing which represents a considerable advance on that of Ben Asher in the direction of more consistent fixing of the details of vocalisation and accentuation of the Biblical text" [1]). Daghesh is used more frequently, every Qames which is to be pronounced as o is specially indicated (ׇ), Metheg is much more frequently inserted, and so on. Even in the pronunciation itself there is an occasional difference between Ben Asher and Ben Naphtali. Thus Ben Asher reads: תַּחְתָּיו, בְּיִשְׂרָאֵל, and Ben Naphtali: תַּחֲתָּיו, בִּישְׂרָאֵל, Of these two rival text-forms, that of Ben Asher acquired the status of authoritative text. In this the support of the great Jewish philosopher Maimonides (1135-1204) may perhaps have been the deciding factor.

Pl. 21

From this historical survey it appears *that we may reckon with the existence of a fairly constant consonantal text even from the beginning of the second century A.D., but that the pointing and accents which now appear in the text were only achieved in the ninth and tenth centuries, after some hundreds of years of study and of tentative preparatory work.*

A question which arises in conclusion concerns the relationship between the pronunciation required by the Masoretes and that of older Hebrew. A number of observations have been made which suggest that the authenticity of the Masoretic pronunciation may be questioned. More than a thousand years lies between the period of the Tiberian Masoretes and the time when Hebrew was still a living speech, and it is highly probable that in this long period the pronunciation of Hebrew,

---

[1]) P. Kahle, *Masoreten des Westens* II (1930), p. 66*.

written as it was without vowels, has undergone a process of change. In fact, older Hebrew texts in Greek and Latin transcription do point in some measure to pronunciation other than that which we find in the Tiberian vocalisation; the same is true of the Samaritan tradition. Further, where differences may be observed among the Masoretes themselves, as with the few texts with Palestinian pronunciation which do not always agree with 𝔐, and as between the pronunciation of Ben Asher and of Ben Naphtali (cf. above), it would appear that tradition varied concerning the pronunciation. It therefore seemed necessary to reckon with a fair number of artificial forms in the Tiberian system, and to relate these to the desire of the Masoretes to produce a correct pronunciation. One of the points of significance about the Dead Sea Scrolls, and especially the Isaiah Scroll, is that the frequent use of vowel-letters in it allows us to see the nature of Hebrew pronunciation at a much earlier stage. From this it emerges unexpectedly that the Masoretic pronunciation is very ancient in certain forms which until recently have often been regarded as innovations. For example, the Masoretic pronunciation of the suffixes of the second person masculine singular as ᵉka is also found in the Isaiah Scroll, whereas other pre-Masoretic texts have the pronunciation āk. In other cases the pronunciation of the Isaiah Scroll is preserved by the Samaritans, while the Masoretes clearly use later formations. Thus, in the forms of the pronouns and suffixes of the second and third persons masculine plural, the Samaritan agrees with the Isaiah Scroll ʾattimma, lakimma, bahimma, ʿᵃlehimma etc., where the Masoretes have ʾattem, lakem, bahem, ʿᵃlehem [1]).

The introduction of pointing met moreover with some opposition. In the ninth century it was still rejected by the head of a Babylonian school, Gaon Natronai II, on the grounds that it did not derive from Sinai. Later its recent origin was disputed. About 1100, the Karaite Hadassi declared that God had not created the Torah without pointing, a view which Johann Buxtorf the Elder (1564-1629) revived in a form of his own. It is not necessary, after the foregoing discussion, to demonstrate further that the pointing does not have the same authority as the consonantal text. This is a matter to bear in mind in textual criticism. At the same time it must be remembered that the Masoretes did not follow their own ideas in vocalising the text, but endeavoured to express exactly the tradition they had received.

---

[1]) R. Meyer, *T.L.Z.* 75 (1950), col. 726 finds in the results he has obtained from an examination of the position of the accent in the language of the Isaiah scroll of Qumran, a proof rather for the view "that the Tiberian system belongs historically to the early Middle Ages. It is therefore not permissible, directly and without careful examination, to draw conclusions from it concerning Hebrew and Canaanite. For in between there lies that great complex, of such tremendous importance for the history of the language, which is normally described as 'pre-masoretic'."

4. The Masora. Alongside the text in BH are printed the notes of
the Masoretes, which are described as Masora, in the narrower sense. Mas
Among the Western Masoretes a distinction is made between the marginal
Masora (Masora marginalis) in the four margins, and the final Masora
(Masora finalis), which is an alphabetic collection at the end of the Bible.
The marginal Masora may be further divided into Masora parva (Mp) Mp
in the side margins and Masora magna (Mm, Mas. M) at the top and Mm,Mas.M
bottom. BH only includes the Mp, following the manuscript L as for the
Hebrew text. The Masora finalis is yet to be added.

The Masora parva contains observations concerning the external form of the text, with the aim of preserving this unaltered. Wherever errors could readily be made in the text, a note is added. Thus it is noted when a word is written defectively which could as well be written *plene*, and vice versa, or when the repeated occurrence of a word like את in a single verse might lead to inadvertent omission. At the same time such occurrences are brought into relation with others of the same kind, with an indication that the same or a similar form is to be found elsewhere. Thus we get frequent enumerations, indications as to how many times a particular form occurs, or the note that it is a *hapax legomenon*. So, for example, it is noted at Gen. i. 1 that בראשית occurs five times, including three at the beginning of a verse, ברא אלהים three times, but that the combination את השמים is only found here. At Gen. i. 11, it is noted that ויהי כן occurs six times in the same section; at Gen.i.12, that ותוצא occurs three times, twice written *plene* and once defectively. Sometimes attention is drawn to curious features of the text; for example in Deut. xxxi.3, that this verse, like two others, begins and ends with the divine name יהוה. In the Masora parva there are further indicated the S^{e}birin, Q^{e}res etc. Often such Masoretic notes seem to us far-fetched, frivolous and without purpose. But we must remember that they are the result of a passionate desire to protect the text and to prevent wilful or careless mistakes by the scribe, even, for example, in the matter of the use of the vowel letters ו and י, in spite of the fact that the use of the *plene* and *defective* forms is in many cases merely a matter of chance, without either consistency of usage or practical significance. The Masora bears witness to an extremely exact revision of the text, which deserves our respect, even though there is always the danger that in the care for the letter of the text its spirit has been missed.

The Masora magna in the top and bottom margins in general provides supplements to the Masora parva. Thus on Gen.i.1 there are noted the five passages in which בראשית occurs. There are in addition such extra notes as required more space.

In the Masora finalis, the Masoretic material is arranged alphabetically. As the basis for the final Masora in his famous Rabbinic

Bible, Jacob ben Chayyim used a mediaeval collection entitled Ochla
Ochla w^e^Ochla (Ochla). This begins with an "alphabetical list of words which only occur twice in the sacred writings, once without and once with ו at the beginning". The first of these is אָכְלָה (I Sam. i.9) וְאָכְלָה (Gen. xxvii.19), from which the whole collection derives its name. It was edited by S. Frensdorff in 1864 from a Paris manuscript.

At first the Masoretic material was transmitted orally. Later as it increased in extent it was gradually added to the manuscripts themselves.

The language of the Masora is Aramaic and, to a lesser extent, Hebrew. Obviously the Masora will vary according to the form of the text for which it was designed. There was therefore an independent Babylonian Masora which differed in terminology and, to some extent, in order from the Palestinian. The wording of the Masora is very terse, using a mass of abbreviations which require considerable knowledge for their understanding. It naturally follows that later scribes no longer understood the Masoretic notes, and these degenerated in the Middle Ages into mere ornamentation of the manuscripts. It was Jacob ben Chayyim who re-introduced clarity and order (cf. pp. 27f.).

A collection of the manuscript material known to him was made by
Gins(burg- C. D. Ginsburg in an unfinished work consisting of four folio volumes:
Mass) *The Massorah compiled from Manuscripts alphabetically and lexically arranged*, London, Vol. I 1880, II 1883, III (Appendices) 1885, IV.1 (Supplement) 1905.

5. Manuscripts. In view of the purpose of this book, the chronological survey which follows includes only those manuscripts, out of the large number that exist, which are utilised in BH or which deserve special mention because of their importance, such as the Nash Papyrus and the Ben Asher Codex of Aleppo.

We may note that Hebrew manuscripts from the tenth and eleventh centuries are very rare. The great bulk of the manuscripts belong to a later period. The most comprehensive collection of Hebrew manuscripts —and the most valuable because of its richness in old ones—is in the Russian Public Library in Leningrad. Two collections were brought there in 1863 and 1876 by the Russian Karaite Abraham Firkowitsch (1785-1874), who had shown unprecedented zeal in gathering them, mainly from Karaite synagogues in the East [1]. Firkowitsch was, however, an active forger, who frequently added new colophons or altered the dates in old ones, in order to prove the antiquity of Karaite Judaism, which

---

[1] The first collection is described by A. Harkavy and H. L. Strack in: *Catalog der hebr. Bibelhandschriften der kaiserlichen öffentl. Bibliothek in St.Petersburg*, (1875). Some variants from individual manuscripts are there quoted (referred to in
V(ar)^F BH as V(ar)^F).

to him was the only true Judaism. Nevertheless, the manuscripts which he collected are of very great importance. The second Firkowitsch collection includes of Bible manuscripts alone 1582 items on parchment and 725 on paper. In the same library there is also a collection of nearly 1200 fragments, deriving probably in part from the Cairo Geniza, made by Antonine, the Russian archimandrite in Jerusalem.

The Hebrew manuscripts found in 1947 in Qumran cave I near the Dead Sea were acquired partly by the Hebrew University of Jerusalem and partly by the Syrian Monastery of St. Mark in Jerusalem. The scrolls belonging to the Monastery of St.Mark were, because of the Israel-Arab war, taken to the United States and there published, with the exception of one which contains an Aramaic version of part of Generis (with additions). In 1954, it was possible for these scrolls too to be acquired for the University of Jerusalem for the sum of 300,000 dollars, so that the whole 1947 find is now re-united [1]).

As a result of the 1947 finds, there must stand first among all Old Testament manuscripts

a) The Isaiah Manuscript from the Dead Sea Cave (Qumran) [2]). A certain date for the manuscript has not yet been reached, but many points suggest a very early origin, probably pre-Christian [3]). As regards the external appearance of the scroll cf. p. 7. It is remarkable that two different text-types are represented in it, which cover exactly two halves of the book of Isaiah, i-xxxiii and xxxiv-lxvi. In the second half the *plene*-forms and full suffix forms are more frequent than in the first. Either one scribe was copying from two different originals, or, more probably, as in Egyptian papyrus scrolls, two scribes with different peculiarities were working at the same time. The text of the scroll is a popular *Pls. 8, 9*

[1]) On the 1952 discoveries, cf. the note on p. 10.

[2]) Published as: *The Dead Sea Scrolls of St. Mark's Monastery*, Vol. I, The Isaiah Manuscript and the Habakkuk Commentary, Edited for the Trustees by Millar Burrows with the assistance of John C. Trever and William H. Brownlee. Published by the American Schools of Oriental Research, (New Haven, 1950).

[3]) The suggested dates range from the second century B.C. to the Middle Ages. The early dating, supported by Albright and others, depends mainly upon palaeographical considerations and upon the archaeological evidence. The jars found in the cave belong to the Roman period (cf. p. 96). The age of a piece of the linen also found has been determined by the radio-active carbon content to be between 167 B.C. and 233 A.D. The results of the excavation of Khirbet Qumran, which has been in progress since 1952, make it appear most probable that the manuscripts were hidden during the first Jewish War (66-70 A.D.). They must all, therefore, have been written earlier, i.e. at the latest during the first half of the first century A.D. This dating is supported by the texts from Wadi Murabaat, which may be dated with certainty, being not later than the time of the revolt of Bar Kochba (132-135 A.D.): 'The script is more developed, the Biblical text definitely that of the Masora, and it must be concluded from this that the documents from Qumran are older, earlier than the second century' (de Vaux, *Revue Biblique*, lx (1953), p. 267). Cf. also p. 94.

text (cf. pp. 12 f.) which essentially confirms 𝔐, but which also contains a very large number of variants. These coincide in a number of cases with variants found in the ancient translations, or with emendations suggested by modern scholars. In view of the fact that real variants are rare in the Geniza fragments and are almost entirely lacking in the later manuscripts, this newly-found manuscript is of special significance in providing such variants in large numbers. The III Apparatus in BH contains about 1375 variants, not including merely orthographical variations, which
Pl. 10 are estimated to be about 4500 in number. A second manuscript of Isaiah, only fragmentary, has a text closer to the Masoretic (cf. p. 102) [1])

Pl. 11 b) The Habakkuk Commentary from the Cave. Only the upper (larger) half of this scroll has survived. It consists of two pieces of leather sewn together. Shorter or longer phrases are quoted seriatim from the first two chapters of Habakkuk, and to these, introduced each time by: "This means", there are added interpretations with reference to the period of the author of the commentary. The national and religious circumstances of this period are thus shown to have been foreseen by the prophet Habakkuk. A number of variant readings to Hab. i and ii are worthy of careful examination (cf. III Apparatus in BH). The divine name Yahweh is written in the old script (cf. p. 5) [2]).

c) The Nash Papyrus [3]). Before 1947 the oldest witness to the
Pl. 5 Hebrew text was reckoned to be the papyrus sheet acquired by W. L. Nash in Egypt in 1902 and presented to the Cambridge University Library—known as the Nash Papyrus. It contains a somewhat damaged copy of the decalogue in a form which follows partly Exod. xx. 2ff. and partly Deut. v. 6ff., and also the Sheᵉma from Deut. vi. 4f. This arrangement shows that we have here not a fragment of a Bible scroll, but a short collection of texts for liturgical, edifying or educational purposes. The papyrus was dated in the second or first century A.D. by those who first examined it. In the *Journal of Biblical Literature* (1937), Albright declared, on the basis of palaeographical indications, which, however, are not undisputed, that it was of Maccabaean origin, whereas Kahle assigns it on internal grounds to the time before the destruction of the Temple in A.D. 70. The sixth and seventh commandments appear in reverse order, and the Sheᵉma is introduced by a phrase not in 𝔐, but found in 𝔊.

d) The Geniza Fragments. The origin of these has already been discussed above (cf. p. 10). The amount of the treasure recovered from

---

[1]) Edition: (1954) אוצר המגלות הגנוזות.

[2]) On this commentary, cf. the thorough investigation by K. Elliger, *Studien zum Habakuk-Kommentar vom Toten Meer* (Tübingen, 1953).

[3]) First published by S. A. Cook in the *Proceedings of the Society of Biblica Archaeology* (1903), pp. 34ff.

the Geniza is enormous. The number of the fragments has been estimated as about 200,000. Besides Bible texts in Hebrew and in Aramaic and Arabic translation, there are passages of Midrash, Mishna, Talmud, liturgical texts, lists, letters, and much besides. Of particular importance was the discovery of the Hebrew original of the Wisdom of Ben Sira, known previously only in Greek, and also of a previously unknown writing in Hebrew, probably originating in the second or first century B.C., to which the name of "Zadokite Fragment" was given. This latter has attracted new interest [1]) because of its relationship with the similar "Manual of Discipline" found in 1947 [2]). The Biblical fragments from the Geniza, of which the earliest may go back as far as the fifth century A.D., have alone made it possible to trace the development of the Masoretic activity before the work of the Tiberian school, and reveal the emergence of the pointing described above. Geniza fragments came into the possession of various libraries, most of the material being in the Cambridge University Library and the Bodleian Library at Oxford.

e) Ben Asher Manuscripts. Five or six generations of the Ben Asher family took a leading part in the work of the Masoretes in Tiberias from the second half of the eighth century until the middle of the tenth. In the two manuscripts which have survived that go back to the last two members of the family, we find a reliable witness to their achievements.

Codex Cairensis (= C). This contains the former and latter prophets and was written and pointed in 895 by Moshe ben Asher. In one colophon (the concluding formula of a mediaeval manuscript, which gives information concerning the scribe and other matters) Moshe ben Asher names the one who commissioned him, and in a second names himself as the scribe. Further colophons relate the fate of the Codex. It was presented to the Karaite community in Jerusalem, and seized by the crusaders in 1099. After its restitution, it came into the possession of the Karaite community in Cairo, where it has remained down to the present day. C, *Pl. 17*

The Aleppo Codex. This contains the whole Old Testament and comes from the first half of the tenth century. According to its colophon, it was not actually written by Aaron ben Moshe ben Asher, but was provided by him with pointing and Masora. It was pointed with especial care, and was regarded as a model codex, only to be used for reading at Passover, Weeks and Tabernacles. It could be consulted by scholars to settle matters of doubt, but not for study. It was originally in Jerusalem, but later was taken to Cairo and thence to Aleppo. The fact that it could not be used for BH is explained there on p. VI. This is the more to be

[1]) Cf. C. Rabin, *Zadokite Documents* (Oxford, 1953), edition and translation.
[2]) Published in Vol. II, Fasc. 2 of the edition mentioned on p. 23 n. 2.

regretted since the latest information is that it has been destroyed by fire.

L, *Pl. 20* Codex Leningradensis (= L). In view of the inaccessibility and now probable final loss of the only complete surviving Bible manuscript which goes back to the youngest member of the Ben Asher family, the Codex Leningradensis, printed in BH, acquires special importance as a witness to the Ben Asher text. According to its colophon, it was a copy completed in 1008 from manuscripts written by Aaron ben Moshe ben Asher. An answer to earlier doubts as to the correctness of this note is to be found in the important discussion in BH pp. VIff.

$\mathrm{V(ar)}^{\mathrm{P}}$ f) The Petersburg Codex of the Prophets (= P) [1]. This contains Isa., Jer., Ezek., and the Book of the Twelve, with Masora magna and parva. The Codex was discovered in 1839 by Firkowitsch, as he maintains, in the synagogue of Tzufutkali in the Crimea. Its importance does not rest only on its age—it belongs to the year 916 A.D.—but most of all in the fact that with its discovery it became possible for the first time to appreciate the nature of the Babylonian system of pointing which had been lost for centuries. But a closer examination and comparison with other Babylonian manuscripts, discovered at the same time or later, have shown that this Codex actually follows the western tradition in its consonantal text, pointing and Masora, while employing the eastern signs. It is thus an impressive symbol of the victory of the western tradition over the eastern (cf. p. 11). On a few leaves (212, 221a) the Tiberian signs have in fact been substituted for the Babylonian; on fol. 1b, both stand side by side.

$\mathrm{V(ar)}^{\mathrm{E\text{-}1.2.3}}$ g) The Erfurt Codices (=E 1.2.3). Three further codices are utilised in BH, described from their former location as the codices "Erfurtensis 1.2.3." They belong to the former Prussian State Library in Berlin (MS. Orient. 1210/11, 1212, 1213), and are at present in the West German Library in Marburg and the University Library in Tübingen. They and others were used by J. H. Michaelis for his edition in 1720 (cf. p. 28). Their peculiarity is that to a greater or less degree—most markedly in E 3—they represent in text and Masora the tradition of Ben Naphtali, or a tradition closely connected with him, though already showing indications of the evolution of the later *textus receptus*.

E 1, fourteenth century, contains the Hebrew Old Testament, Targum, Masora magna and parva.

E 2, probably thirteenth century, contains the Hebrew Old Testament, Targum Onkelos, Masora magna and parva.

E 3, is in age and text the most important of these manuscripts, being one of the oldest German manuscripts (Kahle dates it before 1100). It contains the Hebrew Old Testament, Masora magna and parva, and

[1]) Published in facsimile by H. L. Strack, *Prophetarum posteriorum Codex Babylonicus Petropolitanus*, 1876.

extracts from Ochla weOchla (cf. pp. 21f.). The consonantal text is by two copyists. The pointing, by four different hands, partly follows the text of Ben Naphtali, and partly reveals contacts with it. Kahle comments on this manuscript: "It was, however, valuable to have a Ben Naftali text and a Ben Naftali Masora available when I was editing the Ben Asher text with the Ben Asher Masora" [1]).

h) Lost Codices. Finally, of importance for particular passages are certain codices which no longer exist, but whose peculiar readings have been preserved. A number of such codices are referred to in BH.

Sev

Codex Severi (= Sev). A mediaeval list, found in manuscript form in Paris and Prague, contains 32 variant readings of a Pentateuch manuscript from the Synagogue of Severus in Rome. This manuscript is supposed to have come as part of the plunder brought to Rome in 70 A.D. and presented by the emperor Severus (222-235) to a synagogue which he had built. If this tradition is correct, then it must refer to a scroll, not a codex (cf. pp. 7f.). Cf. in BH the apparatus to Gen. xviii.21; xxiv.7; Num. iv.3.

Hill

Codex Hillel (= Hill). This is supposed to have been written about 600 A.D. by Rabbi Hillel ben Moshe ben Hillel. It is said to have been very accurate and to have been used for the revision of other manuscripts. Readings from this codex are cited a number of times by mediaeval Masoretes and grammarians. Cf. in BH the apparatus to Gen. vi.3; xix.6; Exod. xxv. 19; Lev. xxvi.9.

The mediaeval Masoretes also mention among others the following codices as standard, and cite readings from them:

Codex Muga (already cited in MS. 4445 (cf. p. 30 n. 2) and in the Petersburg Codex of the Prophets). Cf. Lev. xxiii.13; xxvi.39.

Codex Jericho, cf. Gen. xxxi.36; Num. v. 28.

Codex Jerushalmi, cf. Gen. x.19.

Nothing further is known concerning these codices.

6) **Printed editions.** Of the large number of editions only those which are referred to in BH can be described here. In several respects there stands out among the oldest printed editions

𝔅

a) The Second Rabbinic Bible of Jacob ben Chayyim [2]), which was published by Daniel Bomberg in Venice in 1524/5, and is hence called Bombergiana (= 𝔅). This was not the earliest [3]), but was

[1]) P. Kahle, *The Cairo Geniza* (1947), p. 76.

[2]) Jacob ben Chayyim was a Jewish refugee from Tunis and later became a Christian. He died before 1538.

Pl. 22

[3]) It was preceded by editions of separate parts, all with Rabbinic commentaries and to some extent with Targum—Psalms (Bologna(?), 1477), Prophets (Soncino, 1485/6), Writings (Naples, 1486/7), Pentateuch (Lisbon, 1491) etc. Complete Bibles: Soncino, 1488, Naples 1491/3, Brescia, 1494. The first Rabbinic Bible was produced by Felix Pratensis and also published by Daniel Bomberg in 1516/7, a consider-

the most significant of its period, and remained until the twentieth century the standard printed edition of the Hebrew Old Testament. It is a Rabbinic Bible, which means that it includes with the Hebrew text the Aramaic translation (Targum) and commentaries by influential Rabbis (Rashi, Ibn Ezra, Kimḥi etc.), a compendious work in four volumes with altogether 952 folio pages. The special feature of the Bomberg Bible is that it also includes the Masora magna and parva and the Masora finalis, gathered by the editor as a result of enormous labour from a number of manuscripts, mainly faulty and written without any understanding of the Masoretic material (cf. p. 22), and on this the editor shaped his text. In addition there are noted variant readings from manuscripts which Jacob ben Chayyim collated. This text has enjoyed almost canonical authority up to our own day. Even in 1897 Ginsburg wrote that it represented the only Masoretic recension and that deviations from it in modern editions of the Hebrew text must be convincingly established. In his first two editions of the Biblia Hebraica, Kittel too printed this text. But Jacob ben Chayyim based his work on late mediaeval manuscripts or on editions which followed these, and thus provides the late mediaeval *textus receptus*. Nor can we expect from a scholar of the sixteenth century that his edition should fulfil the requirements which we to-day demand of a critical edition, after centuries of development in the science of criticism. This text has therefore been rightly abandoned in the third edition of BH and an older one substituted.

V(ar)M b) The edition of J. H. Michaelis (= M) [1]) (1668-1738, a protestant theologian and orientalist in Halle and a prominent pietist) follows in the main the text of Jablonski's 1699 edition. In its apparatus it notes the most important readings of five Erfurt manuscripts (cf. pp. 26f.) and of numerous printed editions. Often the variants are only a matter of accentuation. Parallel passages are indicated in the margin.

c) Benjamin Kennicott (1718-1783, an Oxford theologian, Librarian 1767, Canon 1770) produced a compendious collection of variants still used today: *Vetus Testamentum Hebraicum cum variis lectionibus*,
V(ar)Ken 2 volumes (Oxford, 1776-1780) (= Ken). Kennicott published the Masoretic text following the edition of the Dutch scholar van der Hooght (1705), the Samaritan text following Walton's London Polyglot (1653-7). In the large apparatus variants are noted from more than 600 Hebrew manuscripts, 52 editions and 16 Samaritan codices in so far as they concern the consonantal text. This enormous work, demanding the colla-

---

able critical achievement which in large measure served as a basis for the Second Rabbinic Bible of Jacob ben Chayyim. (Cf. P. Kahle, *Die Welt des Orients* (1947), pp. 32ff.).

[1]) *Biblia Hebraica ex aliquot manuscriptis et compluribus impressis codicibus, item Masora tam edita, quam manuscripta aliisque hebraeorum criticis diligenter recensita* etc. (Halle, 1720).

tion of these manuscripts, could only be undertaken by Kennicott with the aid of a staff of assistants, not all of whom were competent for the task. In addition, the collated manuscripts were mainly late. On the significance of the edition cf. below.

d) J. B. de Rossi [1]) produced not an edition but merely a collection of variants. This contains a selection of the more important readings from 1475 manuscripts and editions (p. XLV). The material covered is thus much greater than that of Kennicott, and it is more reliably produced. But de Rossi too notes only variations in the consonantal text.

For the recovery of the original text, the actual value of these two collections of variants is very small. The variants noted, apart from orthographical differences and simple scribal errors—haplography, dittography, inversion of consonants—cover such matters as the use of plural or singular with collective words, the insertion or omission of כל, ו etc., the replacing of one preposition by another of the same meaning, or of a word by a synonym (like דבר for אמר), plural for singular (such as דבריך for דברך) and vice versa. These do indeed show that we cannot speak in terms of a complete uniformity in the transmission of the text, as was presupposed by the hypothesis of an archetype. But what is lacking is the really significant variation of meaning, such as is found, for example, in New Testament manuscripts. These collections of variants scarcely help in dealing with a corrupt passage. The manuscripts on which they are based have been so standardised by the work of the Masoretes that no sensational results can come from their use. In view of what has already been said concerning the history of the Masoretic text, we may readily appreciate this disappointing result. It led in its own time to a decline of Masoretic studies. The nineteenth and twentieth centuries have not produced corresponding collections.

e) S. Baer (= B), with the collaboration of Franz Delitzsch, endeavour- VarB
ed, in the years 1869 and following, to produce the Masoretic text of the Old Testament, omitting Exod to Deut., in as correct a form as possible by utilising old editions and manuscript material [2]). "These editions contain much valuable material, but the subjective and unmethodical procedure with which Baer treated the Masora resulted in his constructing a text which never really existed at all. His editions must therefore be used with caution" [3]).

[1]) *Variae Lectiones Veteris Testamenti, ex immensa MSS. Editorumque Codicum Congerie haustae et ad Samar. Textum, ad vetustiss. versiones, ad accuratiores sacrae criticae fontes ac leges examinatae opera ac studio Johannis Bern. de Rossi*, 4 volumes (Parma, 1784/88). As a supplement, de Rossi published in 1798: *Scholia critica in V.T. libros seu supplementa ad varias sacri textus lectiones.*

[2]) *Textum Masoreticum accuratissime expressit e fontibus Masorae codicumque varie illustravit.*

[3]) P. Kahle, in Bauer-Leander, *Historische Grammatik der hebräischen Sprache* (1922), p. 90.

V(ar)^{G} f) C. D. Ginsburg (= G) produced an edition for the British and Foreign Bible Society (1908ff.) [1]. A new edition appeared in 1926. Ginsburg prints "substantially" the text of Jacob ben Chayyim of 1524/5, which he so highly valued, and includes in the apparatus the variant readings of over 70 manuscripts and of 19 printed editions earlier than 1524. The variations cover orthography, vowel signs, accents and divisions of the text. The collated manuscripts, mainly from the British Museum, belong chiefly to the period after the thirteenth century [2]. The unevenness of the material, more or less haphazardly gathered, and the lack of any attempt at assessing and grouping it, lessen the value of this edition, which has however a certain importance as a collection of Masoretic material. By far the majority of the variants are merely trivial and do not affect the sense or interpretation of the text. Variants in the ancient versions are only rarely entered. The reliability of the collations has also occasionally been criticised. This is due to the fact that the task which Ginsburg undertook was so enormous as to be impossible without a great deal of assistance.

V(ar)^{J} g) In BH variants are also cited from the following: V(ar)^{J} = Var codicis Jemensis [3], following R. Hoerning, *Description and Collation of six Karaite Manuscripts of portions of the Hebrew Bible in Arabic Characters* (1889). These are of the tenth and eleventh centuries, the Hebrew text being transcribed into Arabic letters.

V(ar)^{O} V(ar)^{O} = Var secundum Odonem. In the Latin works of a mediaeval scholastic Odo, not yet identified, there are 78 quotations from the Hebrew Bible, of which four are pointed. The work, which aims at the conversion of the Jews, was compiled about the middle of the twelfth century. The existing copy (Trinity College, Cambridge) was written about the end of the twelfth or the beginning of the thirteenth century. The Hebrew quotations, approximately equal in length to the book of Joel, are unusual for their variations from 𝔐 in consonantal form, and in the use of a peculiar pointing, simpler than the Tiberian. Are these in fact examples of "early Masoretic or even non-Masoretic texts", as J. Fischer, their first editor, suggested? [4].

V(ar)^{S} V(ar)^{S} = Var secundum Strack, *Grammatik des Biblisch-Aramäischen* (6th ed. 1921). In the Biblical Aramaic texts appended to the gram-

[1]) *The Old Testament, diligently revised according to the Massorah and the early editions with the various readings from MSS and the ancient versions.*

Pl. 18 [2]) But they also include the Pentateuch Manuscript Or 4445 in the British Museum, which was dated by Ginsburg about 820 to 850 A.D. This manuscript is without colophon, as both beginning and end are lost. The way in which Ben Asher is quoted suggests that it was written in his life time.

[3]) The Jemen (Yemen), an area in south-west Arabia, had a considerable Jewish population.

[4]) Cf. J. Fischer, *Biblica* 15 (1934), pp. 50ff.; 25 (1944), pp. 167ff.; *B.Z.A.W.* 66 (1936), pp. 198ff.

mar there are included the readings of a number of unpublished manuscripts.

V(ar)^{W} = Var secundum Wickes, *A treatise on the accentuation of the three so-called Poetical Books of the Old Testament* (1881, 1888). These are researches into the accentual system on the basis of prolonged study of manuscripts. V(ar)^{W}

C. THE SAMARITAN PENTATEUCH ꙍ

An important event in the history of post-exilic Judaism was the separation of the Samaritans from the Jews. We do not know exactly when the Samaritan community separated itself from Jerusalem and founded its own sanctuary on the ancient holy mountain of Gerizim, near Shechem. It probably happened in the fourth century B.C., as the culminating event of a long process. At the time of the schism the Samaritans took with them the holy scripture of the Jews as it then existed, i.e. the Pentateuch. Thus we possess the Pentateuch in a second Hebrew recension, the Samaritan. We have already observed (cf. p. 5) that the Samaritans retained for their Pentateuch the old Hebrew script, in a somewhat modified form. *Pl. 23*

When the Samaritan Pentateuch (cited in BH as ꙍ) became known to the West in 1616 through a manuscript discovered in Damascus, the liveliest expectations were at first aroused. Some believed that with it a much nearer approach to the original text of the Pentateuch had become possible. Later its reputation waned, and, as a result of the verdict of Gesenius (1815), for a long time it was regarded by many as practically worthless for textual criticism. Gesenius claimed that it was not an independent witness to the text, but was a revision of 𝔐 produced both in language and in matter from the Samaritan point of view. Against this inadequate judgment of the matter protest was made in the nineteenth century by A. Geiger and in this century by P. Kahle [1]).

The problem of the Samaritan Pentateuch is that it deviates from 𝔐 in about 6000 instances. Many of these variants, it is true, are merely orthographic, especially in the more frequent use of *plene*-forms, and many others are trivial and do not affect the meaning. It is, however, noteworthy that ꙍ agrees with 𝔊 against 𝔐 in about 1900 instances [2]). Some deviations from 𝔐 must be regarded as alterations which the Samaritans introduced in the interests of their own cultus. This is especially clear in the introduction after Exod. xx. 17 of a commandment to build

[1]) *Theol. Studien und Kritiken* 88 (1915), pp. 399ff.; *Cairo Geniza* (1947), pp. 144ff.

[2]) The New Testament also agrees with ꙍ in some passages against 𝔐. Cf. Acts vii. 4, vii. 32 and possibly also Heb. ix. 3. Presumably the New Testament depends upon a Greek Pentateuch which was like ꙍ at these points.

a sanctuary on Mount Gerizim; in Deut. xi.30, where to the word מרה (ɯ מרא) there is added מול שכם; and in nineteen passages in Deut. where the choice of the holy place is set in the past and the reference to Shechem is made clear (in the formula הַמָּקוֹם אֲשֶׁר יִבְחַר יְהוָה ɯ has בחר for יבחר) [1]. But such obviously tendentious alterations do not justify our treating all other deviations as deliberate, and especially does this apply to those where ɯ agrees with 𝔊.

The peculiar text-form of the Samaritan Pentateuch is more probably to be explained on the assumption that we have here a popularising revision of the original text, which naturally is not to be equated with 𝔐 (Kahle). Old forms are modernised, difficult constructions simplified, other alterations typical of popular texts are made (cf. pp. 12f.) [2]. Such popularisations were only necessary as long as there was a need for making the Hebrew text as intelligible as possible to the people. They became unnecessary as soon as the method was adopted of translating the text into the popular Aramaic tongue. Thus ɯ must go back to a relatively early date, which makes it impossible to regard it as dependent on 𝔐. It is rather to be regarded as an important witness to a text-form which was once very widely used, as is shown by its agreements with 𝔊, the New Testament and some Jewish texts which escaped the revision undertaken by official Judaism. In these latter we can see especially the effect of the chronology in Gen. v and xi, in which ɯ is independent both of 𝔐 and of 𝔊. Cf. p. 16 above on the survival of the text-form represented by ɯ in mediaeval Masoretic manuscripts.

The latest edition is by A. von Gall, *Der hebräische Pentateuch der Samaritaner* (1914-18). This provides an eclectic text, based on late mediaeval manuscripts. Manuscripts earlier than the thirteenth century are very rare. The oldest known manuscript in *book-form* is in the Cambridge University Library. 'It contains a notice that it was sold A.H. 544 (A.D. 1149-50) and may have been written some centuries earlier. It makes the impression that it is much older than the MSS.written since about A.D. 1200, of which we know a great number' [3]. The sacred scroll of the Samaritan community of Nablus (= Shechem), called the *Abisha-scroll* from its scribe, is very famous. In it the only really old part—older than every other known Samaritan manuscript—is the main part of Num. xxxv-Deut. xxxiv; the remainder was added in the fourteenth century [4].

---

[1]) On the other hand in Deut. xxvii. 4 where 𝔐 has Ebal, ɯ Gerizim, it would seem more probable that we have a later alteration in the Jewish text. A definite decision is not, however, possible. Cf. the commentaries ad loc.

[2]) Cf. S. Talmon, The Samaritan Pentateuch, *J.J.S.* ii (1951), pp. 144-150.

[3]) P. Kahle, *Cairo Geniza* (1947), p. 50.

[4]) Cf. P. Kahle, *Studia Orientalia Ioanni Pedersen dicata* (1953), pp. 188-192.

CHAPTER II

TRANSLATIONS FROM THE ORIGINAL LANGUAGE

A. GENERAL MATTERS CONCERNING THE VERSIONS

The Hebrew text which we have to-day has been altered by many circumstances from its original form, and undoubtedly contains many corruptions. Consequently those translations which enable us to reconstruct an older text of the Old Testament and to correct errors are of considerable importance. But it must be observed at the outset that every translation raises a whole series of problems of its own. For a long period it was customary to treat the versions naively and to use them directly for textual criticism, on the assumption that the nature of the original underlying them could be readily rediscovered. The matter is not, however, so simple. Anyone who translates interprets at the same time. In a translation there appears not only the underlying text but also the translator's own comprehension of it. Every translator is a child of his own time and of his own culture. Each translation must first be considered and valued as an intellectual achievement in its own right. This is especially true in the case of the Bible translations which were produced to meet the practical needs of the community.

With most of the Biblical translations we have to reckon not with one but several anonymous translators. Many different factors leave their mark upon the work—the intellectual presuppositions which the translators inherit from their own age and culture, the religious and other opinions which they hold or to which they have to show deference, the prejudices and desires by which they are bound consciously or unconsciously, their education, their own ability to express themselves and the range of concepts in the language into which they are translating, and other matters besides. We must distinguish between what belongs to the original and what is to be attributed to the translator, a complex task which ought really to be completed before criticism of the Hebrew text is undertaken on the basis of the Versions.

So far as the history of the Versions is concerned, there are still, in most cases, many unsolved and perhaps insoluble problems, especially as regards the earlier part of that history. F. Rosenthal, writing on the

Peshitta, has wisely reminded us that of all linguistic problems that of the translations of the Bible is loaded with such a mass of the most diverse material that there is very little hope of ever arriving at a completely satisfactory solution. We have to reckon, in almost every case, with a series of written stages in the evolution of the translation. These stages cannot be exactly computed and are at present lost to us and never likely to be fully recovered. In addition, allowance must be made for a wealth of oral traditions, which, being based on the one original, may well have evolved in similar forms [1]).

The problems so far considered make for the attraction of the study of the Versions and at the same time urge us on to new researches, but they also make it clear that in many cases we are still a long way from final solutions.

We shall consider first the translations from the original language, which have prior claim in textual criticism, and then the remaining translations, which depend in the main upon the Septuagint. The translation by Jerome, the Vulgate, is nominally also a translation from the original Hebrew, but is at the same time very largely influenced by the Greek translations and by its Latin antecedent, the Vetus Latina. The Vulgate is therefore discussed in the next chapter.

𝔊 B. THE SEPTUAGINT (= 𝔊)

1. Introductory. In accordance with the purpose of this book, we are discussing 𝔊 as a witness to the Old Testament text. But it is appropriate to say a little about its very great significance in the history of culture. For 𝔊 was the book by which for the first time knowledge of the Old Testament revelation came to the Greek world. "The relationship of this book to the Cosmos, and the necessity of their being understood together was commonly felt among Greeks who had come in contact with the Old Testament. However differently they might think about the book, it nevertheless appeared quite certain that it was a creation parallel with the world itself, as great and as comprehensive as the world, and that both must go back to the same originator. What other book has ever at any time been the subject of such a verdict among thinking men?" [2]).

For the early church 𝔊 was the only normative form of the Old Testament. Augustine demanded of Jerome that he should use this canonically accepted text as the basis of his translation, and not the original Hebrew. It may indeed be said with truth that for centuries, almost up to the present day, the Old Testament has influenced Christendom in the form, Hellenistic in language and thought, which it received in 𝔊. We must thus

---

1) F. Rosenthal, *Die aramaistische Forschung* (1939), p. 206.
2) A. von Harnack, *Sitzungsberichte der Berliner Akademie* (1902), p. 509.

agree with V. Ehrenberg in according to 𝔊 the position of a book without which Christendom and the culture of the West would not have been possible.

2. The Letter of Aristeas. We seem at first sight to be well informed concerning the origin of 𝔊, since we possess in the Letter of Aristeas [1]) a record which purports to have been drawn up by one who was actually concerned in its preparation. This tells how Demetrius of Phaleron, who is wrongly described as the director of the famous library of Alexandria, one day reported to his royal master Ptolemy II Philadelphus (285-247 B.C.) that the Jewish Law was worthy of a place in the royal library, but must first be translated into Greek. (The Letter of Aristeas only deals with the Law—the Pentateuch). The king followed up this suggestion immediately. Envoys, among whom was Aristeas, were sent to the High Priest Eleazer in Jerusalem with the request that he should provide men equipped for this work of translation. Eleazer sent to Alexandria seventy-two men, six from each of the twelve tribes, with valuable scrolls of the Law. After being received with honour, they gave the king some examples of Jewish Wisdom, in a series of profound utterances. They were taken to the isle of Pharos, connected by a causeway with Alexandria, and there in quietness and seclusion they translated the Law in seventy-two days, while Demetrius wrote down the text as they agreed upon it. The completed translation was first read out to the Jewish community, and declared to be beautiful, pious and exact. It was to be treated as untouchable. Curses should be upon anyone who added to it, altered it, or omitted anything from it. Only after this approval by the Jewish community did the translation come to the king who had commanded it. He marvelled at the spirit of the Law-giver and sent the translators back to their homes loaded with gifts.

This is the information given by the letter. What is here related was taken up by both Jews and Christians and further developed. Josephus (37/38 to about 100 A.D.) follows it almost word for word, but Philo (c. 25 B.C. till after 40 A.D.) makes the translation into a work of divine inspiration and the translators into prophets. According to him, they worked quite independently, but produced an identical translation. This view is followed by the Church Fathers, who extended it to the whole Old Testament, whereas Aristeas speaks only of the Law. Pseudo-Justin [2]) in the third century even claimed to have seen the remains of the cells in which the translators worked rigidly separated from one

[1]) Text: *Aristeae Epistula*, ed. Wendland (1900); Thackeray in Swete, *Introduction to the Old Testament in Greek* (2nd ed. 1914). Translation: H. T. Andrews in R. H. Charles, *Apocrypha and Pseudepigrapha* II (1913), pp. 83-122; H. St. J. Thackeray (London, 1917); M. Hadas, *Aristeas to Philocrates* (New York, 1951).

[2]) Cohortatio ad gentiles XIII. Edited by de Otto, *Justini Opera*, Vol. 3 (1879).

another. This is clearly a pious legend, but it witnesses to the high value placed upon 𝔊 by the Christian Church.

But even what the Letter of Aristeas itself relates is incredible in many respects. The Letter was not written, as it states, by a heathen, but by a Jew who wished to glorify the Wisdom and the Law of his people through the lips of a heathen ruler. This writer did not live at the time of Ptolemy Philadelphus, but more than a century later. Moreover, the Jewish Law was not translated at the wish of a royal patronof the arts, but because the Egyptian Jews, who no longer understood Hebrew, could not manage without such a translation. Nor does this translation go back to Palestinian Jews, but to members of the Diaspora in Alexandria, for whom Greek was their everyday language.

The legendary character of the Letter of Aristeas has long been recognised. It has nevertheless influenced the conception of 𝔊 right up to recent times in one particular respect, namely in suggesting that we have in 𝔊 a translation (of the whole Old Testament) whose wording was from the first established and authorized, and that this was the only Greek translation possessed by the Jews for a long period. We shall see that this conception is to-day much in dispute.

3. The origin and history of the Septuagint up to the second century A.D. We observed that the Letter of Aristeas assigns the origin of the translation of the Pentateuch to the first half of the third century B.C. In this it may well be right. It further seems probable that the translation is to be associated with the Jewish community in Alexandria, which was the most important in the Jewish Diaspora. Just as in Palestine an Aramaic translation was needed, so there would be a demand in Egypt for a Greek one, and perhaps its origins are to be sought, as in the case of the Targumim, in the oral translations made in worship. Naturally too, that part of the Old Testament which was most vital to Judaism was first translated—namely the Law, followed gradually by the other books. The Prologue to the Wisdom of Ben Sira (Ecclesiasticus) in about 132 B.C. states that, beside that of the Law, translations into Greek existed of the "Prophets and of the other books". We must allow a long period for the translation of the whole Old Testament. For this reason alone, 𝔊 cannot be regarded as the work of one translator or of one group of translators. A detailed study of the work also proves this. The translation of individual books is very unequal. Even within certain books there are such variations that Herrmann and Baumgärtel [1])

---

[1]) Herrmann and Baumgärtel, Beiträge zur Entstehungsgeschichte der Septuaginta, *B.W.A.T.* N.F. V (1923). This view is disputed by J. Ziegler, Die Einheit der Septuaginta zum Zwölfprophetenbuch, *Vorlesungsverzeichnis Braunsberg* (1934), and others. Cf. also the similar views of H. St. J. Thackeray in *The Septuagint and Jewish Worship* (1921. Schweich Lectures 1920).

came to the conclusion that in various books two translators must have been at work. Some books are translated almost word for word; others, like Job and Daniel, quite freely. Certainly when we find that in the Greek translation of Jeremiah some 2,700 words are missing and the arrangement of the material is in some measure different, it appears clear that this is not merely the result of the translator's work, but that the Hebrew original underlying it must have differed from our present Masoretic text. We may sum up by saying that we have no unified translation in 𝔊, but a collection of translations, whose composers varied much in their practice and ability in translating, their knowledge of Hebrew, their style and so on. This variety, which makes it necessary for us to treat each book separately, produces some of the problems of 𝔊, and makes it impossible to use it for text-critical purposes in a completely uniform manner.

𝔊 made it possible for the Jews who were living in the Greek-speaking Diaspora to read their holy writings in the language which was natural to them. But it also gave opportunity for non-Jews to study the Old Testament (cf. Acts viii.26ff.). This was of great importance for early Christianity, since in this way ideas had been spread abroad to which the Christian message could be linked. Furthermore, 𝔊 became the holy book of the Christians of the early centuries. This put the Jewish community in a peculiar position in regard to the translation which it had produced and which it regarded so highly. In disputes between Jews and Christians, the Christians made much use of 𝔊, as for example in the discussion of Isa. vii.14. The Jews affirmed that the reference here was not to a virgin (παρθένος), but to a young woman (νεᾶνις). The Christians could point out in reply that the translation which the Jews themselves had produced did in fact read παρθένος. In the course of time, moreover, Christian interpolations crept into the text, as in Ps. xcv and Ps. xiii. Further, when correct Jewish exegesis began to demand that each and every letter of the text should be properly evaluated, the way in which 𝔊 treated the text in some places with freedom aroused antagonism. Moreover, this translation did not depend upon the authoritative text of the second century A.D., but rather upon an older one to be classed with the popular texts. As a result, the Jews finally gave up 𝔊—they were practically compelled to do so—and condemned what had once been regarded as indispensable and untouchable.

4. The later Greek translations. The need still remained, however, in the Greek-speaking Jewish communities for a translation into their own language. A new translation by Aquila, and the revision by Theodotion, attempted to fill the gap left by the rejection of 𝔊. Symmachus also made a new translation for the Ebionite, Jewish-Christian, community.

a) Aquila (= A), from Sinope in Pontus, was a proselyte and, accord A ing to Jewish tradition, a pupil of Rabbi Akiba, in whose spirit he produced a slavishly literal translation. As he carried the principle of literal accuracy to the absurd point at which the intelligibility of the text suffered, he frequently produced a version which did not sound at all like Greek, although his vocabulary reveals that he had a good knowledge of the language. But it was just this ruthless adherence to the text, and its rather precious quality, as for example in its use of similar sounding words, which endeared his work to his Jewish contemporaries, and his version thus enjoyed considerable popularity among the Jews [1]). It was produced about the year 130 A.D. Our knowledge of Aquila's translation depends, apart from quotations and hexaplaric fragments (cf. pp. 40f.), upon palimpsests from the Cairo Geniza belonging to the sixth century A.D. [2]).

b) Symmachus (= Σ) produced a new translation in about 170 A.D.,
Σ which was designed to be not merely accurate but also in good Greek. According to Eusebius and Jerome, he was an Ebionite; according to Epiphanius, a Samaritan converted to Judaism [3]). Only a few Hexapla fragments preserve his translation.

Θ c) Theodotion (= Θ), who lived about the end of the second century, was also a proselyte according to early church tradition. He did not produce a completely new translation, but revised an existing Greek translation with the help of the Hebrew text. Whether this translation was 𝔊 is disputed, though Rahlfs affirms that it was. The problem arises from the fact that "Theodotionic" readings are to be found in texts older than Theodotion, (the New Testament, Barnabas, Clement, Hermas). Kenyon and Kahle therefore assume that Theodotion revised an older translation which is to be distinguished from 𝔊, but which has disappeared apart from a few quotations in the early period of the church. Theodotion's translation has replaced that of 𝔊 for the book of Daniel in almost all manuscripts. Apart from this, it exists only in fragments [4]).

In addition to these three translations, which have in turn exerted

[1]) Examples of Aquila's translation may be found in *Septuaginta*, ed. by A. Rahlfs (1935), I, pp. VIII-X.

[2]) Cf. F. C. Burkitt, *Fragments of the books of Kings according to the translation of Aquila* (1897); C. Taylor, *Hebrew-Greek Cairo Genizah palimpsests from the Taylor-Schechter collection* (1900).

[3]) H. J. Schoeps, *Aus frühchristlicher Zeit* (1950), pp. 82ff. traces in Symmachus Ebionite theological terms, Greek education, and dependence upon Rabbinic exegesis. There appears thus no doubt that he was an Ebionite Christian. Cf. also A. v. Harnack, *Geschichte der altchristl. Litt.* II, 2 (1904), pp. 164ff.; and H. J. Schoeps, *Theol. und Gesch. des Judenchristentums* (1949), pp. 33ff.

[4]) The Greek text of the Minor Prophets found in 1952 (cf. p. 51) contains many readings of Aquila, Symmachus and Theodotion, although it is older than these. Barthélemy (*R.B.* lx (1953), pp. 25ff.) wishes to see in it the common basis upon which these three translators worked, and to consider them as '*surrecenseurs*' of this old Palestinian recension. But it must not be forgotten that there are many other texts in which an assimilation to the Hebrew text is attempted. A definitive view cannot be adopted until the whole text is published. Cf. also the following notes.

considerable influence upon the transmission of the Septuagint, Origen, in the great scientific study which we shall next consider, made use of yet others, scarcely known to us, the so-called Quinta (= E′) [1]), Sexta E′
and Septima 'The presence of so many different Greek Bible texts among the Jews of that time shows quite clearly how great was the need among the Jews for modern Greek translations of the Bible, and how inadequate were old translations, made centuries earlier, to meet the demands of the time[2]).

5. Origen's Hexapla. The existence of so many translations side by side, in addition to the original text, inevitably produced confusion, especially in discussions with the Jews. Clarification was sought by the production of the Hexapla, the enormous work undertaken by the Hex, hex
Alexandrian theologian Origen somewhere between 230 and 240 A.D. Orig.
Origen declared that the main purpose of his undertaking was to equip Christian theologians for discussions with Jews who had recourse to the original Hebrew. Whether he really had insight into the textual problems of 𝔊 and only modified his expressions because of its prestige in the church—as is repeatedly affirmed—is by no means so certain. Possibly he too did in fact regard 𝔊 as inspired.

Origen arranged the texts in six parallel columns: 1) the Hebrew text (= $\mathfrak{H}^{o}$); 2) the Hebrew text in Greek letters; 3) Aquila; 4) Symmachus; $\mathfrak{H}^{o}$
5) the Septuagint; 6) Theodotion. According to Eusebius, Origen added for the Psalms a fifth, sixth and seventh translation (cf. above). The Hebrew text stands first as the original, while the translations are arranged according to their relationship to that text, with the result that Aquila's stands first as the most literal. The main interest of the Alexandrian scholar was directed towards assimilating 𝔊 to the Hebrew original with the help of other more literal translations [3]). In this he utilised the signs named after the great textual critic Aristarchus (217-145 B.C.), which were in use in Alexandrian philological studies: the obelos (—, ÷, ÷), the metobelos (/., ./·, ✓) and the asterisk (※). These were employed in the following manner:

---

1) Barthélemy (*R.B.* lx (1953), p. 29) wishes to identify this with the text which is attested in the leather scroll containing the Greek text of the Minor Prophets. But he explicitly emphasises that this can only be a provisional suggestion. Cf. P. Kahle's criticism of Barthélemy's attempts to find the newly discovered text everywhere (*T.L.Z.* 79 (1954), col. 89).

2) P. Kahle, *T.L.Z.* 79 (1954), col. 90.

3) The tendency for such assimilations may be observed already before Origen; cf. Sanders-Schmidt, *The Minor Prophets in the Freer Collection and the Berlin Fragment of Genesis* (1927), pp. 25 ff., 265; J. Ziegler, *Duodecim Prophetae* (1943), pp. 33f.; id. *Z.A.W.* 61 (1945/48), pp. 76ff. (cf. below p. 134). P. Kahle has stressed particularly strongly that this tendency was already present in pre-Christian times, and that Origen 'continued the work of the Jews of previous centuries, applying it to the Bible text of the Christians'. (*T.L.Z.* 79 (1954), col. 88).

a) Words in 𝔊, which were lacking in the original text, and which, strictly speaking, ought to be excised, were bracketed with obelos and metobelos: ÷ εἰς φαῦσιν τῆς γῆς ↙ Gen. i.14.

b) Words in the original text, missing in 𝔊, were inserted in the 𝔊 column from another translation, but marked by asterisk and metobelos: ※ καὶ ἐγένετο οὕτως ↙ Gen. i.7.

But Origen did in fact interfere with the text of 𝔊 without indicating it. The form which he gave to 𝔊 in the fifth column of the Hexapla is therefore
𝔊h called the hexaplaric recension: 𝔊h. This soon began to have enormous effect upon the manuscripts. Jerome writes: "vix enim unus aut alter invenietur liber, qui ista (i.e. additamenta hexaplaria) non habeat".

An idea of the appearance of the Hexapla is given by the Milan fragments, discovered by Mercati at the end of the nineteenth century. These are parts of a palimpsest whose lower writing (a minuscule from the tenth century) contains some 150 verses of the Psalter, with all the columns of the Hexapla except the first. The last column contains not the text of Theodotion, but that of Quinta. Unfortunately this valuable, but scarcely legible, text has not yet been published apart from a specimen (Ps. xlvi.1-4) [1]).

Beside the Hexapla, Origen produced a second work, the Tetrapla, which contained only the four Greek translations. Whether the Tetrapla was a later, abbreviated form of the Hexapla, as is usually thought, or its predecessor (so Procksch [2])), is uncertain.

Both works were of enormous size and are not likely to have been copied often in their entirety. The original was in Caesarea in Palestine, and was presumably destroyed during the Islamic conquest. Fortunately the 𝔊-text of the Hexapla was often copied; Pamphilus and Eusebius were actively engaged in circulating it. A genuine manuscript of the Hexapla Septuagint has not, however, survived, but there are certainly manuscripts which represent the text of Origen more or less closely. The situation differs much in the individual books. The important witnesses
Pl. 29 are the Codex Colberto-Sarravianus (G), from the fourth or fifth century, which also preserves the Aristarchian symbols, and a number of minuscules. Of great value too is the very careful Syriac translation of 𝔊h, the
𝔖h *Pl. 31* so-called Syro-hexaplar (= 𝔖h), made very faithfully in 616/7 by Bishop Paul of Tella. The Aristarchian signs were also preserved in this. This translation has survived in the Syro-hexaplar Codex Ambrosianus in Milan from the ninth century, containing the Prophets and Writings [3]).

---

[1]) Cf. *Z.A.W.* 16 (1896), pp. 336f.

[2]) *Z.A.W.* N.F. 12 (1935), pp. 240ff.

[3]) The text of the Psalter in this Syriac version is not, however, the Hexapla text. Cf. Rahlfs, *Psalmi cum Odis* (1931), p. 52. On the Sahidic translation as a textual witness to the hexaplaric Greek, cf p. 68.

In addition to these manuscripts belonging to the Hexapla family ,there are a few belonging to other text-families which are important for the restoration of Origen's text because they note hexaplaric readings in the margin. Among majuscules are Codex Coislinianus (M) and Codex Marchalianus (Q). A collection of all the then known hexaplaric material *Pl. 30* was made by Field, in *Origenis Hexaplorum quae supersunt* (1875). An account of a recent find of hexaplaric material for Isaiah is given by A. Möhle in *Z.A.W.* N.F. 11 (1934), pp. 176ff.

6. Other recensions of the Septuagint. Origen was not the only one who revised 𝔊. Jerome, writing about 400 in his preface to Chronicles, knew of three recensions. "Alexandria et Aegyptus in Septuaginta suis Hesychium laudat auctorem; Constantinopolis usque Antiochiam Luciani martyris exemplaria probat. Mediae inter has provinciae Palaestinos codices legunt, quos ab Origene elaboratos Eusebius et Pamphilus vulgaverunt; totusque orbis hac inter se trifaria varietate compugnat". According to this, the different provinces of the ancient church had their own particular Biblical text. We may not, however, conclude from these words of Jerome's that there were only these three recensions, or that Hesychius and Lucian were anywhere regarded as completely authoritative [1]).

Lucian was a presbyter from Antioch, who died as a martyr in 312. Hesychius is perhaps to be identified with the bishop who was put to death in the persecutions of Diocletian. Whereas the Lucianic recension (= 𝔊 Luc) is mentioned elsewhere, we do not otherwise hear of that of 𝔊Luc Hesychius, and it is thus too shadowy to be described or dated [2]). Nor can we speak of any one principle which applies to the whole of the Lucianic recension. Ziegler has thus described it, with reference to Isaiah and the Minor Prophets: "Lucian took material from the hexaplaric recension, without, however, attempting an exact assimilation to 𝔐. Improvements in accordance with 𝔐, coming from the more recent translators via the hexaplaric recension, are few in number and small in content. Much more important for Lucian were the laws of Greek grammar and style. Most of the improvements belong to this field" [3]).

---

[1]) H. Dörrie, *Z.N.W.* 39 (1940), p. 69.

[2]) J. Ziegler, *Isaias* (1939), p. 23.

[3]) J. Ziegler, *Duodecim prophetae* (1943), p. 89. P. Kahle, in *T.L.Z.* 79 (1954), cols. 83ff., has indicated several older texts which contain Lucianic readings (e.g. Justin Martyr, Philo, Josephus) and reaches this conclusion: 'Text-forms of the Greek Bible, such as Lucian used for his revision, must therefore have been widespread in the early centuries of our era' (col. 85). Indeed, the John Rylands Papyrus Greek 458 and the leather scroll found in 1952 containing the Greek text of the Minor Prophets, prove 'with certainty the existence of text-forms akin to Lucian ... in the pre-Christian era' (col. 86). On the problem of the Lucianic text, which appears 'to become ever more complex' cf. also J. W. Wevers, *Th. R.* N.F. 22 (1954), pp. 98ff.

The recensions which have been mentioned do not represent the final stage in the history of the text of $\mathfrak{G}$, for the development went further. The revised texts tended to fuse and to influence each other. The result is that all surviving manuscripts contain more or less mixed texts. Since manuscripts could be copied from more than one earlier text, it could come about that a single manuscript would follow different recensions. This has, on occasion, led Septuagint research into error. When in 1883
$\mathfrak{G}^{L}$ Lagarde wished to edit the text of Lucian from Genesis to Ruth (= $\mathfrak{G}^{L}$) [1], he worked on the basis of manuscripts 19 and 108, which are clearly Lucianic from the books of Sam. onwards, on the assumption that the text of the previous books was also Lucianic. Rahlfs was able to demonstrate later that these particular manuscripts did not in fact follow Lucian's recension from Gen. to Ruth iv. 10, but another form of text. "Thus Lagarde's supposedly Lucianic text is not Lucianic at all from Gen. to Ruth iv. 10; only the last twelve verses of Ruth (iv. 11-22) are really Lucianic in Lagarde's edition, because of a change of text-form in manuscripts 19 and 108." [2]).

7. The method proposed by Lagarde. It is clear from what has been said that the history of the transmission of $\mathfrak{G}$ is extremely complex. None of the different text-forms which have come down to us preserves the original form of the translation. But is it possible to get back beyond the variety of the existing text-forms to a single form, an 'original Septuagint', assumed once to have existed? Paul de Lagarde (1827-1891), who did so much for Septuagint research in the last century, set out a clearly defined programme of work for it: "It has been my intention for years to recover the three official recensions of the Septuagint known to us from Jerome, to have them printed in parallel columns, and to draw further conclusions from the comparison of these three texts" [3]). Lagarde therefore enjoined the classification of Septuagint manuscripts, and the assignment of them to the separate recensions with the help of quotations in the Fathers and other criteria. From this point it was then proposed to go further back toward the original text. For the recovery of this original, those readings were to be preferred which were furthest from the Masoretic text.

Much has been done towards this end, especially in the Septuaginta Unternehmen der Göttinger Gesellschaft der Wissenschaften under the inspired leadership of A. Rahlfs (1865-1935). But the goal proposed by Lagarde could not be attained. It has already been pointed out that

[1]) *Librorum Vet. Test. Canonicorum pars prior graece* (1883).

[2]) A. Rahlfs, Paul de Lagardes wissenschaftliches Lebenswerk im Rahmen einer Geschichte seines Lebens dargestellt. *Mitt. d. Sept.-Unternehmens d. Ges. d. Wiss. zu Göttingen* 4, 1 (1928), p. 77.

[3]) P. de Lagarde, Septuagintastudien, *Abhandl. d. Göttinger Ges. d. Wiss.* 37 (1891), p. 3.

the Hesychian recension is not recoverable. Moreover, the material itself compelled a modification of Lagarde's principles. The problem differs from book to book, but two examples may suffice:

a) In his edition of Genesis (Stuttgart, 1926), Rahlfs differentiates between two large groups—Origen and the text of the Catena-group [1])—six smaller groups, and in addition one minuscule with the text of Lucian. Seven majuscules and several minuscules could not be fitted into any group.

b) In Ziegler's edition of Isaiah (Göttingen, 1939), the available material was divided into the following four groups: I. The text of Alexandria, represented by Codices Alexandrinus, Marchalianus, some minuscules, Cyril of Alexandria, etc. [2]). This group best preserves the original text of 𝔊, but has been influenced by later material, particularly by the recensions (notably 𝔊^{h}). II. The hexaplaric recension, represented by Codices Vaticanus, Venetus, the Syro-hexaplar, minuscules and the church Fathers Eusebius of Caesarea, Basil the Great and Jerome. III. Lucian's recension may be shown in a main group of five minuscules and in several sub-groups, and further in the commentaries of Theodoret and of (Pseudo-)Chrysostom. The latter explicitly and enthusiastically defends the Lucianic recension against Palestinian attacks. IV. The Catena-group.

From these two examples it appears that the surviving material is much more varied than Lagarde presupposed in his programme. It can, however, be grouped, though admittedly only to a limited extent in Genesis, not indeed in the three classic recensions, but in text-groups whose comparison leads back to an older text. Thus it could be said that the proposals of Lagarde were justified in their essentials, though needing to be modified [3]).

8. Paul Kahle's Thesis. But does the picture of the development of the Septuagint which has guided Lagarde and his followers really correspond to the facts? Does it not depend upon the idea that a translation, to which different laws apply, may be treated on the analogy of an original text? Paul Kahle, in particular, has repeatedly raised this question and

---

[1]) Catena is the name given to a commentary consisting of a chain-like compendium made up of the exegetical comments of various church Fathers, dating from the sixth century onwards. The Catena manuscripts offer their own special, late recension of the text, which is also taken over in other manuscripts with the omission of the Catena itself.

[2]) Cyril, Patriarch of Alexandria 412-444, is an important witness through his commentaries on a number of Old Testament books to the text used in Alexandria (quoted in BH as 𝔊^{Cyr}). 𝔊^{Cyr}

[3]) Cf. on this H. Dörrie, *Z.N.W.* 39 (1940), pp. 57ff. and P. Katz, *Theol. Zeitschrift* 5 (1949), pp. 1ff. (English version in *Actes du Premier Congrès de la Fédération Internationale des Associations d'Etudes Classiques* (Paris, 1951), pp. 165-182). Cf. also P. Katz, *Philo's Bible* (1950).

vigorously challenged Lagarde's method. His views are most fully set out, with the inclusion of much of the evidence, in the Schweich Lectures for 1941 [1]). A somewhat detailed account must be given of this discussion, since it touches upon the central problem of Septuagint research, and, if proved right, would give it a new direction.

Kahle begins from a new interpretation of the Letter of Aristeas. He too regards it as legendary, but suggests that we should consider the purpose for which it was composed. It concerns a translation of the Torah which was regarded as authoritative by the Jewish community of Alexandria. "There cannot be any doubt that the letter was written as propaganda for this standard translation". (p. 134). The letter itself makes clear that this translation was not the first, for it refers to older, unreliable translations (§§ 314-316). For Jews who lived in the Greek-speaking area, Greek translations were as necessary as were the Aramaic Targumim for their Palestinian brethren (cf. p. 56). The first attempts at such translations must go back to about 300 B.C., and cannot have been very satisfactory, so that alterations were continually made to them. Thus arose the desire and the necessity for a reliable and authoritative Greek text, which was produced by a commission set up by the Jewish community in Alexandria [2]). "It is this *revised* version with which the Letter of Aristeas is dealing". (p. 137). As the letter, according to the modern view, was written about 100 B.C. or somewhat earlier, we must set the origin of the standard text (for the Torah alone) in this period.

But this standard text did not succeed in establishing itself immediately or exclusively, any more than has happened in other similar cases. Other translations remained in use, and we find traces of them in the Old Testament quotations in Philo, Josephus, the New Testament [3]) and other texts, even though the original position has been somewhat obscured by later correction in accordance with the text of 𝔊. In the book of Judges too, where the Codex Alexandrinus and the Codex Vaticanus differ so greatly that even Lagarde spoke of two different translations, the explanation is that we have two forms of an Old Testament Targum.

So far as we know, Judaism made no attempt to achieve a standard text for any books beyond the Torah, which represented the real Canon. Even the standard text of the Torah, the Septuagint, was completely

---

[1]) P. Kahle, *The Cairo Geniza* (1947), pp. 132-179; a summary of the conclusions there drawn was published by Kahle in the *Festschrift O. Eissfeldt* (1947), pp. 161-180. The basic hypothesis is to be found already in *Theol. Stud. u. Krit.* 88 (1915), pp. 410ff.

[2]) It seems probable that this commission met on the island of Pharos. Philo tells us (*de Vita Mosis* II. 5-7) that an annual festival was held there to commemorate the completion of the Septuagint.

[3]) Particularly at variance with the text of 𝔊 is the quotation of Isa. xlii. 1-4 in Matt. xii. 18-20.

abandoned in the second century and replaced by new translations (cf. pp. 37ff.) which adhered closely to the authoritative Hebrew text. This Hebrew text was, for Judaism, the final standard of authority.

The Christian Church, however, soon needed a standard text of the Bible in Greek. This was achieved when, after an interim period in which various translations taken over from the Jews were used side by side, only one of these was transmitted further and the others were allowed to lapse. The name "Septuagint", with all the prestige which it carried, was transferred in the second century A.D. to this text of the whole Old Testament, which, as a collection of various translations, could not really give a unified impression. "The manuscripts handed down in the church lead us at best to a standard text used in the church, which had, however, only gradually established itself and does not mark the beginning of the development" [1]).

Thus Kahle, if we may briefly summarise his view, regards 𝔊 on the analogy of the Aramaic Targum. Just as there is no unity at the beginning in the case of the Targum, but a striving after such unity after centuries of development in the hands of unknown persons, so it is also with 𝔊, the Greek Targum. Because of this, Kahle's view of Septuagint research differs essentially from that of Lagarde and his followers: "The task of scholarship here is not the reconstruction of the imaginary original text of this translation, or an approximation to it, but the careful collection and examination of all the fragments and traces of older forms of the Greek Bible which we can discover. Only thus can we be in a position to gain a true picture of the Greek version of the Old Testament.' [2]).

We cannot here undertake to examine the material set out by Kahle and so decide the question as to whether it can or must all be interpreted as he does. T. W. Manson agrees with him [3]), P. Katz has contested Kahle's thesis [4]). We must wait for further competent examinations of

---

1) Kahle, *Festschrift O. Eissfeldt*, p. 177.

2) Op.cit. p. 180. In connection with the discovery of the leather scroll with the Greek text of the Minor Prophets (cf. below p. 51), P. Kahle has re-examined the older material, mainly of Jewish origin. He remarks on this; 'It is a mistake to regard these texts as normative, firmly fixed Bible translations. They can only be properly understood if they are seen as forms of a Greek Targum, which, as has happened with the Aramaic Targums of the earlier period, were circulated in very divergent drafts, which aimed at closer and closer assimilation to the Hebrew original, and which influenced each other in a variety of ways. That this is the case would appear much more clearly if we had more Greek texts of the Bible deriving from the Jews'. (*T.L.Z.* 79 (1954), cols. 89f.)

3) *Dominican Studies* 2 (1949), pp. 183ff.

4) *Theol. Zeitschrift* 5 (1949), pp. 1ff. (English version in *Actes du Premier Congrès de la Fédération Internationale des Associations d'Études Classiques* (Paris, 1951), pp. 165-182); id. *Philo's Bible. The aberrant Text of Bible Quotations in some Philonic Writings and its place in the Textual History of the Greek Bible* (1950). Whereas Kahle sees in those Bible quotations which differ from the normal text of the Septuagint, the remains of an old Jewish translation used by Philo himself, Katz

Kahle's thesis, made on a broad basis. Without anticipating the results of such examinations, we may note that arguments of pure principle do point to the broad conception which he has set out. As with the majority of other Bible translations, we should expect to find a plurality of attempts, especially in that part of the Old Testament where no text could claim absolute authority, i.e. in the Prophets and Writings. If Judaism possessed a translation, and that not a very satisfactory one, for so important a text as the Old Testament, it would be natural to find a second and third attempt being made. Kahle therefore rightly differentiates between an original text and a translation, and in the examination of the material which he has set out the fundamental question which he asks must also be seriously considered: "The editor of a dialogue of Plato must naturally endeavour to come as near as possible to the original text written by Plato. But can we speak of such an original text in the case of a translation of the Bible?" [1]).

9. The Septuagint and the Hebrew text. No other translation has received such attention in the work of textual criticism as that of 𝔊. Not only was it highly valued in antiquity, but in the nineteenth century it was in practice regarded by many scholars as more valuable than 𝔐. As its tradition goes back to pre-Christian times, it was thought possible to reconstruct with its help an older, pre-Masoretic text, which would stand closer to the original than 𝔐. But to-day we can see that 𝔊 is not, and was never intended to be, simply a philologically exact translation. Many different factors and motives played their part in its formation. An uncritical use of it, without sufficient regard to these factors, inevitably leads to erroneous conclusions. In what follows a few important points are indicated and it may again be recalled that 𝔊 differs so much from book to book that generalisations can only be made with considerable reserve.

a) If we are tempted to prefer 𝔊 to 𝔐 as an older witness to the text, we must at once recall how lacking in unity is its transmission. Whereas 𝔐 has clearly remained very nearly constant in its consonantal text from the second century onwards, the Septuagint manuscripts, even centuries later, differ widely. Lagarde was from his own standpoint quite right in demanding the establishment of a unified "original text" as a preliminary to the use of 𝔊 in textual criticism. Kahle has now fundamentally

believes that these quotations are to be traced to a late recension of the Septuagint influenced by Aquila, which have displaced those from the original Septuagint text in some of the Philo manuscripts. Cf. on this the review by G.D. Kilpatrick, who expresses this judgment: 'Thus while Dr. Katz has made an important contribution to the study of Philo's text, he has not convinced us that the aberrant text is a recension of the LXX and not the remains of a distinct translation. The question remains open'. (*J.T.S.* N.S. 2 (1951), p. 89). Kirkpatrick agrees with Katz 'that the aberrant text in the Biblical quotations does not come from Philo'.

[1]) Kahle, *Festschrift O. Eissfeldt*, p. 162.

questioned this procedure. But even those who disagree with him must admit that we are to-day still very far from an original text which can be set over against 𝔐 as a unified whole.

But even if we did possess this original text, could we then prefer it to 𝔐 merely on the grounds of its age? This raises the question of the Hebrew text used by 𝔊. Is it necessarily better because it is older than 𝔐? We have already noted that in hundreds of cases 𝔊 agrees with the Samaritan (pp. 31f.). This and other observations have led to the view that the Hebrew text used by 𝔊 was one of those popular texts mentioned earlier (pp. 12f.). This view, which is held by Kahle, is most forcefully argued by Nyberg in reference to the book of Hosea: "𝔊 and 𝔖 both go back to old popular recensions which were in circulation among the Diaspora Jews, whereas 𝔐 offers a careful recension which stands in relation to the Diaspora text just as the texts of the classical authors established by the scholars of Alexandria stand in relation to the popular texts of those authors which are now available to us in the Egyptian papyri" [1]).

At this point a word may be added concerning the script of the text used by the Septuagint, since this problem touches closely upon textual criticism and has already led to far-reaching consequences. The question has been much discussed since 1923, when in an essay F.X.Wutz put forward his theory, developed later in larger works [2]), that the translators of the Septuagint worked with a Hebrew text transcribed into Greek letters. This transcribed text is supposed to have been much corrupted by scribal and other errors, or to have been wrongly understood by the translators. Working from these assumptions, Wutz believed he could re-establish the original Hebrew text. It cannot be denied that transcribed texts did exist. But there are so many points which militate against the assumption that 𝔊 depends upon such a text that Wutz' hypothesis has not found acceptance. Only for a few isolated instances is it perhaps applicable. By and large the parent text of the Septuagint was probably written in the new Aramaic script, which already in many of its forms approximated closely to the square script [3]).

b) How is 𝔊 to be assessed as a translation? What presuppositions did the translators bring to their work, by what tendencies were they influenced, how accurately does their work reflect the original? The answers to these questions are important for deciding in what way and how far 𝔊 may be utilised in textual criticism. We can here indicate only a few characteristic features which may be taken as examples:

---

[1]) H. S. Nyberg, *Z.A.W.* N.F. 11 (1934), p. 254.

[2]) F. X. Wutz, *Th. Bl.* 2 (1923), cols. 111ff.; later *Systematische Wege von der Septuaginta zum hebräischen Urtext* (1937), etc.

[3]) Cf. the various works of J. Fischer, e.g. In welcher Schrift lag das Buch Isaias der Septuaginta vor? *B.Z.A.W.* 56 (1930).

i) The language of 𝔊 is the so-called Koine, the common Greek of the Hellenistic period. Naturally in a translation made by Jews from the Hebrew there appear Hebraisms and Aramaisms, but these are fewer in number than used to be assumed. The discovery of the papyri in Koine Greek since the end of the nineteenth century has made this clear.

Even where the translators were most concerned to depart as little as possible from the original, there must inevitably be alterations due to the character of the Greek language. Thus sentences were subordinated to one another rather than co-ordinated. One example may serve (Gen. xxiv.28): 𝔐 ותרץ הנערה ותגד לבית אמה; 𝔊 καὶ δραμοῦσα ἡ παῖς ἀπήγγειλεν εἰς τὸν οἶκον τῆς μητρὸς.

In the case of a word so broad in meaning as the Hebrew דבר, the translators did not merely give the literal equivalent (ῥῆμα, λόγος etc.), but sought out expressions suitable to Greek language and thought. Thus for דבר we find in Exod. i.18 πρᾶγμα; xii.35 συντάσσειν; xviii.16 ἀντιλογία; xviii.22 κρίμα; xxiv.14 κρίσις; viii.8 ὁρισμός; iv.10 ἱκανός; v.13, 19 καθῆκον; xvi.4 τὸ (τῆς ἡμέρας); xviii.11, 14 τοῦτο; xxix.1 ταῦτα; v.11 οὐδείς (with negative) [1]). It would be quite wrong to assume that the translators had a different Hebrew text before them at these points.

Often the Hebrew demanded more in lexicographical and grammatical knowledge than the ancient translators possessed. Thus they clearly did not understand the exact meaning of the comparatively common word דֶּבֶר (pestilence), but either rendered it as θάνατος or read it as דָּבָר (Hos. xiii.14 δίκη; Hab. iii.5; Ps. xc.3 λόγος; Ps. xc.6 πρᾶγμα) [2]).

Ziegler's verdict on the translator of the book of Isaiah is that he "was not over-concerned to reproduce his original exactly, word for word; he had no hesitation in simply omitting difficult or rare words if the sense of the sentence was not thereby disturbed, or dividing up phrases or joining them together differently if he could not make sense of his original. Often he appears to have been governed by a particular thought, and translates the sections in question in accordance with this thought. Thus in Isaiah we meet with many translations which can properly be described as 'free' " [3]).

ii) The Jews of the Greek Diaspora did not differ only in language from those to whom we owe the Hebrew Old Testament. They lived in a world where social conditions, thought and not least belief were different. This environment changed them. It 'Hellenised' them. Thus they speak of God in more abstract, philosophical terms than the 'Hebrews', and

---

[1]) G. Bertram, *Th.R.* N.F. 10 (1938), p. 153 where further examples may be found.

[2]) G. Bertram, *loc.cit.*, pp. 155f.

[3]) J. Ziegler, *Untersuchungen zur Septuaginta des Buches Isaias* (1934), pp. 7f. Cf. also I. L. Seeligmann, *The Septuagint Version of Isaiah* (1948).

try to avoid the anthropomorphic and anthropopathic expressions which are so characteristic of the Hebrew Old Testament. In Exod. xix. 3, Moses does not climb up to God, but to the mount of God; in Exod. xxiv. 10 f., the elders do not see God, but the place where God stands. In Jos. iv. 24 the phrase יד יהוה is translated δύναμις τοῦ κυρίου. The expression that 'God repented' of something is avoided by circumlocution [1]).

Of particular significance is the enlarging of the conception of God by the use of κύριος for the divine name יהוה. "The Bible, in which God is called Yahweh, is the Bible of one nation; that, in which God is called κύριος, is the Bible of the world" [2]).

In other places the translators, by avoiding literal translation, tried to exclude the possibility of a theological misunderstanding. Thus they did not employ the common Old Testament picture of God as 'the Rock' (צור), but substituted other expressions. Since in Hellenistic religions, rock and stone were used as symbols, abodes, or even as representations of the godhead, "the use of this picture in the Greek Old Testament, the Septuagint, which, in contrast to the Hebrew original, was always directed towards missionary, propagandist and apologetic purposes, would have led to serious misunderstandings, as if a rock were worshipped as God in the Old Testament. So the metaphor is sacrificed to the literal meaning. The Septuagint gives a new stamp to the text of the Old Testament, but in this preserves the spirit of the Old Testament revelation of God" [3]).

iii) The efforts of the translators to make the Old Testament intelligible to the circle of readers living in Egypt, led them to use concepts belonging to the Egyptian and Alexandrian environment which were by no means exact equivalents of the Hebrew expressions. Thus the נגשים (slave-drivers) of Exod. v. 6, 10, 13 become the ἐργοδιῶκται (overseers of work, taskmasters) known to us also from papyri of Hellenistic Egypt [4]). Similarly in the extremely difficult list of articles of female attire in Isa. iii. 18-24, which the translator did not exactly understand, he solved the problem by including suitable articles from his own time and environment. "We cannot indeed here describe his work exactly as 'translation'; the equivalent is not found for most of the expressions, but some other object is set in its place. Thus it comes about that the Greek translation

---

1) E. Stauffer, *Th.W.B.z.N.T.* III (1938), p. 110; where further examples may be found. Cf. C. T. Fritsch, *Anti-anthropomorphisms of the Greek Pentateuch* (1943), and the review by T. W. Manson, *J.T.S.* xlvi (1945), pp. 78f.; and, for a discussion of the problem, J. W. Wevers, *Th.R.* N.F. 22 (1954), pp. 174ff.

2) A. Deissmann, *Neue Jahrbücher für das klassische Altertum* 11 (1903 I), p. 174. Cf. C. H. Dodd. *The Bible and the Greeks* (1934).

3) G. Bertram, *Z.A.W.* N.F. 16 (1939), p. 101.

4) Cf. I. L. Seeligmann, *Jaarbericht ex Oriente Lux* II, 6-8 (1939/42), p. 388.

often contains quite different objects and cannot be used for the exact rendering of the Hebrew words" [1]).

Finally, we may indicate the effort to show the relevance of the ancient words by pointing to the circumstances of Egyptian life. In Deut. xxiii. 18 (E.V. 17), we read: There shall not be a sacred prostitute (קדשה, 𝔊 πόρνη) of the daughters of Israel, neither shall there be a sacred prostitute (קדש, 𝔊 πορνεύων) of the sons of Israel". The choice of the words πόρνη and πορνεύων instead of the word ἱερόδουλος corresponding to קדש already changes the sense of the passage. But it is even more significant that 𝔊 adds: οὐκ ἔσται τελεσφόρος ἀπὸ θυγατέρων Ισραηλ, καὶ οὐκ ἔσται τελισκόμενος ἀπὸ υἱῶν Ισραηλ. τελεσφόρος and τελισκόμενος refer to taking part in the Mysteries. In ancient Israel, sacred prostitution was the temptation which must be resisted; in Hellenistic Egypt, it was the Mysteries [2]). Like the translators of the Targumim, the Egyptian translators felt themselves justified in bringing out the relevance of the text by expansion [3]).

We may summarise the position by saying that the language and content of 𝔊 must be understood against the particular historical and religious situation in which it came into being and on which it was intended to make its impression. This makes its use in textual criticism more complex. Certainly it is an important, indeed indispensable witness to the text. But it is only after careful assessment of its nature, its particular method of translation, and its history, that it may be used for text-critical work. Bertram has rightly said: "The Septuagint belongs more to the history of Old Testament exegesis than to that of the Old Testament text. It can only be used as a witness to the text if its own understanding of the Old Testament text has first been made clear" [4]).

10. Manuscripts. The manuscript material for 𝔊 is very extensive. In making their edition (cf. below p. 55), Holmes-Parsons collated 311 codices according to their reckoning (actually 297), including 20 majuscules. A. Rahlfs in 1914 in his "Verzeichnis der griechischen Handschriften des Alten Testaments" [5]) counted more than 1500 complete and fragmentary manuscripts (up to and including the sixteenth century). In addition there are quotations in the Fathers and translations from 𝔊 into other languages as indirect evidence. Recent decades have brought a valuable enrichment of the material

[1]) J. Ziegler, *Untersuchungen zur Septuaginta des Buches Isaias* (1934), p. 208.

[2]) Cf. Seeligmann, *op.cit.* p. 390 d.

[3]) Influences of Jewish tradition as it can be found set out in Talmud and Midrash, may also be observed in 𝔊. Cf. most recently on this L. Prijs, *Jüdische Tradition in der Septuaginta* (1948).

[4]) G. Bertram, *B.Z.A.W.* 66 (1936), p. 109.

[5]) In the *Nachrichten der K.Ges. d. Wiss. zu Göttingen*, Phil.-hist. Kl. (1914), Beiheft.

in the finds of papyri, which are older than anything that was known hitherto.

a) Papyri.

i) Papyrus Greek 458 of the John Rylands Library in *Pl. 24*
Manchester [1]), from the middle of the second century B.C., provides the oldest surviving Greek Biblical text. The six fragments, extracted from the wrapping of a mummy, belong with Papyrus Fouad 266 (cf. p. 132) *Pl. 25*
and the leather scroll containing the Greek text of the Minor Prophets found in 1952 [2]), to the few surviving fragments of the Greek Bible from pre-Christian times, whose Jewish origin is probable or certain. They contain parts of Deut. xxiii.24-xxiv.3; xxv.1-3; xxvi.12, 17-19; xxviii.31-33, some fifteen verses in all. They include a number of unusual readings, either unique or shared with very few other authorities [3]).

ii) The Chester Beatty Papyri (= 𝔊 Beatty) are, from their age 𝔊 Beatty
and extent, the most important papyri. They were described at the time as *Pl. 26*
the most important discovery for Biblical textual criticism since that of the Codex Sinaiticus. There are fragments of eleven codices, which contain parts of nine Old Testament and fifteen New Testament books, of the book of Enoch, and of a Homily of the Church Father Melito of Sardis. They belong to the second to fourth centuries A.D., and form presumably the remains of a Christian library, probably situated in the Fayyum. The main part of these manuscripts, discovered by the local inhabitants, was purchased about 1929 by the Englishman Chester Beatty; other sections came into the possession of the University of Michigan and of the American John H. Scheide. Smaller fragments are in Vienna, in Italy and in private possession [4]). Of Old Testament material there are considerable portions of Gen., Num., and Deut.; fragments of Isa. and Jer., parts of Ezek., Dan., Esther and fragments of Sir. The text of Daniel is particularly valuable, since in Daniel the translation of Theodotion

---

[1]) C. H. Roberts, *Two Biblical Papyri in the John Rylands Library* (1936).

[2]) This scroll, to which reference has been made several times already, was found in August 1952 by Beduin of Taʿamira in a cave in the Wilderness of Judaea whose exact location has not been specified. It was acquired by the Palestine Museum of Archaeology in Jerusalem. The surviving sections belong to the books of Mic., Jon., Nah., Hab., Zeph., and Zech. Barthélemy, who has given a provisional report, including readings from it, dates it towards the end of the first century B.C. C. H. Roberts would assign it to the century from 50 B.C. to 50 A.D. From texts and coins which were found with it, it can be deduced that it was deposited during the revolt of Bar Kochba (132-135 A.D.), but it had already been much used by then. The whole scroll has not yet been published, but what has so far been disclosed shows that it is to be rated of very high importance. Cf. D. Barthélemy, *R.B.* lx (1953), pp. 18-29 and P. Kahle, *T.L.Z.* 79 (1954), cols. 81-94. Cf. also above pp. 5, 38f., 45.

[3]) Cf. the detailed examination by J. Hempel, *Z.A.W.* N.F. 14 (1937), pp. 115ff.

[4]) Publications: F. G. Kenyon, *The Chester Beatty Biblical Papyri*, 7 vols. (1933-37); A. C. Johnson, H. S. Gehman, E. H. Kase, The John H. Scheide Biblical Papyri: Ezekiel, *Princeton University Studies in Papyrology* 3 (1938).

superseded that of 𝔊 (cf. p. 38), with the result that only one eleventh century manuscript with the text of 𝔊 was known.

Pl. 27 There must further be mentioned the Berlin fragments of a Genesis manuscript (end of the third century: Gen. i.16-xxxv.8), which was published in 1927 together with parts of a codex of the Minor Prophets from the late third century [1]. Of relatively late date is the papyrus
$\mathfrak{G}^{\text{Pap Lond}}$ book in the British Museum (= $\mathfrak{G}^{\text{Pap Lond}}$) from the seventh century, containing Ps. x.2-xviii.6 and xx.14-xxxiv.6.

b) Manuscripts. Among Greek manuscripts a distinction is made between Majuscules or Uncials (in capitals) and Minuscules (in small letters). In antiquity only the capital letters were used, placed side by side in books without joining, though in ordinary use, in letters and such like material, they were joined together (cursive). From the cursive script there developed in the Middle Ages the so-called small letters. Up to the eighth century there were only Majuscules; in the ninth and tenth centuries Majuscules and Minuscules side by side; from the eleventh century onwards, only Minuscules. But even though the Minuscules are thus later, they may nevertheless be valuable witnesses to the text if the lost Majuscules, from which they were copied, were good texts. It is important to realise, for purposes of textual criticism, that up to the eighth century the letters were written with no word division, no accents, breathings or punctuation.

As sigla for the manuscripts, Holmes-Parsons used Roman numerals
$\mathfrak{G}^{\text{XI}}$ for the Majuscules (e.g. $\mathfrak{G}^{\text{XI}}$), Arabic numerals for the Minuscules (e.g.
$\mathfrak{G}^{62.147}$ $\mathfrak{G}^{62.147}$). Later, Lagarde introduced Roman capitals for the Majuscules, of which many have come into common use and are employed in BH.

Here are mentioned, in chronological order, the manuscripts to be found cited in BH [2]:

$\mathfrak{G}^{\text{B}}$ i) Codex Vaticanus (B). Fourth century. Vatican Library. Complete for the Old Testament, but Gen. i-xlvi.28 and Ps. cv.27-cxxxvii.6 were added in the fifteenth century. This manuscript enjoys very great authority. Rahlfs thought that its content and text suggested Lower Egypt as its place of origin.

Pl. 28 $\mathfrak{G}^{\aleph}$ ii) Codex Sinaiticus (א, also S). Fourth century. Discovered in 1844 and 1859 by Tischendorf in the Monastery of St.Catherine on Mount Sinai. A small part in Leipzig (Codex Friderico-Augustanus), the bulk in the British Museum (since 1933, formerly in Leningrad), place of origin possibly Palestine. According to recent research, the manu-

[1]) H. A. Sanders and C. Schmidt, *The Minor Prophets in the Freer Collection and the Berlin Fragment of Genesis* (1927).

[2]) It is not possible here to go into questions of the form of text or the value of the surviving papyri and manuscripts. For this cf. the introductions to the Göttingen Septuagint, H. B. Swete, *An Introduction to the O.T. in Greek* (2nd ed. 1914), and F. G. Kenyon, *Our Bible and the Ancient Manuscripts* (4th ed. 1948).

script was written by three scribes, of whom two were also active as correctors. Later correcting hands may also be discerned. The correctors are indicated in BH as $\aleph^{c.a,\,c.b,\,c.c.}$ Of the Old Testament there survives Gen. xxiii.19-xxiv.46, Num. v.26-vii.20 (both with gaps), I Chron. ix.27-xix.17, Ezra-Neh. from Ezr. ix.9 onwards, Esther, Tobit, Judith, I, IV Macc., Isa., Jer., (to Lam. ii.20), Joel to Mal. (in Greek order), Pss., Prov., Ecc., Songs., Wisd., Sir., Job.

iii) Codex Alexandrinus (A). Fifth century. British Museum. $\mathfrak{G}^{A}$
Presented to Charles I of England in 1627, formerly in the Patriarchal Library of Alexandria (whence its name). Of the Old Testament there is wanting: I Sam. xii.17-xiv.9; Ps. xlix.20-lxxix.11.

iv). Codex Colberto-Sarravianus (G). Fourth/fifth century. *Pl. 29* $\mathfrak{G}^{G}$
Largest part in Leyden, a smaller section in Paris, one leaf in Leningrad. Contains Gen. xxxi.5 to Judg. xxi.12 in the Hexaplaric recension with Aristarchian signs (cf. pp. 39f.).

v) Codex Ambrosianus (F.). Fifth century. Ambrosian Library $\mathfrak{G}^{F}$
in Milan. Contains Gen. xxxi.15 to Jos. xii.12 (with gaps).

vi) Codex Freer (Θ). Fifth century. Bought by Freer in 1906 in $\mathfrak{G}^{\Theta}$
Gizeh, now in the Smithsonian Institution in Washington. Contains Deut. (v.16-xvi.18 missing), and Jos. (iii.3-iv.10 missing).

vii) Codex Ephraemi Syrus rescriptus (C). Bibliothèque $\mathfrak{G}^{C}$
Nationale, Paris. A palimpsest, named from the upper writing which belongs to the thirteenth century and contains the works of Ephraem Syrus. In the lower writing, from the fifth century, are fragments of Job, Prov., Ecc., Songs, Wisd., Sir., New Testament.

viii) Codex Cottonianus (D). Fifth/sixth century. British Museum. $\mathfrak{G}^{D}$
150 fragments of a manuscript destroyed by fire in Ashburnham House in 1731, of which an old collation also exists from before the fire. Only contains Gen.

ix) Codex Marchalianus (Q). Sixth century. Vatican Library. *Pl. 30* $\mathfrak{G}^{Q}$
Contains Isa., Jer., Ezek., Dan. and the XII. Hexaplaric readings in the margin, which enhance the value of the manuscript (cf. p. 41).

x) Codex Coislinianus (M). Seventh century. Bibliothèque Natio- $\mathfrak{G}^{M}$
nale, Paris. Contains Gen.—I Kings viii.40 (with some gaps), with scholia and Hexaplaric notes (cf. p. 41).

xi) Codex Lipsiensis (K). Seventh/eighth century. University $\mathfrak{G}^{K}$
Library, Leipzig, formerly in the Sabas Monastery near Jerusalem. Bought by Tischendorf in 1844. A palimpsest, written over in Arabic in 885-886. The lower writing contains rather small parts of Num. to Judg. To this manuscript belong also six leaves in Leningrad, also with fragments of Num. to Judg.

xii) Codex Basiliano-Vaticanus (N) Eighth century. Vatican $\mathfrak{G}^{N}$
Library. Formerly belonged to the Basilians in Rome. Belongs with $\mathfrak{G}^{V}$

and with it contains large sections of the Old Testament apart from the Psalms. Gen. i-Lev. xiii.59 is missing, among other sections.

𝔊V xiii) Codex Venetus (V). Second part of the foregoing.

𝔊Γ xiv) Codex rescriptus Cryptoferratensis (Γ). Palimpsest, lower writing eighth century, upper writing thirteenth. Grottoferrata in the Alban Hills. The lower writing contains fragments of some of the Minor Prophets and of Isa., Jer., Ezek. and Dan.

𝔊E xv) Codex Bodleianus Geneseos (E) Ninth/tenth century. Bodleian Library, Oxford. Contains Gen. i-xlii.18 (with gaps), written in Majuscule. To the same manuscript belong leaves written in Minuscule, containing Gen. xlii.18 -I Kings xvi.28; these are in Cambridge (one leaf), Leningrad (146) and London (16). The manuscript was found by Tischendorf and presumably comes from the Monastery of Sinai.

𝔊W xvi) Codex Atheniensis (W). Thirteenth century. National Library, Athens. Contains the historical books and Esther, Judith and Tobit.

11. Editions. In theory there are two possible procedures open to the editor of an ancient text which has been transmitted in different forms in various manuscripts: a) It is possible to print the text of one manuscript and note variant readings from other manuscripts in the apparatus. The reader must then examine all the material included and make his own judgments. b) It is possible to attempt to reconstruct a text by choosing from the various readings those which appear to be the oldest attainable. By this eclectic procedure we get a scientific recension which can be checked by the examination of the material offered in the apparatus. The first method was used in all the earlier great editions; the second for the first time in the Göttingen Septuagint. The method which best suits the Septuagint material is still being discussed.

The main editions are the following:

Pl. 41 𝔊C(om)pl a) The edition in the Complutensian Polyglot (1514-1517: 𝔊C(om)pl). The material upon which it is based has not survived. For the Book of the Twelve, J. Ziegler [1]) has demonstrated frequent coincidence with the Lucianic text-form, with the third century papyrus codex edited by Sanders (cf. p. 52), with the margin of minuscule 86, and with the Coptic and Old Latin translations. From this it appears that the Complutensian Polyglot had as the basis for its Greek text one 'which transmitted quite ancient readings, lacking to us in the manuscripts which we know' [2]).

Its text is therefore of particular value.

𝔊Vn b) The Aldine (Venice, 1518: 𝔊Vn) offers a late text of little value. J. Ziegler [3]) has demonstrated for the Book of the Twelve that the text of the Aldine edition derives from a manuscript now lost of which the

[1]) *Biblica* 25 (1944), pp. 297-310.
[2]) J. Ziegler, *op.cit.* p. 309.
[3]) *Biblica* 26 (1945), pp. 37-51.

larger part was derived from minuscule 68, and the small remaining part from 97. 'It was unfortunate that the editor based the Aldine edition upon a manuscript which transmitted a late text, dependent upon the Catena group, strongly influenced by hexaplaric and Lucianic readings, as this is to be found in the two manuscripts 68 and 97. [1]).

c) The Sixtine (Rome, 1587), an official edition produced at the order of Pope Sixtus V. In the main it offers the text of $\mathfrak{G}^{B}$; where this is wanting, several Vatican manuscripts are used. There is also a rich collection of variants. The use of $\mathfrak{G}^{B}$ marks a real step forward, though this is impaired by dependence upon the Aldine edition [2]). The Sixtine edition provided the standard for many editions up to the nineteenth century, including that of the London Polyglot (1654-57), Holmes and Parsons (1798ff), van Ess (1824 and later), the Polyglot of Stier and Theile (1847-55), Tischendorf (1850 and later), and the edition of the Clarendon Press (Oxford, 1875), on which is based the concordance by Hatch and Redpath (1897ff.).

d) Holmes and Parsons, *Vetus Testamentum Graecum cum variis lectionibus* (1798-1827). The text is based upon the Sixtine, and to this are added the variants of about 300 specially collated manuscripts. In addition references are given to quotations in the Fathers, and to daughter translations. The wealth of material in this collection in five large folio volumes has not been surpassed. It is referred to in BH ($\mathfrak{G}^{\text{MSS}}$ (Holmes-)Parsons = manuscripts according to Holmes-Parsons).

$\mathfrak{G}$ MSS (Holmes-) Parsons

e) H. B. Swete, *The Old Testament in Greek*, 3 vols. (1887-1891 and several later editions). A convenient, much used edition, which prints $\mathfrak{G}^{B}$ (the gaps filled from A and א) and contains in the apparatus the readings of several important uncials.

f) Brooke-McLean-Thackeray: *The Old Testament in Greek according to the Text of Codex Vaticanus, supplemented from other Uncial Manuscripts, with a critical Apparatus containing the Variants of the chief ancient Authorities for the Text of the Septuagint* (Cambridge, 1906ff.). The editors, considering that the time had not yet come for a critical edition, offer the material quite objectively. The text, with the correction of obvious mistakes, is that of $\mathfrak{G}^{B}$ (gaps filled from A and א) [3]). In the apparatus there are noted all the uncials, about thirty selected minuscules, daughter translations, Philo, Josephus and early Christian writings. Up to the present Gen. (1906) to Tobit (1940) have appeared.

g) The second alternative—the provision of the text in a critical

---

[1]) J. Ziegler, *op.cit.* p. 51.

[2]) According to Lagarde and Rahlfs, with whom Ziegler agrees, the Sixtine presents an Aldine edition corrected from $\mathfrak{G}^{B}$ (and other manuscripts). Cf. J. Ziegler, *Biblica* 26 (1945), pp. 49f.

[3]) From Exod. onwards, instead of the first hand, the text of the corrector of B is utilised where it agrees with the main line of trdition.

edition—was first achieved in the Göttingen Septuagint: *Septuaginta, Vetus Testamentum Graecum auctoritate Societatis Litterarum Gottingensis editum.* Here is printed not the text of one single manuscript, but at each point the reading which appears the best in the light of the manuscript tradition as a whole, with due consideration of the Hebrew text. The apparatus offers a comprehensive body of manuscript evidence, arranged according to text-groups (recensions). This makes it possible for the reader, independently of the decisions of the editor, to gain a picture of the transmission. The goal is the best text attainable, which does not involve the claim that the original has been discovered in every case. The editions are provided with valuable introductions. For the plan of this undertaking, which ultimately goes back to Lagarde, and for criticism of it, cf. above pp. 42 ff. There have appeared so far: *Psalmi cum Odis*, edited by Rahlfs (1931), *I Macc.* by Kappler (1936), *Isaiah* (1939), *The Twelve Prophets* (1943), *Ezekiel* (1952), *Susanna Daniel, Bel et Draco* (1954) by Ziegler. Rahlfs produced the book of *Ruth* in 1922 and *Genesis* in 1926 in a smaller form.

h) A convenient critical edition of the whole Septuagint, especially intended for the use of students and clergy, and modest in price, was produced by A. Rahlfs in 1935 at the Privilegierte Württembergische Bibelanstalt. It depends in the main on the three chief manuscripts B, א, A.

As an indispensable aid to work on 𝔊 there must further be mentioned: Hatch and Redpath, *A Concordance to the Septuagint*, 2 vols. (1897); Supplement (1906).

12. The Samaritikon. The Samaritan Pentateuch was also translated into Greek. Origen several times quotes this as *Samareiticon.* Some small fragments belonging to the fifth or sixth century have been assigned by Rahlfs to this translation. (cf. P. Glaue and A. Rahlfs, Fragmente einer griechischen Übersetzung des samaritanischen Pentateuchs [*Mitteilungen des Septuaginta-Unternehmens*, 2 (1911)]).

C. THE ARAMAIC TARGUMS (= 𝔗)

1. Origin and character. It is well known that in post-exilic Judaism, Hebrew ceased to be generally spoken and was replaced by Aramaic, which had become the official language of the Persian Empire. Hebrew was, of course, still understood and used in intellectual circles, particularly among theologians. But for the benefit of a large part of the Jewish community it became necessary to combine the normal readings in Hebrew from the scriptures in worship with a translation into Aramaic. This translating was called *targem*, the translator *turgeman*(*a*) or *meturgeman*(*a*), and the translation itself *targum*. Since the need was felt at an early date, the custom must be old and certainly pre-Christian. The Jewish tradition which connects it with Ezra may be right.

In worship the translation might only be given orally, not read from a scroll, presumably in order that a distinction should be preserved between the translation and the really sacred text, the Hebrew. It is clear, however, on various grounds—for example, that a Targum scroll of the book of Job was laid before Rabbi Gamaliel, the teacher of Paul—that in the pre-Christian era there were already written Targums. But the development from oral translations makes it natural to believe that the Targums varied from place to place. It is true that the Hebrew text and its normal interpretation in Judaism remained determinative, but it was possible for individual characteristics to appear in the form of words, the extent of paraphrase, interpretation, re-presentation etc. Thus there was not at first one sole, authoritative Targum, but a series of different Aramaic translations.

These translations have in varying measure certain features in common, indicative of their practical purpose. The community was to be educated and edified, to have an explanation of the contemporary message of the text. Thus the interpretative element is nowhere so strong as in the Targums. They paraphrase, they explain by insertions, they re-interpret the text, often rather boldly, in accordance with the prevailing theology of their time. They indicate its relevance to contemporary life and political circumstances, and so forth. More particularly, they endeavour to avoid anthropomorphic and anthropopathic statements about God. This method of treating the text in the Targums, in which in certain cases little note is taken of the actual meaning of the Hebrew, reduces their value as witnesses to the text, but makes them important documents in the history of Old Testament exegesis [1]).

2. The various targums. a) Only a fraction has survived of the many and various translations which once existed. The first group of Targums described here did not undergo an official redaction, and reveal particularly clearly the characteristics of the older Targum type just mentioned. α) Remains of an old *Palestinian* Targum on the Pentateuch have survived in fragments of seven manuscripts of the seventh to ninth centuries (edited by P. Kahle, *Masoreten des Westens* II (1930), quoted in BH as 𝔗P-Targum palaestinense). This is not a simple translation from the Hebrew, but rather one with considerable explanatory material of a midrashic or homiletical nature. Variants in passages which have survived in duplicate show that there is no question of a 𝔗P

[1]) A particularly bold re-interpretation was necessitated under the influence of anti-Christian polemics in Isa. lii. 13-liii. 12. The translation is now conveniently to be found in J. Jeremias, *Th. W. B. z. N. T.* V(1952), pp. 691ff. English translation in J. F. Stenning, *The Targum of Isaiah* (1949).

𝔗 J II definitive text. β) The Targum *Jerusalem II* (quoted in BH as 𝔗 J II), also called the *Fragment-Targum,* contains only the midrashic elaborations to individual verses, so that the continuous translation is lacking. As a comparison with the Palestinian Targum just mentioned shows, the Fragment-Targum is 'nothing else than a collection of the midrashic explanations of single verses taken from the Palestinian Targum to the Pentateuch' [1]). (Edition: M. Ginsburger, *Das Fragmenten-Targum* (*Targum Jeruschalmi zum Pentateuch*) 1899). γ) The Targum on the Pentateuch known as *Pseudo-Jonathan*, or *Jerusalem I* (edited by M. Ginsburger
𝔗 J in 1903 from a manuscript in the British Museum, quoted in BH as 𝔗 J) also has special characteristics. It contains the text of the official Targum Onkelos, amplified with midrashic material such as was customary in Palestinian Targums, but which was found to be wanting in the Targum Onkelos. It received its present form only in the Islamic period.

b) The Targums which are best known and of greatest importance for Judaism are markedly different from those so far mentioned. They are the Targum *Onkelos* on the Pentateuch, and the Targum *Jonathan* on the Prophets. Here we are dealing with *official* Targums, whose wording was finally established definitively in Babylonia, and not before the fifth century A.D. Their names have possibly been erroneously derived from those of the Greek translators Aquila (= Onkelos) and Theodotion (= Hebrew Jonathan), for it was known that they had endeavoured to produce literal translations to correspond to Jewish understanding of the Old Testament. Actually these two Targums can hardly be the work of individuals, but were presumably created by commissions, which established an official translation conforming to Jewish standards, revised according to the Hebrew text, and considerably purged of midrashic additions, to replace the various forms of text which were in circulation. They thus mark a definitive point in the history of the Targums. They established themselves firmly in Palestine only at a later period. Both these Targums attempt a fairly literal rendering of the Hebrew text, and as a result, as earlier with Aquila, the language—a literary form of Aramaic which was understood in all Aramaic-speaking lands [2])—had to suffer.

Of these two, the greater authority was accorded to the Targum Onkelos
𝔗 O (𝔗 O), and to this, as to the Hebrew original itself, a Masora was supplied [3]). The text was edited by A. Berliner (1884-1886), following the Editio Sabioneta of the year 1557.

The Targum Jonathan, which contains much more haggadic material, was published by P. de Lagarde from the Codex Reuchlinianus (*Prophetae*

[1]) P. Kahle, *The Cairo Geniza* (1947), p. 125.
[2]) Cf. P. Kahle, *The Cairo Geniza* (1947) p. 119.
[3]) Edited by A. Berliner (Leipzig, 1877), and by S. Landauer (Amsterdam, 1896).

chaldaice (1872), quoted in BH as 𝔗 L). The Targum on Joshua and 𝔗L
Judges in the Yemenite tradition was edited by Fr. Praetorius in 1899
and 1900 (quoted in BH as 𝔗 Pr). 𝔗Pr

c) Reference is made in BH to the following editions, as well as to those
already mentioned: the Targum on the Writings edited by P. de Lagarde
in 1873 (*Hagiographa chaldaice*, quoted in BH as 𝔗 L); a selection of 𝔗L
Targum texts from old manuscripts and editions which was edited by
A. Merx in 1888 with notes and a glossary (*Chrestomatia targumica*,
quoted in BH as 𝔗 M); the Targums of the Rabbinic Bible published in 𝔗M
1524-25 by Jacob ben Chayyim (quoted as 𝔗 B), and the rich collection 𝔗B
of material in the London Polyglot of Brian Walton (1654-57, quoted
as 𝔗 W). 𝔗W

3. The Samaritan Targum (quoted in BH as ш 𝔗). Among the шT
Samaritans also the sacred text, the Pentateuch, was translated into Aramaic. No official edition was, however, produced. The result is that almost every surviving manuscript offers its own particular text. "We have here an excellent example of a Targum in its earlier stage, through which generally translations of the Bible pass before a definite text is created" [1]).

Editions: The Paris Polyglot (1645) and the London (1657) from a manuscript of the year 1514; C. Petermann, *Pentateuchus Samaritanus* (1872-91, not satisfactory from a scholarly point of view) [2]). P. Kahle has edited and explained fragments in the *Zeitschrift für Assyriologie* XVI (1902) and XVII (1903).

D. THE SYRIAC TRANSLATION (PESHITTA = 𝔖) 𝔖

1. Name and Literary problems. The Syriac Church, at a fairly late date, described the translation of the Old Testament in normal use as the Peshitta (pronounced in Jacobite Syriac Peshitto), that is, the "simple" (translation). It is not clear in what sense this word is used. It may be that the translation is thus indicated as the normal (vulgaris), or perhaps as one which does not paraphrase. Alternatively it may be intended to differentiate between the "simple" and that which goes back to the Hexapla, that is, the "Syro-hexaplar" (cf. p. 40).

The literary problems of the Peshitta are rather complex and are made more difficult because we have no critical edition which sets out the manuscript tradition. Nor is there information from antiquity concerning the origin of the Peshitta.

---

1) P. Kahle, *Cairo Geniza* (1947), p. 37. Cf. also Lea Goldberg, *Das Samaritanische Pentateuchtargum* (1935).

2) The curious story of the origin of this edition has been revealed by P. Kahle, *Z.D.M.G.* lxi (1907), pp. 909 ff. Cf. also *Cairo Geniza*, pp. 37f.

The text of the Peshitta, especially that which is to be regarded as its oldest form, agrees in the main with the Masoretic text. This is particularly true of the Pentateuch, but applies also to such other books as have been examined in detail. Intimate acquaintance with the Hebrew original and with Jewish tradition is so clear that there is no doubt of Jewish influence on the Peshitta. How far this goes in detail, and also how it is to be explained historically, is still being discussed. Recently Kahle has declared decisively in favour of actual Jewish origin, for at least part of the Peshitta [1]. In the first Christian century the royal house and leading circles of the kingdom of Adiabene (east of the Tigris) were won over to the Jewish faith for several decades (approximately 40 to 70 A.D.). Hence they needed a translation into their own language, Syriac, of the Old Testament, especially of the Pentateuch. Thus the origins of the Syriac translation would fall in the middle of the first century A.D. Kahle assumes that for the Pentateuch an older form of West Aramaic translation (Targum) was transcribed into East Aramaic (Syriac), and Baumstark and Peters have endeavoured to show that in other books too there are close contacts with the Targums.

According to other scholars the Peshitta is of Christian origin. But even so its character can only be explained if it is assumed that to some extent older Jewish translations were used or that the translation must have been done by Jewish Christians.

In either case we must reckon with considerable later work on the translation. The Septuagint especially had a very great influence upon it and this must be borne in mind when the Peshitta is evaluated for textual criticism. Agreements between the Peshitta and the Septuagint against the Masoretic text may have been occasioned by the later intrusion of Septuagint readings. In such cases the twofold witness has no more value than that of the Septuagint alone.

Undoubtedly the Peshitta goes back to various hands. It reveals considerable unevenness between the different books and has a complex inner history to which the existence of two text types in the manuscripts also bears witness. Further researches are necessary to establish satisfactorily the history and textual importance of the Syriac version of all the Old Testament books. But even so it may be affirmed that among witnesses to the text the Peshitta holds an important place and must most certainly be taken into account in textual criticism.

2. Manuscripts and editions. As the Syriac Church divided in the fifth century into Nestorians and Jacobites, we have to differentiate between the Nestorian (East Syriac) and Jacobite (West Syriac) traditions.
Pl. 33 tions. From the fifth century onwards there appears a series of ancient

[1]) P. Kahle, *The Cairo Geniza* (1947), pp. 179ff.

Peshitta manuscripts. The most important is the West Syriac Codex Ambrosianus in Milan from the sixth or seventh century, published photolithographically by A. M. Ceriani, *Translatio Syra Pescitto Veteris Testamenti* (1867, $= \mathfrak{S}^{A}$). Its text is especially close to $\mathfrak{M}$. This is not, $\mathfrak{S}^{A}$ however, the result of late revision, but may well go back to the original Syriac text-form.

The quotations of the Syriac Church Fathers are also of importance, as, for example, Ephraem Syrus († 373) and Aphraates, who belong to the time before the division of the Church. The readings of Aphraates, whose 23 letters, belonging to the years 337 and 345, form the oldest surviving original work in Syriac, are indicated in BH by $\mathfrak{S}^{Aphr}$. $\mathfrak{S}^{Aphr}$

There is no edition of the Peshitta which is completely satisfactory from a textual point of view. The text of the Paris Polyglot of 1645 became the standard for other editions, but it depends upon a bad manuscript of the seventeenth century as its main source. Although the deficiencies of this edition were recognised, it was reprinted in an even worse form in the London Polyglot by Walton ($= \mathfrak{S}^{W}$). The sixth volume of this $\mathfrak{S}^{W}$ supplied also the readings of a few Syriac manuscripts. The following editions were all prepared for practical purposes, for the use of the surviving Syriac communities in the mountains of Kurdistan, at Lake Urmia and in North Persia. Their textual value is small. The edition by Lee (1823, quoted as $\mathfrak{S}^{L}$), depends in the main upon the London Polyglot. $\mathfrak{S}^{L}$ The edition of Urmia (1852, quoted as $\mathfrak{S}^{U}$), by the American Protestant $\mathfrak{S}^{U}$ Missionary Society, and that prepared by the Dominicans at Mosul in 1887-91, differ from the above mentioned in that they depend upon the East Syrian tradition.

Editions of individual books were made by W. E. Barnes. In 1904 there appeared "*The Peshitta Psalter according to the West Syrian text with an apparatus criticus*, and in 1914 the *Pentateuchus Syriace*, intended for practical use but taking into account his study of the manuscripts.

CHAPTER III

THE REMAINING TRANSLATIONS

𝔏 A. THE OLD LATIN (= 𝔏)

a. Origin and problems. In Rome itself Greek rather than Latin was used in religion and philosophy until a movement in the reverse direction began in the third century A.D. But Latin was in a much stronger position in Southern Gaul and in North Africa, and it is here that we first, about 150 A.D., come across Latin texts of the Bible. Tertullian (born in Carthage about 160) obviously employed a written Latin translation of the Bible of which the language was definitely different from his own. The Latin translation, like others, was the result of practical needs in worship and private use. At first the texts read in Greek in worship would be translated orally into Latin for those who could not understand; later the translation was written down and extended to all the Biblical books. It is clearly established that Cyprian († 258) took his Bible quotations from an Old Latin text.

The basis for this version—called Vetus Latina to distinguish it from the later translation by Jerome— was naturally the Septuagint customarily used in the Christian communities. The Vetus Latina forms an important witness to the Septuagint text, since it takes us back before the period of the recensions. But there are very great preliminary difficulties in the way of its use for textual criticism, and these must first be overcome by researches based upon an edition which gathers together all the material. The basic problem of Vetus Latina research is the question as to whether we are dealing with a single original translation or with several. Various statements by the Fathers suggest a plurality of translations, as when Augustine distinguishes the Itala from several other Latin translations. The problem is made all the more difficult since, even if an original translation did exist, it was not regarded as official and unalterable. Work upon it, particularly to improve its popular Latin and to bring it closer to its Greek basis, may have altered its original form in such diverse ways that the resulting texts would hardly reveal their common ancestry. We may definitely distinguish an African type and a European, and the latter may be further sub-divided. The name

Vetus Latina must therefore be regarded rather as a general term than as the name of an individual text. In view of the wealth of the tradition, which reveals continuous work on the texts, we cannot expect that more than a fraction of the material is uninfluenced by the recensions of the Septuagint.

2. Editions and manuscripts. As the Vetus Latina was superseded in the early Middle Ages by the Vulgate, interest in the manuscript tradition declined. Thus we find that it does not survive in complete manuscripts like 𝔊. We have rather to gather the material from fragmentary manuscripts, from liturgical books, quotations by the Fathers in commentaries, sermons and letters, and so forth. The Benedictine Pierre Sabatier (1682-1742) gathered together the material then known in *Bibliorum sacrorum latinae versiones* etc. (1739-49; = 𝔏). Sabatier prints 𝔏
in one column the most complete text of the Vetus Latina which he could find for each section, then the Vulgate, and various additional material for 𝔏 in the notes. There remained naturally many gaps in the 𝔏-text.

A series of unpublished Old Latin texts of the Old Testament was collected by S. Berger in *Notices et Extraits des Manuscrits de la Bibliothèque Nationale et autres Bibliothèques*, Tome 34, II (1893), pp. 119-152 (= $\mathfrak{L}^{L}$ (Berger)). 𝔏 (Berger)

A new edition conforming to modern standards and utilising the material available since Sabatier was begun in 1949: *Vetus Latina. Die Reste der altlateinischen Bibel nach Petrus Sabatier neu gesammelt und herausgegeben von der Erzabtei Beuron* (Editor: P. Bonifatius Fischer). This large edition is to include: 1. all Old Latin Bible manuscripts and fragments; 2. all quotations in the writings of the Church up to the time of Isidore of Seville (c. 560-636), and the important material from the later writers up to the Carolingian period. So far there have appeared: Vol. I (Sigla); Vol. II, Genesis.

In BH reference is made to the collections of Sabatier and Berger and also to the following manuscripts:

a) *Konstanzer altlateinische Propheten- und Evangelienbruchstücke mit* *Pl. 34*
Glossen, edited and arranged by P. Alban Dold (1923, = $\mathfrak{L}^{D}$). This is a $\mathfrak{L}^{D}$
complete edition and examination of the fragments of a manuscript of the Prophets, formerly in Constance, probably written in the fifth century in Northern Italy, which came to light in the binding of 26 parchment manuscripts from 1856 onwards. It contains fragments of Hos., Amos., Mic., Joel, Jonah, Nah., Ezek., Dan.

b) The Würzburg Codex, a palimpsest first published by Ernst Ranke, *Par palimpsestorum Wirceburgensium* (1871, = $\mathfrak{L}^{h}$). The lower $\mathfrak{L}^{h}$
writing belongs to the fifth century (probably from the centre of eastern France) and contains fragments of the Pentateuch and of the Prophets.

c) Codex Lugdunensis, in the city Library of Lyons (= $\mathfrak{L}^{L}$). $\mathfrak{L}^{L}$ *Pl. 35*

Editions: U. Robert, *Pentateuchi versio latina antiquissima e codice Lugdunensi* (1881); *Heptateuchi partis posterioris versio latina antiquissima e codice Lugdunensi* (1900). An uncial of the seventh century, probably written in Lyons. The manuscript, now damaged, contains parts of Gen. xvi.9 to Judg. xx.31.

𝔏Lg d) Codex Gothicus Legionensis, Léon, S. Isidoro (= 𝔏Lg). A Vulgate from the year 960. This contains numerous Old Latin readings in the margin by the same hand. As far as the Old Testament is concerned, they cover the Heptateuch, I and II Sam., I and II Kings, Chron.

e) Palimpsestus Vindobonensis, since 1919 in the Biblioteca
𝔏Vind Nazionale in Naples (= 𝔏Vind). The lower writing belongs to the fifth century, probably from Italy. Parts of Gen., Exod., Lev. survive. The part of it edited by Belsheim, *Palimpsestus Vindobonensis* (1885), is faulty (Dold, Fischer).

𝔙

B. THE VULGATE (= 𝔙)

1. Jerome's translation. We have seen that in the Latin-speaking Churches the Biblical text was in circulation in very different forms. For theological discussion and liturgical use a uniform and reliable text was badly needed. So it came about that Pope Damasus I (366-384) commissioned the preparation of a reliable text by Jerome, who, with his knowledge of Latin, Greek and Hebrew, seemed particularly suited to the task. Jerome was born somewhere between 330 and 340 in Dalmatia, had studied grammar and rhetoric in Rome, and had then dedicated himself to ascetic practices and theological studies, living in various places in the West and the East of the Empire. As a hermit in the desert of Chalcis, he had learnt Hebrew from a Jewish Christian, and later, already a priest, had studied under Apollinarius of Laodicea and Gregory of Nazianzus. He was called back to Rome in 382 and entrusted with the work on the Latin Bible, which he carried out first in Rome and then, from the autumn of 386, as head of a monastery in the neighbourhood of Bethlehem. His final work went far beyond the limits of the original plan. We can here only discuss his work on the Old Testament.

Various stages are to be distinguished:

a) Jerome first revised the Psalter rapidly (cursim) according to the Septuagint, which, in his day, enjoyed canonical authority. This revision was introduced into the liturgy of the city of Rome and hence received the name Psalterium Romanum. It is still used to-day in the office at St.Peter's and in the Psalm-texts of the Roman Mass [1]).

---

[1]) Edition: R. Weber, *Le Psautier Romain et les autres anciens Psautiers Latins* (Collectanea Biblica Latina X, 1953). The theory of de Bruyne (*Rev. Bénéd.* 42 (1930)) that the Psalterium Romanum has nothing to do with this revision by Jerome has not been generally accepted, so far as I am aware.

b) Jerome undertook a second revision of the Psalter in Palestine, using the Hexapla of Origen which was in Caesarea. This Psalter, which was first used in worship in Gaul and hence is called Psalterium Gallicanum, was soon adopted generally and still appears to-day in the official Roman edition of the Vulgate. It is essentially a revision of the Old Latin in accordance with the fifth column of the Hexapla. It appears that Jerome revised in this manner the rest of the Old Testament as well as the Psalter, but only the book of Job and fragments of Prov., Songs and Ecc. have survived.

c) The work which represents the real achievement of Jerome and marks his significance for the history of the text, and which exerted the most far-reaching cultural influence, was the translation of the Old Testament from the Hebrew, which he accomplished in the years 390-405. He alone among Western Christians, thanks to his knowledge of Hebrew, was capable of making this translation from the original. Quite apart from the severe attacks of those to whom he appeared as a "falsarius", we may judge how unprecedented this undertaking was from the disquiet felt even by Augustine at Jerome's setting aside the Septuagint, inspired and canonical in its authority, and going back to a text which no one in the Church but himself could understand. Augustine feared that this would bring about a division between the Greek and Latin Churches, and never gave up his objections to the ecclesiastical use of this translation from the Hebrew.

Jerome was, however, no iconoclast, and the independence of his translation must not be exaggerated. Having no dictionaries or grammars available to him, he had inevitably to depend most upon the Greek translations, the Septuagint, Aquila, Symmachus and Theodotion, and upon the instruction which he received from the Jewish side. As a result he was kept very much on traditional lines, and the influence of the material on which he depended is clearly observable in his work [1]. Moreover the distrust shown against his work by the majority of theologians, as well as his own churchmanship, would lead him to take careful account of the current Latin text. Many passages are re-interpreted in a completely Christian manner. On the other hand, the translation reveals the Graeco-Roman education of its author, even if much in the language must be regarded as due to the activity of later revisers. Thus the Rome edition now appearing (cf. below p. 67) points out "that the Ciceronic style of the Vulgate comes in large measure from Alcuin. Jerome did indeed approach classical Latin at many points, but nevertheless preserv-

[1]) How much Jerome was indebted to the later Greek translators, especially Aquila and Symmachus, is revealed by the amply illustrated study of J. Ziegler, Die jüngeren griechischen Übersetzungen als Vorlagen der Vulgata in den prophetischen Schriften, *Vorl.-Verzeichnis Braunsberg*, Wintersemester (1943/44).

ed more 'vulgarisms' (real or supposed) than the text hitherto available would suggest" [1]).

The work of Jerome thus presents from the beginning a very complex appearance and the later developments, which can only be briefly indicated in the next section, increased this complexity. This considerably impairs its value for textual criticism; to discover from the translation the Hebrew which Jerome used is difficult, and only possible after detailed study. Stummer rightly states: "Where Jerome agrees with the Septuagint or with the later translators over against our present Masoretic text, he is, in my opinion, to be disregarded. For that proves at most that the Septuagint at his time, or one of the later translators, read the text thus, but cannot prove without further ado that the Hebrew text which he used was also different from our own" [2]).

2. The history of the Vulgate. It was only over a period of centuries that Jerome's translation attained the general recognition which is indicated from the sixteenth century onwards in the name 'Vulgate' [3]). At the beginning of the seventh century it stood on a par with the Old Latin in respect and usage, and in the eighth and ninth it gained the lead. During the period when these two Latin texts of the Bible existed side by side, they must inevitably have influenced each other. The restoration of a pure text was attempted in the revisions made by Cassiodorus, formerly statesman of Theoderic the Great, in the sixth century [4]), and by Alcuin (730/5-804), a close associate of Charlemagne. The latter, as has already been pointed out, made considerable stylistic alterations. About the year 1100, Abbot Stephen Harding produced an important scholarly edition for the Cistercian monasteries. In the later Middle Ages great influence was exerted by a Paris recension which, from the scholarly point of view, was not entirely satisfactory. It was through this recension that the division into chapters, made by the Paris teacher Stephen Langton (afterwards Archbishop of Canterbury † 1228), found general acceptance.

For the later history of the Vulgate the decree of the Council of Trent of April 6th 1546 was of epoch-making significance; it declared the Vulgate to be the authoritative Bible of the Catholic Church, over against the many new translations "that is, in matters of belief and morals it is conclusive, though this does not meant that the Septuagint, or the original Hebrew text, and the Greek New Testament, are rejected or forbidden" [5]).

---

[1]) F. Stummer, *Z.A.W.* N.F. 17 (1940/41), p. 258.

[2]) F. Stummer, *Einführung in die lateinische Bibel* (1928), p. 123.

[3]) On the history of the name Vulgate, cf. E. F. Sutcliffe, *Biblica* 29 (1948), pp. 345 ff., and A. Allgeier, pp. 353 ff.

Pl. 37 𝔙A [4]) Possibly the famous *Codex Amiatinus* (= 𝔙A) of the eighth century, now in Florence, bears witness to this recension.

[5]) F. Stummer, *Einführung in die lateinische Bibel* (1928), p. 172.

The distinction thus given to the Vulgate necessitated an official edition of the text, which did not however appear for half a century. After a variety of preliminary attempts, there appeared the hastily drawn up edition made by Sixtus V himself (Sixtina, 1589), which was withdrawn after his death and replaced by the edition of Clement VIII (Clementina: first ed. 1592; the second and third editions of 1593 and 1598 included some improvements). Although even this edition cannot claim to have restored Jerome's text, it has remained the official text up till the present time. The edition commonly in use to-day, made by Hetzenauer and first issued in 1906, also contains the same text.

The Benedictine Order has been commissioned, since 1907, with the preparation of a comprehensive edition taking full account of the wealth of manuscript material (approx. 8,000 mss.), so as to give a complete picture of the textual tradition. After detailed preparatory work, it began to appear in 1926 under the title: *Biblia Sacra iuxta latinam vulgatam versionem ad codicum fidem iussu Pii PP. XI cura et studio Monachorum Abbatiae Pontificiae S. Hieronymi in urbe ordinis S. Benedicti edita.* So far there have appeared the Pentateuch, Josh., Judg., Ruth, Sam., Kings, Chron., Ezra, Tobit, Judith, Esther, Job, Pss. [1]).

A critical edition of Jerome's translation of the Psalter from the Hebrew which was not taken up into the Vulgate, has been made by De Sainte-Marie, *Sancti Hieronymi Psalterium iuxta Hebraeos* (Collectanea Biblica Latina XI, 1954).

C. THE COPTIC TRANSLATIONS (= 𝔎) 𝔎

Coptic is the language of the native Egyptian Christians and is written
mainly in Greek letters. Greek played a very great part in Egypt, but *Pl. 38*
not among the native peasant population. Christianity, as it spread at an early date in these circles, had therefore to use the popular language, Coptic, enriched by Greek words. As Coptic consists of various dialects, there were several linguistically different translations which are gathered together in BH and referred to as Coptic (= 𝔎). The oldest is undoubtedly the *Sahidic* (Upper Egyptian [2])) translation made from the Greek, Sah
which was undertaken probably by official ecclesiastical circles about the middle of the third century. This was followed by the *Achmimic*, made

---

1) It must be added that several books contained in the Vulgate were not revised by Jerome because he did not regard them as canonical — Baruch (with the Epistle of Jeremy), Wisdom, Sir., I and II Macc. These books appear therefore in the Old Latin translation.

2) According to P. E. Kahle, Jr., *Balaiza* (Oxford, 1954), Sahidic was the official dialect of the native population of Egypt, and the official language of Alexandria long before the spread of Christianity.

from the Sahidic, and later, perhaps in the fourth century, the *Bohairic* (Lower Egyptian), which was translated from the Greek independently of the Sahidic. For text-critical work, especially in the study of the Septuagint, these translations are important because of their ancient stamp. Many manuscripts and fragments of manuscripts which were written before the end of the fifth century A.D. have survived, and not a few which go back to the third or fourth century. On the basis of the material which Groussow and Ziegler have set out for the Minor Prophets [1]), Kahle has made the suggestion 'that the official text of the Septuagint which Origen established for the fifth column of the Hexapla, formed the basis of the Sahidic translation'. 'In the Sahidic version of the Minor Prophets, we may therefore very probably see a witness to Origen's Septuagint text, which was perhaps translated even in the life-time of Origen, or at any rate very shortly after his death, and which is attested for us in manuscripts from as early as the fourth century (Jonah in Budge, *Biblical Texts* [2])). It is a witness almost 400 years older than the Syro-Hexaplar translated by Paul of Tella in 616-617, which has ranked till now as the main source for Origen's Septuagint' [3]). From these statements it can be seen that the Coptic texts, and the Sahidic translation in particular, deserve special attention.

𝔄̈

D. THE ETHIOPIC TRANSLATION (= 𝔄̈)

Pl. 39 About the middle of the fourth century, the king of the kingdom of Aksum in Abyssinia and his people were won over to Christianity. A translation of the Bible from Greek must have been started soon after, but its completion certainly took a long time, possibly several centuries, as is thought by some scholars. How far this original translation survives in the existing manuscripts is open to question, for the earliest of these belongs to the thirteenth century. We must in any case reckon with considerable later revision. Ziegler has established the fact that the Ethiopic version of the Minor Prophets frequently agrees with the Alexandrian group of witnesses to the Septuagint. "The Ethiopic often has a very free rendering, partly because the translator was not altogether familiar with the Greek vocabulary, partly from a desire to make it smoother and to make the difficult Greek original easier to read" [4]).

---

[1]) Groussow, *The Coptic Versions of the Minor Prophets. A contribution to the Study of the Septuagint* (Rome, 1938); Ziegler, *Biblica* 25 (1944), pp. 105ff.

[2]) Cf. Plate 38.

[3]) P. Kahle, *T.L.Z.* 79 (1954), col. 94.

[4]) J. Ziegler, *Duodecim Prophetae* (1943), p. 25. Cf. also below p. 160.

E. THE ARMENIAN TRANSLATION (= Arm)

Arm

After an early period during which the Armenian national Church used Greek and Syriac as languages for literature and worship, the Armenian alphabet was created in the fifth century, and thereafter an Armenian literature came into being. In the course of this movement, the Bible was also translated. The first translation, at the beginning of the fifth century, was based, according to Armenian Sources, on the Peshitta. The final, official translation, which has come down to us and is supposed to have been made by Mesrob in about 430, depends upon the Septuagint, but shows clear Peshitta influence. It may be that this official translation was really only a revision of the first, in accordance with 𝔊, at least so far as some books are concerned [1]).

F. THE ARABIC TRANSLATIONS (= 𝔄)

𝔄

With the victory of Islam, Arabic spread widely and became the every-day language of Jews and Christians in the conquered lands. The need thus arose for Arabic translations of the Bible, and it was satisfied by several, mainly independent versions. The translation by Saadia Gaon, (a native of Egypt, who became in 928 head of the Jewish school at Sura in Babylonia), which depended upon the Hebrew text, survives in part. It was also taken over by the Samaritans in its original form, but has been continually subject to alterations, as we can recognise from surviving manuscripts. The *textus receptus* of the Arabic translation used to-day among the Samaritans is ascribed to a certain Abu Saʿid, who lived in the second half of the thirteenth century [2]). *Pl. 40*

Translations were also made into Arabic from the Septuagint, the Peshitta and other versions. The manuscripts and editions (especially in the Polyglots) contain in the main translations of very diverse origin. It is not therefore a unified Arabic translation which is indicated in BH by the sign 𝔄.

1) So in a private communication from Professor A. Vööbus of Chicago.

2) Cf. Paul Kahle, *Cairo Geniza* (1947), pp. 38f.

CHAPTER IV

TEXTUAL CRITICISM

A. THE AIMS OF TEXTUAL CRITICISM

The history of the text has shown that all our witnesses to it are far removed from the original text both in time and by long processes of transmission. They therefore contain a great variety of scribal errors such as any manuscript transmission occasions, and in addition some actual transformations of the original, deliberate or accidental. Scholarly study of the Old Testament cannot remain satisfied with this state of affairs. In the work of textual criticism the attempt is made to detect all such alterations and to restore the oldest text which can be recovered. This does not mean the recovery of the actual form in which the individual sentences were first conceived, but the form of the text which the Old Testament books had when they had already attained their present shape, as regards extent and content, and were becoming canonical, which happened with differences in detail from the fourth century B.C. onwards. Even if the goal of textual criticism is thus limited, there must be no illusions concerning the possibility of its attainment in detail. There are, on the one hand, corrupt passages whose correction must always remain uncertain unless new discoveries open up new possibilities. On the other hand, it must be observed that it was only when the process of canonisation reached its close that such a mechanical attitude was observed with regard to the text as may permit us to reckon with complete accuracy in the work of the copyists. Before this there was a period during which small alterations in the wording clearly evoked no adverse comment provided the sense was preserved [1]).

The pre-history of our existing Old Testament books is outside the province of textual criticism. Thus the reconstruction of the *ipsissima verba* of the prophets in what may be considered their original form, the separation of the strands of the Pentateuch, the investigation of questions of integrity, and such like, are all matters which are the concern of

---

[1]) Cf. what has been said about the 'popular' texts, and G. Douglas Young, *Oudtestamentische Studiën*, VIII (1950), p. 295, and earlier J. Wellhausen, *Der Text der Bücher Samuelis* (1871), pp. 16ff.

'Higher Criticism', literary criticism and exegesis. Even though in practice textual criticism, literary criticism and exegesis frequently come into contact with each other, and sometimes inevitably overlap, it is nevertheless desirable to preserve in principle the basic division of their different spheres of application.

B. CAUSES OF TEXTUAL CORRUPTION

1. General remarks. Since the goal of textual criticism consists in the removal of textual errors and the recovery of original readings, the textual critic must have a clear picture of the kind of errors which he may expect to find. Errors in the copying of a text can occur in all sorts of ways, as we know in our own experience. Sometimes it is not even quite clear afterwards to ourselves how, in our writing down or copying, this or that error did in fact occur. We can therefore scarcely expect to correct and explain every error which has slipped past the ancient scribes—perhaps simply as a result of fatigue. Moreover a gap in the text due to damaged writing material, or a word or group of words already illegible, may have given rise to a text which must now be regarded as doubtful or corrupt. One mistake may have occasioned several others, so that it is now impossible for us to trace the development exactly. It is justifiable therefore in many cases to assume that there is textual corruption which cannot now be explained. But naturally this assumption should be made as rarely as possible.

In addition to those corruptions which can no longer be explained because they depend on mere chance, there is a whole series of errors which occur over and over again when texts are circulated in manuscript form. If we can demonstrate the presence of such typical errors, we are on reasonably sure ground in restoring the text. For a reasoned diagnosis of the trouble points the way to the remedy. There are two main groups of such typical errors: those which are to be regarded as due to unconscious, mechanical mistakes by the copyist (errors in reading and writing); and alterations which are the result of deliberation, leading to a deviation from the text being copied (deliberate alterations).

2. Errors in reading and writing. [1]). These include all textual errors which result from misreading or miswriting (and also mishearing in the case of dictation). In order to demonstrate that such errors are not merely assumed by modern textual criticism, but really did occur, the examples are taken as far as possible from a comparison of 𝔐 and the newly discovered Isaiah Scroll (DSIa: cf. pp. 23f). We may then reckon

[1]) F. Delitzsch, *Die Lese- und Schreibfehler im Alten Testament* (1920) provides a wealth of material. Cf. also J. Kennedy, *An Aid to the textual Amendment of the O.T.* ed. N. Levison (1928).

with their occurrence elsewhere too. As we are only concerned here to prove the possibility of such errors by means of examples, the variants are simply set out without any detailed discussion.

a) The interchange of letters which look alike is the commonest cause of copyists' errors. In the square script interchanges took place most often between:

i) ב and כ: Isa. xxviii.20 𝔐 כהתכנס — DSIa בהתכנס; Is. xxviii.21 𝔐 כהר, כעמק — DSIa בהר, בעמק.

ii) ד and ר: Isa. ix.8 𝔐 וידעו — DSIa וירעו; Isa. xiv.4 𝔐 מדהבה — DSIa correctly מרהבה; Isa. xlvii.10 𝔐 ברעתך — DSIa בדעתך; Isa. xxxiii.8 𝔐 ערים — DSIa correctly עדים.

iii) ה and ח: Isa. xxx.33 𝔐 תפתה — DSIa תפתח; Isa. xlii.16 𝔐 מחשך — DSIa מהשוכים; Isa. xlvii.13 𝔐 (K) הברו — DSIa חוברי (having at the same time י for ו as Q); Isa. li.9 רהב — DSIa רחוב.

iv) ה and ת: Isa. xlii.25 𝔐 חמה אפו — DSIa correctly חמת אפו; in Judges vii.8 read צדת העם for צדה העם.

v) ו and י: Isa. v. 29 𝔐 ושאג — DSIa ישאג (so also Q); Isa. xi.6 𝔐 ומריא — DSIa ימרו; Isa. xxxiii. 13 𝔐 ודעו — DSIa ידעו.

vi) ע and צ: II Kings xx.4 𝔐 העיר nonn MSS Q Vrs חצר (confusion at the same time of ה and ח).

vii) כ and נ: Isa. xxxiii.1 𝔐 כנלתך — DSIa ככלותך.

For a large part of the Old Testament we must also reckon with the possibility of interchanges in the Old Hebrew script. Thus in Ps. xix.5 בהם may well have arisen from בים through the confusion of the Old Hebrew י and ה which are similar in form. As the Lachish Ostraka reveal, the letters א and ת, כ and נ, ע and ד are also much alike in the Old Hebrew alphabet.

In the assessment of readings in 𝔊 it is often important to remember that the Greek capitals may be confused in writing. This also occurs in the transmission of the New Testament text.

b) Inversion of letters is made easier by the lack of vowel signs and is therefore not uncommon. Isa. ix.18 𝔐 נעתם — DSIa נתעם; Isa. xxxii. 19 𝔐 העיר — DSIa היער; Isa. xxviii.1, 4 𝔐 גיא — DSIa גאי (as proposed also by L. Rost *Z.A.W.* N.F. 12 (1935), p. 292).

haplogr c) Haplography (= haplogr; single writing). This is where an omission is made when the same letter occurs twice together, or two similar letters, groups of letters or words follow each other directly.

i) *Omission of a single letter*: Isa. v.8 𝔐 בית בבית — DSIa בית בית; Isa. viii.11 𝔐 בחזקת היד — DSIa בחזקת יד; Isa. viii.19 𝔐 בעד החיים — DSIa בעד חיים.

In the Lachish Ostraka (III.9) we find the form חיהוה = חי יהוה which suggests that when two identical letters followed one another they were frequently written only once, even if they belonged to two different words. The reader could easily supply the correct reading. It may well be that we should consider the many cases of haplography in the Old Testament in the light of this possibility.

ii) *Omission of one of two identical or similar words*: Isa. xxvi.3f. 𝔐 בך בטוח בטחו — DSIa בך בטחו; Isa. xxxviii.11 𝔐 יה יה' — DSIa יה.

d) Dittography (=dittogr.). This is the accidental writing twice of a letter, a group of letters, a word or a group of words: Isa. xxx.30 𝔐 והשמיע—DSIa השמיע השמיע; in Isa. xxxviii.20, DSIa has repeated the whole of the previous verse. dittogr

e) Omission due to Homoeoteleuton (= homoeotel: similar ending). If two words stand near together and are the same, or have similar or identical endings, it is possible for the eye of the copyist to stray from the first of these words to the second and so to leave out several words. Isa. iv.5f. ... ברא יהוה ... ענן (יומם ועשן ונגה אש להבה לילה כי על כל כבוד חפה וסכה תהיה לצל) יומם מחרב. The words in brackets are missing from DSIa; the eye of the copyist passed from יומם in v.5 to יומם in v.6. Further examples may be seen in DSIa in Isa. xvi.8-9; xxiii.15; xxxvii.29; perhaps also in xl.7f. where the omitted section was later inserted. Less common is an omission due to similarity of the beginnings of words (Homoeoarchton). homoeotel

f) Incorrect joining or dividing of words. By contrast with Greek which was written up to the Middle Ages without gaps or dividing marks between the words (*scriptio continua*), there is no real proof that *scriptio continua* was used for Hebrew. In the Siloam Inscription and the Samaria Ostraka a word-divider is used regularly, and it is frequent also in the Lachish Ostraka. In the square script it was customary, as may be seen from the newly found manuscripts, to leave a gap between words, though admittedly this was sometimes so small that it could become doubtful where one word ended and another began. Two words could thus be wrongly joined together. The Lachish Ostraka also provide examples of a scribe writing two words without a gap between them in order to fit them into the space available. (IV.9; V.10). On the other hand a single word might be divided between two lines. Both of these can easily lead to misunderstanding and to words being wrongly joined together or divided.

The *wrong joining together of words* can clearly be seen in Amos vi.12. The reading usually adopted, בבקר ים for בבקרים, restores both the parallelism and the sense.

The *wrong division of a word* is found in 𝔐 in Isa. ii.20 לחפר פרות: DSIa correctly לחפרפרים. In Jer. ii.21 the text has been made unintelligible by the wrong division לי סורי הגפן; read with Duhm and many others לסוריה גפן (= into a stinking vine).

g) Errors due to vowel letters. Consonants were used as vowel letters from an early date, and, as the newly found manuscripts indicate, for a certain period they were employed in great profusion. If a vowel letter was later wrongly thought to be a consonant, this would naturally lead to an error in the text. Thus it appears from DSIa that א was used as a vowel letter for a (e.g. i. 17, 23 יאתום for יתום; i. 15 עאון for עון; and so frequently). In Amos ii. 7 such an א was wrongly treated as a root letter; read השפים for השאפים.

3. Deliberate alterations. Since the text of the Old Testament was not regarded as unalterable before the authoritative fixing of the consonantal form, we must clearly expect that those who were concerned with its transmission would from time to time make alterations, consciously and for some deliberate purpose. If we are to evaluate such alterations rightly, we must avoid the idea of 'falsification'. They were undertaken in good faith, and their purpose was not by any means to bring anything foreign into the text. The intention was to restore the correct reading, or to avoid what the copyist thought might lead to misunderstanding. They must belong to a time when it was still permissible to alter the letter of the text in order to make its spirit more readily understandable to the circle of readers or hearers for whom it was intended.

Many of these alterations can only be recognised with great difficulty, or presumably remain undetected, since the transmission of 𝔐 has only preserved variant readings to a very limited extent. Others belong in the realm of higher criticism, for the line of demarcation is here very fluid. Some part of the material may, however, be included at this point.

Thus certain small, common words were readily inserted into the text: e.g. ו, כל, אחד, עתה, אשר, שם, לאמר. This has already been indicated as characteristic of the popular text, but the manuscript tradition of 𝔐 has also preserved examples of it. "These words are nearly always inserted in support of an interpretation which is, in itself, quite possible. But the harm done is quite sufficient if as a result one of the possible interpretations of the passage now becomes obligatory, especially when the construction and relationship of whole sentences are influenced" [1]).

It is also understandable that a text which was not only the subject of learned study, but was read and heard repeatedly in the whole Jewish community, should be assimilated to the linguistic needs of this community. A rare word, or one used in an unusual sense, would give place to a more common one. For example in Isa. xxxix. 1 in 𝔐 חזק is used in the sense of 'become well'; but the usual word for this is חיה and this has in fact replaced חזק in DSIa at this point. Other cases of assimilation to everyday usage have been mentioned above (pp. 12f.). We have not suffi-

---

[1]) J. Wellhausen, *Der Text der Bücher Samuelis* (1871), p. 26.

cient ancient material to make comparisons and to demonstrate such alterations in 𝔐 in large numbers. But the parallel texts show that it was not free from such changes. It is a general rule that where the tradition has parallel versions of the same passage, the one with rarer, the other with more common words, the one with an involved text and the other reading smoothly, the former is in each case to be regarded as original.

Since the wording of the text varied before it was finally fixed, it was also possible to replace expressions which were religiously or morally repugnant. It has already been shown how this happened with the divine name בעל (cf. p. 14). Here is another example. In Job. i.5, 11, ii.5, 9 we read now ברך 'bless' (with God as object), where we should expect קלל 'curse' or some similar word; the scribes replaced the objectionable phrase 'to curse God' by a euphemism [1]).

Among deliberate alterations must be included also additions and glosses to the text [2]). Thus in I Kings xviii.19, 400 prophets of Astarte are mentioned with 450 prophets of Baal. The former are not mentioned in vv.22 and 40, where they ought not to be omitted if they really belonged to the original story. It therefore appears that they were added later, as the result of learned reflection.

Sometimes an expression was given a further explanation in the margin or between the lines, and the gloss was later taken up into the text. In I Kings viii.6 we find, together with the older expression דביר הבית the common later one קדש הקדשים. Often a gloss betrays its presence because it has not been taken into the text at exactly the right place, and it now interrupts the context. Thus, for example, in Gen. x.14 the marginal note 'from whom the Philistines came' was placed before the relevant words 'the men of Caphtor', whereas if it were original to the text it would stand after.

These alterations in the text give us a glimpse of an activity which is in many respects official, and goes back to an early date [3]). This wide field of study has unfortunately not yet been as systematically examined as is desirable.

C. THE METHODS OF TEXTUAL CRITICISM

1. General remarks. Textual criticism, like any other science, cannot lead to convincing results unless it is adapted to its subject matter and follows the methods demanded by it. Arbitrary procedure which hastily and unnecessarily sets aside the traditional text and puts

---

[1]) Cf. A. Geiger, *Urschrift und Übersetzungen der Bibel* (1857, new ed. 1928), pp. 267ff. This contains a great deal of material relevant to this subject.

[2]) On the glosses cf. now the instructive essay by G. Fohrer, Die Glossen im Buche Ezechiel, *Z.A.W.* N.F. 22 (1951), pp. 33ff.

[3]) P. Volz, *Z.A.W.* N.F. 13 (1936), pp. 103f.

personal conjectures in its place, results in a subjective form of text which remains historically unsound, and cannot claim any theological relevance. It is further likely to lead to a basic distrust of textual criticism as such, even where it is justifiable and necessary.

A strictly prescribed method for Old Testament textual criticism has never yet been laid down. It is indeed questionable whether it is possible to do so, since the state of the tradition is very varied, and what is proper to one case may not give results in another. There are, however, certain basic points, which are generally recognised, if not always in practice at least in theory, and these help to place textual criticism on a firm basis and to avoid the excesses of arbitrariness and subjectivity. These basic points are not specifically theological, but have developed from the application of the normal methods of scientific textual criticism to the particular needs of the Old Testament. Even the beginner is well-advised to be acquainted with them, for they provide him with certain standards for the assessment of the results of the textual criticism which he meets continually in his exegetical studies, and can then lead him on to his own consideration of the problems and to actual practice. They are therefore briefly outlined here.

2. The establishing of the traditional text. The starting point for all textual work must be the tradition itself. It must therefore first be determined which text is to be regarded as traditional. The various witnesses to the text must be examined, first 𝔐, and then the others, in approximately the following order of importance for textual criticism: ɯ, 𝔊, A, Σ, Θ, 𝔖, 𝔗, 𝔙, 𝔏, Sah, 𝔎, 𝔄, 𝔄, Arm. (For the reasons underlying this arrangement, compare the remarks made concerning each in the section on the history of the text). In each case the whole manuscript material should be considered, in so far as it is available.

In the case of 𝔐, for which the manuscript variants are to be found in Kennicott, de Rossi and Ginsburg, it is possible to give in the main a fairly simple picture, since real variants are very rare. A first sifting of the material may be undertaken as it is collected, by setting aside readings which are to be regarded as due to carelessness on the part of the scribes (misreading, miswriting, omission, dittography etc.), or to readily recognisable alterations (insertion of ו, כל, etc.). To obtain as objective a basis as possible for the later assessment of the readings which survive this preliminary sifting, it is necessary to attempt to create a picture of the general character of the manuscripts in which they occur. The fewer errors a manuscript reveals, the more likely it is to be reliable as a whole, and dependent upon a good tradition. Further, in general, the older it is, the more does a particular reading, which is possible both as regards language and meaning, merit attention: manuscripta ponderantur, non numerantur. The method adopted in BH of counting Hebrew manuscripts, following Kennicott or de Rossi, was unavoidable for the sake of brevity. But it has the disadvantage that it does not show which manuscripts favour a particular reading. In general, the Hebrew manuscripts have not yet been as fully examined with regard to their value, their special characteristics, and their interrelationships, as is desirable.

In the Versions, especially 𝔊, the manuscript tradition is much more complex. This must therefore first be clarified, before conclusions are drawn concerning the Hebrew original underlying them. For 𝔊, the editions of the Göttingen Septuagint, used intelligently, provide a valuable guide through the maze of variants. Here too a sifting of the material should accompany its collection. Variants within the tradition of 𝔊, for example, which can be recognised as corruptions within the Greek itself (e.g. confusion of letters), or as deliberate alterations (perhaps to obtain better Greek), may be set aside immediately. In assessing the manuscript variants of a particular translation, it must also be remembered that many texts of the translations have been assimilated to 𝔐. It may be suspected that a reading which agrees with 𝔐, side by side with one which diverges, is the result of such later assimilation. For the rest, the principle 'manuscripta ponderantur non numerantur' applies here as with the Hebrew manuscripts.

It is self-evident that translations which are dependent upon one particular version (normally 𝔊), or are influenced by it, can only be regarded as independent witnesses to the text if in a particular case it appears probable or certain that they have preserved the original text of a translation which has later been altered, perhaps by assimilation to 𝔐. Hence a reading which is, for example, attested by 𝔊 and 𝔏, is really only attested once, because 𝔏 is a daughter translation of 𝔊.

3. Examination of the traditional text. After the establishing of what may be regarded as the traditional text — a task which, as we have seen, is by no means a matter of mechanical collecting, but demands critical sifting of the material—the real examination of the tradition begins. It is convenient to divide this into two parts—the consideration of language and of matter. The main interest is centred upon 𝔐. Since 𝔐 depends upon direct transmission in the original language, and was handed down with great care, it deserves special attention in every case. To-day, the earlier tendency to underestimate the value of 𝔐 in favour of the Greek translation, or even in favour of modern conjectures, has been almost entirely given up, since 𝔐 has revealed itself repeatedly as the best witness to the text. Every deviation from it must therefore be justified. But this does not mean that we hold to 𝔐 in all circumstances, since it undoubtedly contains errors which can to some extent be corrected with the help of the other witnesses. It is clear from the history of the text that the vocalisation of 𝔐 has not the same significance as the consonantal basis, and that alterations of the vowel signs do not really rank as emendations (cf. pp. 17 ff.).

The general rule must be that where 𝔐 is unobjectionable, both as regards language and matter, it deserves to be preferred to all the rest of the tradition, unless there are in individual cases special reasons for favouring some other testimony. But the question whether 𝔐 is unobjectionable in language and matter can often be decided only after very detailed examination. Moreover the rejection of a reading of 𝔐 demands as a preliminary that every possible interpretation has been fully examined. It is not at all scientific to reject a reading in 𝔐 because it does not happen to conform to the particular point of view of the interpreter of the text. Where there is conflict, it is the scientific theory which must give way to the textual tradition and not vice versa.

The linguistic investigation means first a consideration of grammatical and lexical possibilities. Since research in these fields is still continuing, we must often look for new interpretations which are not yet included in the standard grammars and dictionaries. The possible meanings which, for example, a single word includes, can often only be seen if a concordance [1]) is used and every occurrence of the particular word in the Old Testament is examined. Not infrequently such 'internal interpretation', in which particularly the parallelismus membrorum is often useful, suggests possibilities of understanding the text which had not before been noticed, and enables good sense to be made of the traditional Hebrew text. Many generally accepted emendations have in this way been shown to be unnecessary. A further important aid to linguistic study is the consideration of the related Semitic languages. Light is often shed by them on words whose meaning is still obscure in the Old Testament. In addition to Arabic, which has been used for a long time, there have come into use Accadian, Old South Arabic, and Ugaritic among others, and Egyptian, a mixed Hamito-Semitic language, is important for loanwords in the Old Testament. This work, the material for which is being constantly increased by excavations, (recently, for example, by the texts from Ugarit and Mari), is naturally still being actively prosecuted, and many useful results may be expected from it. An example may be quoted from Hab. iii.6b, 7a: in the incomprehensible form לו תחת און

---

[1]) The concordance commonly used is S. Mandelkern, *Veteris Testamenti Concordantiae Hebraicae atque Chaldaicae* (2nd ed. 1937). The references in the *Handwörterbuch* of Gesenius-Buhl (17th ed. 1915), *Lexicon in Veteris Testamenti Libros* by L. Köhler (1953) and F. Brown, S. R. Driver and C. A. Briggs, *Hebrew and English Lexicon of the O.T.* (Oxford, 1907; corrected ed. 1952). take the place of a concordance for many words. The Privileg. Württ. Bibelanstalt is at present preparing a concordance to the Hebrew Bible.

there is concealed the word תחתאן 'destruction' with the preposition ל; this has been recovered from Ugaritic [1]).

Lastly in this connection it must be noted that a text may or may not appear probable on stylistic, metrical, form-critical or other grounds. Peculiarities which thus appear often lead to the recognition of additions, glosses, displacements or other dislocations of the original text. As our knowledge in several of these fields, for example that of metre, is still limited and open to discussion, and subjective judgments are particularly easy to make, it would be a good thing if there were more restraint and self-criticism than is normal.

The consideration of the matter of a passage concerns the question as to whether a particular point, an idea or a statement, can really be regarded as original to it in view of what is known to us of the very varied aspects of the world of the Old Testament. This approach leads to the recognition of later alterations, and to the setting aside of later additions. This is a point at which textual criticism comes into close contact with literary criticism and exegesis. It is therefore all the more necessary, from the point of view of method, to be clear whether objection is made to a text on textual, literary or exegetical grounds. The boundary of textual criticism which was indicated on pp. 70 f. may be recalled here and re-emphasised. As a final point in the consideration of the subject-matter, it must be recalled how fragmentary is our knowledge of the world of the Old Testament. We must reckon therefore with the possibility that a phrase is as yet incomprehensible to us because our knowledge is limited. As it increases — as it does with every excavation — we may hope one day to establish a good sense in passages which are still obscure. It is essential for the student to consider every new discovery connected with the world of the Old Testament, and to be ready to allow earlier attempts at a solution to be corrected by new knowledge.

Beside 𝔐 the translations must also be subjected to detailed examination, since it is possible that even where 𝔐 does offer an unobjectionable or at least a possible meaning, a translation which deviates from it may have preserved the original text. It is particularly important in the evaluation of the ancient versions for textual purposes that they should not be used piece-meal. We should not merely consider isolated readings, without taking into account the whole character of the relevant translation, its translation method, its bias, its intellectual background, and so forth. The references in the apparatus of BH are therefore to be regarded only as pointers, which are to be followed up by thorough study of the translations themselves. Only those readings which are not to be

[1]) cf. K. Elliger in *A. T. Deutsch* ad loc.; the suggestion goes back to Albright. For further material, cf. A. M. Honeyman, Semitic Epigraphy and Hebrew Philology in *The O.T. and Modern Study*, ed. H. H. Rowley (Oxford, 1951), pp. 264-282.

regarded as errors of translation, careless mistakes or deviations due to the language, spirit, bias, or technique of translation, may—re-translated into Hebrew—be placed beside 𝔐 as real variants.

4. Making a decision. After the evidence of the tradition has been collected and examined, the decision must be taken as to which text is to be regarded as the original, or the nearest approximation to it. When the various witnesses to the text are placed side by side, we find, in the main, the following patterns:

a) 𝔐 and the remaining witnesses offer the same intelligible and unobjectionable text. Here we may naturally assume that the original has been handed down, and the tradition may be followed without question. It may perhaps seem rather strange that this point should be made, since it appears so obvious. But anyone who knows anything of the history of Old Testament scholarship will recognise that it is not a superfluous statement.

b) Where 𝔐 and some or all of the other textual witnesses, properly assessed, deviate from one another, giving real variants, the following possibilities may be envisaged:

i) 𝔐 can be seen to be certainly or probably the original text, whereas the variants of the other witnesses are secondary (due to misreading, misunderstanding, deliberate or unconscious correction). Here 𝔐 is to be followed.

ii) The readings of 𝔐 and of the other witnesses offer different but equally good or at least passable sense, without it appearing that one or other of the readings is clearly secondary, or even probably so. In this case, it will be normal to give the preference to 𝔐 as a matter of first principle. But other points must also be considered. The rule may apply of preferring the reading which is more difficult from the point of view of language and subject-matter (*lectio difficilior*). Or the other rule may apply that of two readings that one is to be chosen which most readily makes the development of the other intelligible. Often in such cases it will be necessary to say that there can be no certainty (*non liquet*).

iii) The text of 𝔐 is doubtful or impossible on grounds of language or content, whereas the other witnesses offer a satisfactory reading. If there are reasons for showing the originality of this reading, and more particularly if it is possible to show how the text of 𝔐 could have become thus corrupted, we may legitimately correct 𝔐 from it. The objection that in this case 𝔐 offers the more difficult reading does not operate, because there is not here a contrast of easier and more difficult readings, but of meaningless, corrupt readings and meaningful ones. If, however, the intelligible reading in a version has come about only because the translator had the Hebrew text before him already in a corrupt form, and tried to improve it in his own way —that is to say, if the version offers nothing more than an ancient conjecture—then we must recognise that the original text of the passage has not been preserved at all.

c) In this case, and similarly when neither 𝔐 nor the other witnesses offer a possible or probable text, improvement may be attempted by conjecture, or it may be noted that such improvement can hardly be expected (*crux interpretum*). We are justified in making a conjecture because the corruption of the text has crept in so early that it already faced the earliest translators. If such a conjectural improvement is attempted, it must be with as near an approach as possible to the existing text-form, and with due consideration of the causes of textual corruption sketched above pp. 71 ff. (cf. for example, the conjecture on Jer. ii.21, p. 73). The scholar must further be aware of the uncertainty of a text established by such means.

5. Psychological considerations. Finally, it may be stressed that in all work of textual criticism due note must be taken of the psychological aspect. That is to say, wherever an error is assumed, we must consider how the error could have originated, and for this the possibilities of corruption noted already (cf. pp. 71 ff.) may serve as pointers, though they do not by any means exhaust the subject. If we can discover how an error originated, we are on the way to the establishment of the original text with some certainty. Thus the careful observance of the psychological aspect gives to textual criticism the necessary assured basis, makes proposed emendations more convincing, and provides a proper finish to the work. Not the least of its services may also be the prevention of too drastic a handling of the text.

No book of the world's literature has been so often copied, printed, translated, read and examined as the Bible. To none has so much attention been given, to hand it on faithfully, to understand it, and to make it intelligible to others. We may think of the Sopherim and Masoretes, with their strict principles and precise investigation, of the translators, the mediaeval monks drawing letter after letter in their quiet cells, and the exegetes, for example, Luther, who devoted the greater part of his activity as an exegete to the Old Testament.

What was the real motive behind all this concern for the Biblical record? Certainly not mere interest in a valuable antiquity, which it was desired to preserve because of its age. So much literature as old or older than the Old and New Testaments has been lost and only sparse records or occasional fortunate discoveries of fragments bear witness to its existence. It is for quite another reason that men have been so continuously concerned with the Bible, to ensure that it should be preserved for their contemporaries and for those who came after. It was the recognition of its value for every generation, the knowledge that here is the source of Life, because God himself speaks in it.

It is this which makes us to-day concerned with the Bible. It would be quite wrong if our discussion, concerned with the actual fortunes of the Old Testament text, were to be understood as if it were written merely as a matter of academic interest in antiquities, or even to show the deficiencies which belong to the Bible because of its transmission by men. There is indeed a profound theological significance in thinking of the Word of God expressed in the 'form of a servant', as this, its human form, is revealed in the history of its transmission. But we are not concerned so much with its deficiencies and errors as with endeavouring to overcome them. We are concerned to discover the original form of the Old Testament record, and of that of the Bible as a whole, because we wish to be confronted with the Word itself, and not merely with that which fallible men have made of it in the process of transmission. The history of the text, and the textual criticism which depends upon it, belong therefore inseparably with any Old Testament study which is intended to be consciously theological. "Without textual criticism there can be no understanding of Old Testament religion, and no real Old Testament theology. Everyone who penetrates more deeply into the problems of textual criticism knows that theology and textual criticism are not two separate fields of study, but interdependent, even at the deepest level" [1]).

But, the modern reader may ask, does concern for the letter actually lead to our being confronted with the real matter of the Bible? Shall we not rather find this in quite a different manner? Someone may be tempted to appeal to that misunderstood remark of Luther's "that no one can understand even one iota of the Scriptures unless he has the Spirit of God". (De Servo Arbitrio. W.A. 18, 609). But we must remember that it was the same Luther who so forcibly contrasted the 'Spirit' of the Enthusiast (Schwärmer) with his insistence upon the 'Word', and that he also pointed out repeatedly that God "gives neither Spirit nor faith without the external Word and Sign in which he has enshrined it". (W.A. 18, 136). Luther means, by these apparently contradictory sayings, that God has linkedhis Spirit to the written and spoken Word; but he controls the working of his Spirit in the Word by his own unlimited sovereign will [2]). "Literal understanding and spiritual understanding are therefore not to be separated. We cannot acquire the one without at the same time having the other" [3]). Since this is so, the concern for the letter, to which this book seeks to contribute, has real theological significance.

---

1) P. Volz, *Z.A.W.* N.F. 13 (1936), p. 113.
2) H. Bornkamm, *Das Wort Gottes bei Luther* (1933), p. 12.
3) K. Holl, *Gesammelte Aufsätze* I (6th ed. 1932), p. 558.

PLATES

Plate 1

THE STONE OF MESHA, KING OF MOAB (C. 840 B.C.)

cf. p. 4. Illustration from Kenyon, *Bible and Archaeology* (2nd ed. 1949).

In 1868 a missionary named Klein discovered this victory inscription on black basalt in Diban (= Dibon), the capital of Mesha, north of the river Arnon in Transjordan. The stone was later broken up by Beduin, but the text was put together again and restored from a paper squeeze made beforehand. Height 1 metre, breadth 0.6 metres, now in the Louvre in Paris.

27 of the 34 lines, written in Phoenician-Old Hebrew script (cf. p. 4), have survived. They celebrate the victory of Moab over Israel after a period of Moabite submission (cf. II Kings iii.4 ff.), and record Mesha's building of various cities.

"This stele of Mesha king of Moab is of great importance as the sole historical monument of the Moabite kingdom and a record of historical relations between Moab and Israel which are glossed over or omitted from the Old Testament. It further reveals Moabite as a Semitic dialect almost identical with Hebrew and proves the advanced stage of writing in a petty kingdom lying off the main historical routes in the 9th century B.C." (G. R. Driver, *Semitic Writing* (London, rev. ed. 1954), p. 109).

The script is remarkably developed, with a tendency towards cursive forms and simplification. It is of special note that the words and sentences are divided, the words by dots, the sentences by strokes.

Transliteration into the square script: K. Galling, *Textbuch zur Geschichte Israels* (1950), pp. 47ff. Translation: H. Gressmann, *Altorientalische Texte zum Alten Testament* (2nd ed. 1926), pp. 440ff.; W. F. Albright in *Ancient Near Eastern Texts relating to the Old Testament*, ed. by J. B. Pritchard (1950), p. 320. Cf. also S. R. Driver, *Notes on the Hebrew Text of the Books of Samuel* (2nd ed. 1913), pp. lxxxivff., and G. A. Cooke, *A Text-book of North-Semitic Inscriptions* (1903), pp. 4ff.

Plate 2

THE SILOAM INSCRIPTION FROM JERUSALEM (c. 700 B.C.)

cf. p. 4. Illustration from D. Diringer, *The Alphabet* (1948).

In 1880 there was found, on the wall of the rock at the opening of the rock channel which runs from the spring of Gihon (now Mary's well) to the Pool of Siloam, an inscription in Old Hebrew letters (cf. p. 4). It relates the successful completion of the making of the channel. The original was later cut away and is now in the Museum in Constantinople (Istanbul).

The narrative, which does not include any names or dates, most probably refers to the water-channel made by King Hezekiah (725-697 B.C., cf. II Kings xx.20; II Chron. xxxii.30), and thus belongs to the period about 700 B.C. The palaeographical evidence confirms this. "The writing may fairly be assigned to the same general stage of development as that represented by the Moabite Stone but is lighter and more flowing, while some of the letters have considerably altered their shape". (Driver, *Semitic Writing* (rev. ed. 1954), p. 119).

The text consists of six lines and is 38 cms. high and 72 wide. The rock surface was smoothed for it over an area about 70 cms. square, the inscription being on the lower half. Was a pictorial representation to be added in the space (Gressmann), or has the first part of the inscription been lost (Albright)?

Transliteration into the square script: K. Galling, *Textbuch zur Geschichte Israels* (1950), p. 59. Translation: H. Gressmann, *Altorientalische Texte zum Alten Testament* (2nd ed. 1926), p. 445; W. F. Albright in Pritchard, *Ancient Near Eastern Texts relating to the Old Testament* (1950), p. 321, where references may be found to the literature on the inscription. Cf. also S. R. Driver, *Notes on the Hebrew Text of the Books of Samuel* (2nd ed. 1913), pp. viiiff.; G. A. Cooke, *A text-Book of North-Semitic Inscriptions* (1903), pp. 15ff.; J. Finegan, *Light from the Ancient Past* (1947), Plate 69.

Plate 3

LACHISCH LETTER NO. IV

cf. p. 4. Illustration from *Lachish* I (*Tell ed-Duweir*): *The Lachish Letters* by H. Torczyner, L. Harding, A. Lewis, J. L. Starkey (1938).

During the course of excavations in a room in the gate-building at Tell ed-Duweir, the site of Biblical Lachish, there were found in 1935 eighteen fragments of pottery (ostraka), inscribed in Old Hebrew script, and a further three in 1938. (cf. pp. 5 f.). They were found in a stratum of burnt material clearly the result of the destruction of the city by the Babylonians at the time of the fall of the state of Judah (588-587), and so they belong to the latest period of the southern kingdom. Their contents form, in the main, part of a military correspondence, which gives us a picture of the distressed state of Judah during the Babylonian invasion.

"As in other countries where potsherds were used for messages, the writer begins his letter on the outside of the sherd and continues only where necessary on the less smooth inner surface. The scribe of the Lachish Letters used a reed-pen, and wrote in an iron-carbon ink, as the chemical analysis has shown". (H. Torczyner, *Lachish* I (1938), p. 204).

The script is beautiful and cursive, the result of centuries of literary tradition. The word-divider is used very irregularly. On the writing of **חיהוה** in III.9 cf. p. 72. The language is Biblical Hebrew, especially reminiscent of the styles of Jer. and Deut. This proves that the Biblical books in 𝔐 are written predominantly in the language of pre-exilic Judah. The ostraka are of great philological, palaeographical and historical significance since they are the only known examples of documents in classical Hebrew. They are now in Jerusalem and London.

Transliteration into the square script (in selection): K. Galling, *Textbuch zur Geschichte Israels* (1950), pp. 63ff. Translation: J. Hempel in *Z.A.W.* N.F. 15 (1938), pp. 126ff.; W. F. Albright in *Ancient Near Eastern Texts relating to the Old Testament* (1950), pp. 321ff. Full edition: H. Torczyner, **תעודות לכיש**, *Library of Palestinology of the Jewish Palestine Exploration Society* XV/XVII (1940), not accessible to the author. Cf. *Lachish* III (1953), pp. 331-339.

IV 6025

Plate 4

ELEPHANTINE PAPYRUS

Cf. pp. 3 f. Illustration from Ed. Sachau, *Aramäische Papyrus und Ostraka aus einer jüdischen Militär-Kolonie zu Elephantine* (1911), Plate 1.

During excavations undertaken in 1907 and 1908 by the Berlin Papyrus Commission on the island of Elephantine, in the Nile opposite Assuan, there were found, among other things, numerous papyri in the Aramaic language and script. They belong to the fifth century B.C., and include letters, legal documents, fragments of the Story of Ahikar, and fragments of an Aramaic translation of Darius' Behistun inscription. They provided the first information concerning the existence of a "Jewish military colony" in Elephantine, which had a temple, where, besides Yahu (= Yahweh), there were worshipped a goddess Anathbethel and a god (אשמביתאל—the pronunciation is not certain). (Cf. M. Noth, *Geschichte Israels* (1950), pp. 254f.).

These papyri attest the widespread use of the Aramaic language and script under the Persian empire (cf. p. 3). The Aramaic script, from which, in addition to the square script, there developed the scripts of the Nabataeans, Palmyrenes, Syrians (Estrangela) and others, represents, as does the Phoenician-Old Hebrew script, a branch of the north-Semitic alphabet. The oldest known examples of it are in ninth century inscriptions from the Aleppo area. "The Aramaic script gradually assumed a distinctive character which is marked by the following main tendencies: (1) The opening of the tops and the sides of a few letters (the beth, the daleth and resh, the ʿayin) is a prominent feature. (2) The endeavour to reduce the number of separate strokes, in the kheth and teth, for instance, is also noticeable. (3) Angles become rounded and ligatures develop. These tendencies were completed during the Persian period. By the fifth century B.C. the transformation is complete, as we can gather ... especially from the cursive Aramaic writing on papyrus used in Egypt between 500 and 200 B.C.". (D. Diringer, *The Alphabet* (1948), p. 259).

Cf. A. E. Cowley, *Aramaic Papyri of the Fifth Century B.C.* (1925); *Jewish Documents of the Time of Ezra* (1919). Also *The Brooklyn Museum Aramaic Papyri*, ed. E. G. Kraeling (1953).

THE NASH PAPYRUS

Cf. p. 24. Enlarged infra-red photograph from *B.A.S.O.R.* 115 (1949). The sections in brackets have been completed from Exod. xx and Deut. v.

(אנכי י)הוה אלהיך אשר (הוצא)תיך מארץ מ(צרים)
(לוא יהיה ל)ך אלהים אחרים (על־פנ)י לוא תעשה (לך פסל)
(וכל תמונה) אשר בשמים ממעל ואשר בארץ (מתחת)
(ואשר במים) מתחת לארץ לוא תשתחוה להם (ולוא)
(תעבדם כי) אנכי יהוה אלהיך אל קנוא פק(ד עון אבות)
(על בני)ם על שלשים ועל רבעים לשנאי (ועשה חסד)
(לאלפים) לאהבי ולשמרי מצותי לוא ת(שא את שם)
(יהוה א)להיך לשוא כי לוא ינקה יהוה (את אשר)
(ישא את ש)מה לשוא זכור את יום השבת ל(קדשו)
(ששת ימים) תעבוד ועשית כל מלאכתך וביום (השביעי)
(שבת ליהוה) אלהיך לוא תעשה בה כל מלאכ(ה אתה)
(ובנך ובתך) עבדך ואמתך שורך וחמרך וכל ב(המתך)
(וגרך אשר) בשעריך כי ששת י(מי)ם עשה י(הוה)
(את השמי)ם ואת הארץ את הים ואת כל א(שר בם)
(וינח ביום) השביעי עלכן ברך יהוה את (יום)
השביעי ויקדשיו כבד את אביך ואת אמ(ך למען)
ייטב לך ולמען יאריכון ימיך על האדמה (אשר)
יהוה אלהיך נתן לך לוא תנאף לוא תרצח לו(א)
(תג)נב לוא תענה ברעך עד שוא לוא תחמוד (את)
(אשת רעך לו)א תתאוה את ב(י)ת רעך שד(הו ועבדו)
(ואמתו וש)ורו וחמרו וכל אשר לרעך
(ואלה החק)ים והמשפטים אשר צוה משה את (בני)
(ישראל) במדבר בצאתם מארץ מצרים שמ(ע)
(ישרא)ל יהוה אלהינו יהוה אחד הוא וא(הבת)

Plate 6

THE ENTRANCE TO QUMRAN CAVE I

Cf. p. 10. Illustration from Sukenik, אוצר המגילות הגנוזות (1954).

In the Spring of 1947 there came to light in Jerusalem the now famous manuscripts from a cave in the neighbourhood of the Dead Sea. The war in Palestine prevented the rediscovery of the cave until early in 1949. It was then investigated under the guidance of L. Harding and P. de Vaux, but no further texts of any considerable size were found. The cave is situated in a particularly dry area of Palestine, 12 km. south of Jericho, 1 km north of Khirbet Qumran. It was found accidentally by a herdsman searching for a lost goat. Later searches revealed the existence in the same area of about 30 other caves, which were used at the same period as hiding places or stores. In four of these there were also hidden remains of manuscripts, some of which were of considerable length (cf. p. 10).

All these caves were very closely connected with the ancient settlement of Khirbet Qumran. Excavations have been carried out at Qumran since 1951 under the guidance of P. de Vaux and L. Harding, and in the course of these, about 250 coins were also found, of great importance for the dating of the finds. They range from the period of John Hyrcanus (135-104 B.C.) to that of the second Jewish War (132-135 A.D.). These excavations show that Qumran—a sort of monastery—was founded in the time of John Hyrcanus or Alexander Jannaeus (103-76 B.C.), and was 'the administrative centre, the place of assembly and also of burial, for a community which lived scattered about the neighbourhood' (de Vaux), until it was destroyed in the time of the first Jewish War (66-70 A.D.). It is very probable that the scrolls found since 1947 were hidden because of these military events. Qumran appears later to have served as a Roman military post, and finally as a stronghold of the Jewish rebels of the second Jewish War.

We may conjecture that Khirbet Qumran is the place in the Judaean Desert 'above Engedi' which Pliny the Elder describes as the centre of a community of pious Jews, celibates, who lived in solitude—the Essenes. The results of the excavations and many details in the literature discovered favour this identification [1]).

---

[1]) On the excavations of Khirbet Qumran, cf. the provisional reports by P. de Vaux, *Revue Biblique* 60 (1953), pp. 83-106; 61 (1954), pp. 206-236, 567 f.

Plate 7

TWO JARS FROM QUMRAN CAVE I

Cf. p. 7. Illustration from Sukenik מגילות גנוזות II (1950)

The undamaged jars here illustrated were taken from cave I by the Beduin when it was discovered, and were later bought by Professor Sukenik of Jerusalem. Their heights (without lid) are 65.7 and 47.5 cms. respectively, and their diameters 25 and 26.5 cms. They were designed to protect the scrolls from damage.

During the archaeological investigation of the cave, broken pieces of about 50 other jars of the same or similar pattern were found. Since each jar could contain three or more scrolls, cave I could at one time have sheltered 150-200 scrolls, a whole library. But not all the jars will have contained scrolls, as was at first assumed. 'The only solid evidence for the possible quantity is the number of different books which can be identified, and these amount to about seventy-five. How or when so many of these documents were removed or damaged is a question which is at present unanswerable'. [1]) If we think in terms of the removal of scrolls centuries ago, then a letter from the Nestorian Patriarch Timotheus I of Seleucia (726-819) may be compared. Here it is recorded that an Arab huntsman was led by his dog into a cave in which were many books. 'The huntsman went to Jerusalem and told the Jews. They came in large numbers, and found the books of the (Old) Testament, and others in Hebrew script' [2]). No definite statement can be made on this however.

Jars of the same or similar pattern have also been found in the neighbouring caves and in Khirbet Qumran itself. From the results of the excavations, they are to be dated in the first century A.D. 'This does not prejudice the discussion of the date of the manuscripts, which may be much older, but it is decisive for the date of the deposit. It was made during the first century of our era, that is to say, in the Roman period, during the Jewish War of 66-70'. (de Vaux, quoted by Rost, *Theol.Lit. Zeit.* 77 (1952), cols. 278f.).

---

[1]) L. Harding, *Qumran Cave* I (1955), p. 3.

[2]) Attention was drawn to the letter by O. Eissfeldt, *Theol. Lit. Zeit.* 74 (1949), cols. 597f.

Plate 8

THE FIRST ISAIAH SCROLL

Cf. pp. 7, 23 f. Illustration from Sukenik, מגילות גנוזות II (1950)

The first Isaiah scroll is here shown opened at cols. 32 and 33 (Isa. xxxviii.9-xl.28). It can clearly be seen that the scroll is made up of separate pieces of leather. The way in which it was handled is also plain: on the right is the beginning of the scroll, and on the left the end. For easier use, and to reduce wear, rollers were used, on which the scroll could be rolled up, one at each end for Torah scrolls, but for other books only one at the beginning. A section of the scroll had to be left plain at the end to serve as a protective wrapping.

Now that the place of their discovery has been determined and investigated (cf. pp. 94, 96), it may be accepted as certain that the scrolls are old and genuine. Doubts as to this, such as have been repeatedly raised by, for example, S. Zeitlin in the *Jewish Quarterly Review* (1949f.), may now be regarded as removed, in consequence of this examination. The absolute dating is, however, a more difficult question. A *terminus ad quem* is perhaps now provided by the period 66-70 A.D. suggested by de Vaux (cf. pp. 94, 96). But the scrolls could, of course, already be of considerable age at the time of their deposit in the cave, and they do in fact show signs of much use in antiquity (cf. the outside of the scroll in the illustration). Absolute dating on palaeographical evidence has been attempted by Albright, Trever, Birnbaum, Sukenik and others. Though the details vary, their suggestions all point to the second and first centuries B.C. A sufficient body of comparative material of known date is lacking for a final decision. We must for the present agree with Kahle when he says: "It seems certain to me that we cannot at present arrive at a satisfactory objective dating of the newly discovered Hebrew manuscripts on the basis of palaeographical evidence". (*Handschriften aus der Höhle* (1951), p. 8). Nevertheless we may claim that the first Isaiah scroll is older than the others in its style of writing. Most of the final letters are missing here—as also in the "Manual of Discipline". Thus the square script is not yet so fully developed as in the Nash Papyrus and in the other scrolls from the cave.

Plate 9

AN EXTRACT FROM THE FIRST ISAIAH SCROLL (ISA. xl.6-20)

Cf. pp. 23 f. Illustration, somewhat enlarged, from the edition referred to on p. 23 n. 2

As may be seen from the illustration, the following words of 𝔐 were missing from vv. 7f. in the original text of the Isaiah scroll: כי רוח יהוה נשבה בו אכן חציר העם יבש חציר נבל ציץ. They were added in poor script by a later hand between the lines and in the left-hand margin of the column. It is simplest to explain the omission as due to homoioteleuton; they eye of the scribe passed from נבל ציץ in v.7 to the same words in v.8. But it is noteworthy that the same passage is also missing in 𝔊, and Origen marks it with an asterisk (cf. p. 39). It is possible that the agreement between the original text of the Isaiah scroll and that of 𝔊 is accidental: homoioteleuton could in each case have led to the omission. But it is also possible that the text of 𝔐 is the result of later amplification, not yet to be found in the text underlying 𝔊 and in the Isaiah scroll. Objections have frequently been made to the phrase אכן חציר העם.

In the passage which has been added four dots appear instead of the divine name Yahweh. Did the scribe feel such awe that he did not dare to write the divine name? It is more likely that we should assume that the space was thus marked so that the divine name could be added later, no doubt in another script. Thus in the Habakkuk Commentary the name Yahweh is always written in Old Hebrew letters (cf. pp. 104f.).

In verse 7 דבר has a dot under each letter, which presumably means that this word is to be omitted.

In xl. 14-16 (from the second וילמדהו to the end of 16) the script is different from that in the preceding and following verses. But this does not indicate that a passage originally missing from the text was added later. "Either another scribe has taken over the copying for a short time, or the scribe has simply sharpened his pen or taken a new one". (Burrows, *B.A.S.O.R.* 113 (1949), p. 32).

Of the many variants in this extract, two are of special importance: in xl.6 ואומרה (𝔐 ואמר) confirms the correctness of the emendation often proposed *wa'omar* (so 𝔊 𝔙); in xl.17 וכאפס (𝔐 מאפס) supports the conjecture כאפס (cf. the II Apparatus of BH).

Plate 10

THE SECOND ISAIAH SCROLL

Cf. p. 24. Illustration from Sukenik, מגילות גנוזות II (1950)

The second Isaiah scroll, as the illustration shows (1st col. Isa. xlviii. 17-xlix. 7; 2nd col. Isa. l. 7-li. 8), is in bad condition. The leather has rotted so that some part of every column is lost. Opening the scroll was particularly difficult because the leather was stuck together in many places. The surviving portions belong to Deutero-Isaiah, with only fragments of Proto-Isaiah.

The script is relatively small, but beautiful and clear. By contrast with the first Isaiah scroll, it is surprising to find how much the text of the second agrees with 𝔐. To some extent the vowel letters are used even more sparingly than in 𝔐: **שלמך** (𝔐 שלומך) xlviii. 18; **צר** (צור) xlviii. 21; **כלתי** (כליתי) xlix. 4. Conversely, additional vowel letters are also found where they are lacking in 𝔐: **יוצרי** (יצרי) xlix. 5; **גואל** (גאל) and **קדוש** (קדש) xlix. 7.

Variants from 𝔐: xlviii. 17 **מדרכיך** (מדריכך); xlix. 4 **אך** (אכן); xlix. 6 **הנקל** (נקל) and **ארץ** (הארץ): xlix. 7, agreeing with the first Isaiah scroll, **אדני יהוה** (אדני); **יקומו** (וקמו); l. 11 **ומאזרי** (מאזרי). The second Isaiah scroll thus offers considerably fewer variants from 𝔐 than the first. Kahle regards this scroll as a popular text. "But whereas the first Isaiah scroll is an example of a really typical popular text, the second Isaiah scroll has already been considerably assimilated to the definitive consonantal text, broadly presupposes its existence, and can therefore only have been written when this consonantal text was already available". (*Handschriften aus der Höhle* (1951), p. 81). The more developed form of the script, particularly in the final letters, also points to a later date. But cf. p. 96 on the date of the deposit in the cave.

Plate 11

THE HABAKKUK COMMENTARY (COLS. IX and X —Hab. ii.7-14)

Cf. p. 24. Illustration from the edition referred to on p. 23 n. 2

This scroll is of considerable religious importance because, like the Manual of Discipline, it gives us new information concerning a religious movement in pre-Christian Judaism. It is important for the textual history and criticism of the Old Testament because the words of prophecy in Hab. i and ii are here quoted and commented upon, phrase by phrase. The text quoted in this scroll deviates from 𝔐 in a way similar to that of the first Isaiah scroll. The III critical Apparatus in BH mentions about 60 variants, not including those merely of an orthographic kind, such as *scriptio plena.* In a few places the text and commentary differ as between themselves with regard to the text of Habakkuk (cf. i.8, 11; ii.16).

It is particularly of note that the divine name Yahweh is written in the Old Hebrew script (cf. left-hand column lines 7 and 14). In other scrolls **אל** and **אלי** are similarly treated. This peculiar writing of the divine name is also referred to by Origen and by Jewish tradition. Among the fragments found in the Cairo Geniza, some contain parts of the translations of Aquila and Symmachus, in which Yahweh is written in Old Hebrew script in the middle of the Greek text. This must therefore have been a widespread practice at one time. In the text of the Commentary itself, the tetragrammaton is avoided and **אל** used instead. In the period of these manuscripts, it is clear that *'adonai* was already being pronounced instead of Yahweh, for the first Isaiah scroll, for example, sometimes has **אדני** where 𝔐 has **יהוה** (iii.17) and vice versa (vi.11; vii.14; ix.7; xxi.16; xxviii.2). **יהוה**, whether in Old Hebrew or square script, had thus become merely an ideogram for **אדני** (cf. Eissfeldt, *Theol.Lit.Zeit.* 74 (1949), col. 225; Kahle, *Handschriften,* pp. 63 ff.).

In the illustration, horizontal lines on which the letters are suspended, and vertical lines which mark off the columns, may be clearly seen. Scribes of the third century A. D. regarded these lines as an essential part of a book. They traced the practice back to Adam, considering it as of extreme antiquity (L. Blau, *Studien zum althebr. Buchwesen* (1902), pp. 142ff.).

Plate 12

FRAGMENTS OF LEVITICUS IN THE OLD HEBREW SCRIPT

Cf. p. 4. Illustration (with transliteration) from Sukenik, מגילות גנוזות II (1950)

The texts illustrated contain parts of Lev. xix. 31-34; xx.20-23; xxi.24-xxii.3; xxii.4-5. They came to light during the investigation of the cave by P. de Vaux and Lankester Harding in February 1949. These fragments offer us the first examples of the Old Hebrew script written upon leather. A dot is used as word-divider. There is one variant from 𝔐: in xx.21 היא is found instead of the Masoretic הוא with *Qere perpetuum*.

The suggestion that the fragments were of Samaritan origin was a natural one since the Samaritans are known to have preserved the Old Hebrew script for their Torah. But Kahle has pointed out that in Lev. xx.22, where the Jewish and Samaritan traditions differ, these fragments contain the Jewish text. The dating raises great difficulties, and has been placed between the fifth and the first centuries B.C. The use of the Old Hebrew script does not in itself indicate the date, since there were still scrolls in this script in the first Christian centuries (cf. p. 5). "The fragments are, without question, of the utmost interest as examples of a Jewish Torah scroll in the Old Hebrew script. They may be older than the fragments in square script, but this is not absolutely necessary. We must reckon with the possibility that they come from the same period. Here too palaeography does not help, since we have no comparable datable material". (Kahle, *Handschriften*, p. 21).

אלהיכם . מפנ[י]

מאלהיך . אני . יהו[ה]

את[ו] כאזרח . מכם

ישאו

[א]חיו . נדה . היא . [ער]ות

[ושמרת]ם . את . כל . חקתי . ואת . כל .

אתכם . הארץ . אשר . אני .

תלכו

אל[ה]

ישראל

. בניו .

. אשר .

[לדרתיכ]ם . כל . איש . אשר .

[א]שר . י[קדישו] . בני .

[מלפ]ני . [א]נ[י]

נפ[ש]

בכל . ש[רץ]

Plate 13a

A FRAGMENT CONTAINING PARTS OF DEUT. xxix.14-18 and xxx.20-xxxi.5

Illustration from L. Harding, *Palestine Exploration Quarterly* (1949)

The fragment was obtained from an 'outside source' (Harding). It has aroused particular interest because of its text in Deut. xxxi.1. This verse reads:

𝔐; וילך משה וידבר את[1] הדברים
Fragment: ויכל משה לדבר את כל
𝔊: καὶ συνετέλεσεν Μωυσῆς λαλῶν πάντας τοὺς λόγους τούτους.

𝔊 and the fragment agree completely against 𝔐. "Thus, for the first time in Biblical history, we were confronted with a Hebrew scroll of Deuteronomy, where practically a whole verse followed the Septuagint reading". (Leveen, Newly Found Hebrew Scrolls from Palestine, *The Listener* (Aug. 25. 1949), p. 323). The belief that 𝔊 here depends upon a Hebrew text which differs from 𝔐 thus becomes a certainty. Bertholet, Marti and Steuernagel had already emended 𝔐 on the basis of 𝔊, whereas König maintained the originality of 𝔐 (cf. the commentaries). The variants arose by the transposition of letters in the first word. In favour of the reading of 𝔐 is the fact that it is the *lectio difficilior*; against it, that it gives a forced meaning. In my opinion this latter argument is here so strong that the text of 𝔐 must be abandoned.

1) 28 Hebrew manuscripts add כל.

Plate 13b

PART OF AN UNOPENED SCROLL

From the 1949 discoveries

Illustration from L. Harding, *Palestine Exploration Quarterly* (1949)

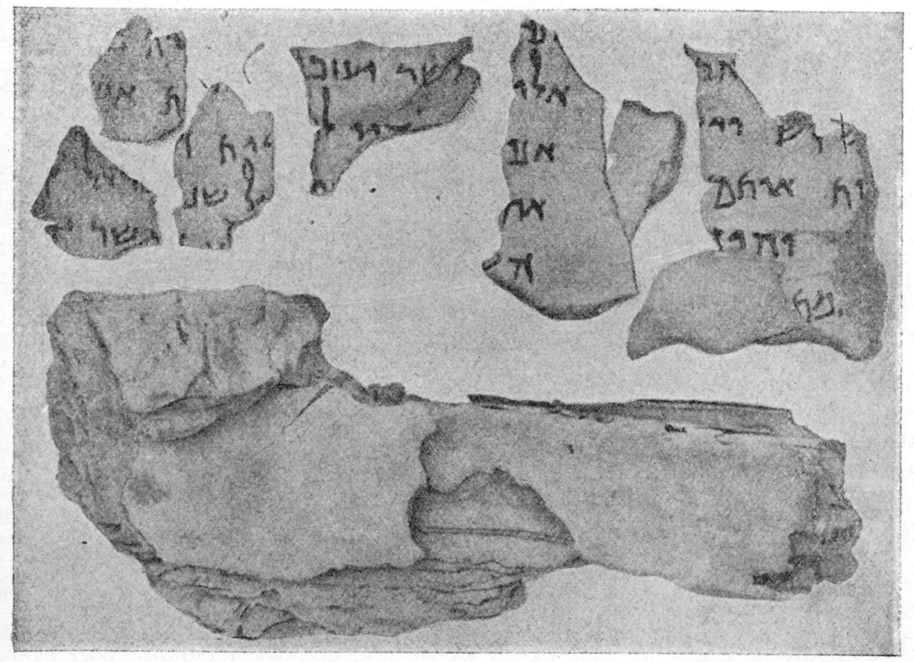

Plate 14

A PAGE WITH BABYLONIAN POINTING

(Job xxxvii.17-xxxviii.15: Berlin Ms.or.qu.680 = Ec 1)

Cf. p. 18. Illustration from Kahle, *Masoreten des Ostens* (1913)

94 parchment sheets, now in Berlin, form the remains of a once complete manuscript of the Writings. 7 further sheets are in the Glaser collection in New York. The original, purely Babylonian, punctuation was later worked over by a Yemenite hand. "In the reproduction, the original punctuation is often difficult to discern, whereas the working over stands out clearly". (Kahle). The *Masora parva* has, for the most part, been written in the text above the word to which it refers. In the lower margin is the *Masora magna,* which cannot be seen on the page illustrated because it has been destroyed by mildew. A detailed discussion is to be found in Kahle, *Der masoretische Text des Alten Testaments nach der Überlieferung der babylonischen Juden* (1902); cf. also *Masoreten des Ostens* (1913), p. 140.

Plate 15

FRAGMENT OF HAPHṬARAH WITH BABYLONIAN POINTING

(Isa. lxii.8f.; Hos. xiv.2f. with Targum; Cambridge B 15_1 = K b, 7,1)

(Cf. p. 18. Illustration from Kahle, *Masoreten des Ostens* (1913)

In Jewish worship, certain sections from the Prophets were read in addition to the Torah. Such a section was called a Haphṭarah. The name (from the Hebrew הפטיר—conclude) is probably to be explained from the fact that the reading from the Bible was concluded with the reading from the Prophets. (I. Elbogen, *Geschichte des jüdischen Gottesdienstes* (2nd ed. 1924), pp. 174ff.). The Haphṭaroth were collected into special scrolls or books at an early date.

The page illustrated contains verses from the Haphṭarah for the Sabbath before New Year and verses from the Haphṭarah for the Sabbath after New Year. According to Kahle, it belongs to the remains of a particularly beautiful manuscript like the Petersburg Codex of the Prophets, and provides an example of the most developed form of the eastern system of pointing.

As is usual, each verse in Hebrew is followed by its Targum. A later hand has added in the margin Isa. lxiii.7-16, which also has a verse by verse Targum.

אשר בגדיך חמים | בהשקט ארץ מדרום

תרקיע עמו לשחקים | חזקים כראי מוצק

הודיענו מה נאמר לו | לא נערך מפני חשך

היספר לו כי אדבר | אם אמר איש כי יבלע

ועתה לא ראו אור בהיר הוא בשחקים | ורוח עברה ותטהרם

מצפון זהב יאתה | על אלוה נורא הוד

שדי לא מצאנהו | שגיא כח

ומשפט ורב צדקה | לא יענה

לכן יראוהו אנשים | לא יראה כל חכמי לב

לח

כ״ד 24

ויען יהוה את איוב מן הסערה ויאמר:

מי זה מחשיך עצה במלין | בלי דעת

אזר נא כגבר חלציך | ואשאלך והודיעני

איפה היית ביסדי ארץ | הגד אם ידעת בינה

מי שם ממדיה כי תדע או מי נטה עליה קו | או מי ירה אבן פנתה

ברן יחד כוכבי בקר | ויריעו כל בני אלהים

ויסך בדלתים ים | בגיחו מרחם יצא

בשומי ענן לבשו | וערפל חתלתו

ואשבר עליו חקי | ואשים בריח ודלתים

ואמר עד פה תבוא ולא תסיף | ופא ישית בגאון גליך

המימיך צוית בקר | ידעתה השחר מקמו

לאחז בכנפות הארץ | וינערו רשעים ממנה

תתהפך כחמר חותם | ויתיצבו כמו לבוש

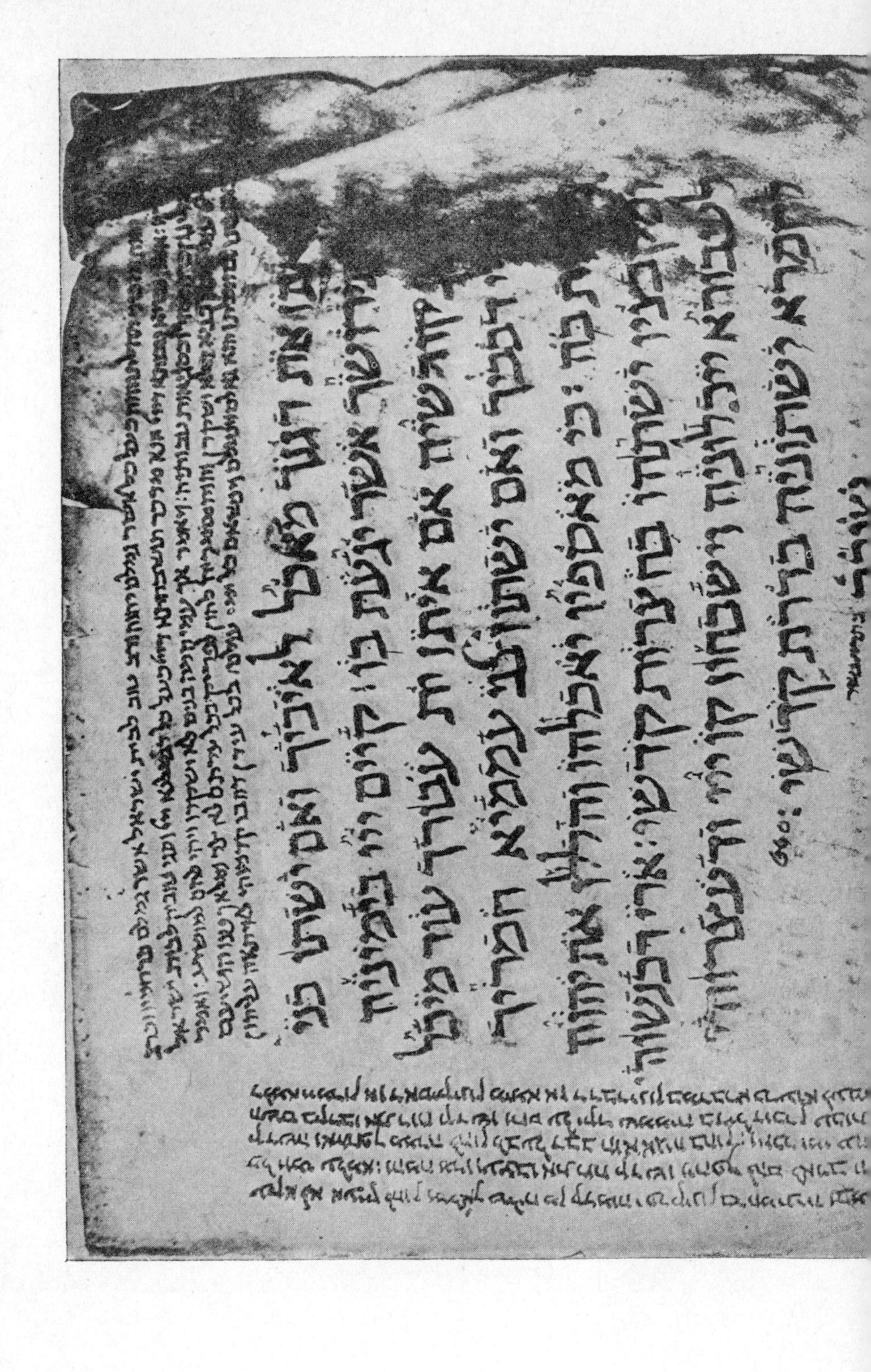

תוב ישראל לדחלתא דיוי אלהך ארי

איתקילתא בחובך: קחו עמכם דברים

ושובו אל יהוה אמרו אליו כל תשא עון וקח

טוב ונשלמה פרים שפתינו: קריבו

עימכון פיתגמין דאודאה

Plate 16

A FRAGMENT WITH PALESTINIAN POINTING

Cf. p. 18. Illustration (Isa. vii. 11-ix. 8) from Kahle, *Masoreten des Westens* II (1930)

The fragment (Oxford Ms Heb. e 30, fol. 48b), together with a few other leaves, forms all that remains of a manuscript of the Prophets, and led at the end of last century to the re-discovery of the Palestinian system of pointing (cf. Kahle, *Z.A.W.* 21 (1901), pp. 273ff.).

It is also remarkable in that it offers a Hebrew text in the form of abbreviations. Only the first word of each verse is written in full; the remainder are indicated by a single consonant (not always the initial), with its appropriate vowel and accent. Such abbreviations are already mentioned in the Talmud under the name of סירוגין. They were probably intended as reminders for the reader in the synagogue, or for students in school.

While abbreviation is used in this text consistently, abbreviations for certain common words were occasionally used in Biblical manuscripts from an early date. If they were not recognised as such in copying, they could naturally lead to textual corruption. F. Perles, in particular, has attempted to prove that such abbreviations in the pre-Masoretic text were a source of error in many passages (F. Perles, *Analekten zur Textkritik* (1895); New Series (1922).).

שאל-א עה מ א אחד
ויאמר ח ל-א אס
ויאמר מכ חא כתא ג
לכו תתה כמר ל תתמ ש
המאח פ כ תמא בה ת בט
[illegible] נ א ה ח בתומ שלם נמל
[illegible] א יל עך בם י ר ט א
והוה י ר לב שצ לר ש הבת
ובאו לקל לנתמ׳ כנ עכ בה נל
בינסה לגת תשכר עחבר של לכ תפ
והיה חו-א עלכ ת-
והיה ר של כב כ כ-ת
והיה ק שש אג למ ל ש
בחצים ב ש כ-ש-מ ו ש
ולר ד י ע בשאו י למ מ
אמר ו לך ג ו ת ל מפ לחב
ועורח לה נ א א-ר ב-יבר
[illegible] ב ב תת ק מ מקל תב
[illegible] ש מ א [illegible]
[illegible] ל ע
ישע מ א מ של חה לא מש צב
[illegible] לה ה חת שע פה ל ע-
[illegible]

רעו מ ו חזוכ מלק ה זק ו חת ה ו ה
עצו ע תפד ב כפ
כי ל חק י ושר נמ ד נ ז
לאק ק כמצ קא-ר א א ה
אתנ א מ ד כ מ רע
והיה ל א נ עש נק אפ ל
ובשלוב קב נקש נכ
עד ע חת ה למר
וחכיתי תנ ק
הנח כר שתת עשכ ת
וכיבר א ב א-ה הצ מנ לע עה
לתורח ע א-ר של שה
וטבר כ שע יע עקכ ה
ואל-א נ וכ מע ו ל נ ר
כי עש צכע שק אלה יע ג
חעס ח אב א נג
הדרית ג לשנ כב יצ ג חלל
כי א-עס ל אש נג החת י
כי סא סא ר של גל נפ תכל
כי [illegible]
ס ן למ [illegible]
ע- דבר לה עפ
[illegible]

Plate 17

CODEX CAIRENSIS

Cf. p. 25. Illustration (Jer. ii. 16-33) from a photograph kindly lent by P. Kahle.

Here is an extract from the second colophon at the end of the manuscript:

"I, Mosche b. Asher, have written this Maḥzor (Codex) of the Scriptures, according to 'the good hand of my God upon me' (Neh. ii.8), 'very plainly' (Deut. xxvii.8), in the city of Ma'azya-Ṭabariyya, (= Tiberias) 'the renowned city' (Ezek. xxvi.17) ...

It was written at the end of the year 827 after the destruction of the Second Temple (= 895 A.D.) ...

Whoever alters a word of this Maḥzor or of this writing, or erases from it a letter, or tears off from it a leaf—except that he understands and knows that there is in it a word in which we have erred, in writing, or in punctuation, or in Masora, or in defective or in plene, let him not have pardon or forgiveness, neither let him behold the beauty of the Lord (Ps. xxvii.4), nor let him see the good that is reserved for those who fear Him (Jer. xxix.32). He shall be like a woman in impurity, and like a leprous man who has to be locked up, so that his limbs may be crushed, the pride of his power be broken, his flesh be consumed away that it cannot be seen, and his bones that are not seen stick out (Job xxxiii.21). Amen.

Whoever reads shall hear, whoever hears shall understand, whoever sees shall perceive! Peace!"

Complete text of the colophon with English translation in Kahle, *The Cairo Geniza* (1948), pp. 110ff.; German translation in Kahle, *Masoreten des Westens* I (1927), pp. 15f.

356

קדקד הלוא זאת
תעשה לך עזבך את
יהוה אלהיך בעת
מוליכך בדרך ועתה
מה לך לדרך מצרים
לשתות מי שחור ומה לך
לדרך אשור לשתות
מי נהר תיסרך רעתך
ומשבותיך תוכחך
ודעי וראי כי רע ומר
עזבך את יהוה אלהיך
ולא פחדתי אליך נאם
אדני יהוה צבאות כי
מעולם שברתי עלך
נתקתי מוסרותיך
ותאמרי לא אעבוד
כי על כל גבעה גבהה
ותחת כל עץ רענן
את צעה זנה ואנכי
נטעתיך שורק כלה
זרע אמת ואיך נהפכת
לי סורי הגפן נכריה
כי אם תכבסי בנתר

ותרבי לך בורית נכתם
עונך לפני נאם אדני
יהוה איך תאמרי לא
נטמאתי אחרי הבעלים
לא הלכתי ראי דרכך
בגיא דעי מה עשית
בכרה קלה משרכת
דרכיה פרה למד מד
בר באות נפשו
שאפה רוח תאנתה
מי ישיבנה כל מבקשיה
לא ייעפו בחדשה
ימצאונה מנעי רגלך
מיחף וגורנך מצמאה
ותאמרי נואש לוא כי
אהבתי זרים ואחריהם
אלך כבשת גנב כי
ימצא כן הבישו בית
ישראל המה מלכיהם
שריהם וכהניהם
ונביאיהם אמרים לעץ
אבי אתה ולאבן את
ילדתני כי פנו אלי ערף

ולא פנים ובעת רעתם
יאמרו קומה והושיענו
ואיה אלהיך אשר
עשית לך יקומו אם
יושיעוך בעת רעתך
כי מספר עריך היו
אלהיך יהודה
למה תריבו אלי
כלכם פשעתם בי נאם
יהוה לשוא הכיתי
את בניכם מוסר לא
לקחו אכלה חרבכם
נביאיכם כאריה משחית
הדור אתם ראו דבר
יהוה המדבר הייתי
לישראל אם ארץ
מאפליה מדוע אמרו
עמי רדנו לוא נבוא
עוד אליך התשכח
בתולה עדיה כלה
קשריה ועמי שכחוני
ימים אין מספר מה
תיטבי דרכך לבקש

Plate 18

BRITISH MUSEUM CODEX OR. 4445

Cf. p. 30 n. 2. Illustration (Num. xxvi.12-27), smaller than original, by kind consent of the British Museum.

This is a pointed and accented manuscript of the Pentateuch from which the beginning (Gen. i-xxxix.19), the end (from Deut. i.34 onwards), as well as Num. vii.47-73 and Num. ix.12-x.18 are missing. Some of this material was added later. The manuscript is written in good, clear lettering. Each page contains three columns. *Masora parva* appears in the margins, *Masora magna* at the top and bottom of the page. Ginsburg (*Introduction to the Hebrew Bible* (1897), pp. 469ff.) regarded this manuscript as the oldest known, and dated the consonantal text and the pointing about 820-850 A.D. According to him, the Masora was added about a century later by a Nakdan (cf. p. 12) who also revised the text. Since the Masora mentions the Masorete Ben Asher without using the normal formula of blessing for one who has died, we may assume that it was written during his lifetime. Kahle, however, places the origin of the whole manuscript in the lifetime of Ben Asher. "Ben Asher was obviously the great authority for the copyist, and that he really copied a Ben Asher text, is confirmed by the book of Mishael b.'Uzziel". (Kahle, *Vetus, Testamentum* I (1951), p. 167; cf. also *Masoreten des Westens* I (1927), pp. 17f.; on Mishael ben 'Uzziel cf. above p. 19 and BH pp. VIff.).

משפחת הנמואלי
לימין משפחת
הימיני ליכין משפחת
היכיני לזרח משפחת
הזרחי לשאול משפחת
השאולי אלה
משפחת השמעני
שנים ועשרים אלף
ומאתים בני
גד למשפחתם
לצפון משפחת
הצפוני לחגי
משפחת החגי
לשוני משפחת
השוני לאזני
משפחת האזני
לערי משפחת
הערי לארודי
משפחת הארודי
לאראלי משפחת
האראלי אלה

משפחת בני גד
לפקדיהם ארבעים
אלף וחמש מאות
בני יהודה
ער ואונן וימת ער
ואונן בארץ כנען
ויהיו בני יהודה
למשפחתם לשלה
משפחת השלני
לפרץ משפחת
הפרצי לזרח
משפחת הזרחי
ויהיו בני פרץ
לחצרן משפחת
החצרני לחמול
משפחת החמולי
אלה משפחת
יהודה לפקדיהם
ששה ושבעים
אלף וחמש מאות
פ

בני יששכר למשפחתם
תולע משפחת
התולעי לפוה
משפחת הפוני
לישוב משפחת
הישבי לשמרן
משפחת השמרני
אלה משפחת
יששכר לפקדיהם
ארבעה וששים
אלף ושלש מאות

בני זבולן למשפחתם
לסרד משפחת
הסרדי לאלון
משפחת האלוני
ליחלאל משפחת
היחלאלי אלה
משפחת הזבולני
לפקדיהם ששים
אלף וחמש מאות

Plate 19

A TORAH MANUSCRIPT FROM THE YEAR 930 A.D.

Cod. 17 of the 2nd Firkowitsch Collection (cf. pp. 22 f.). Illustration (Deut. ix. 15-23) from Kahle, *Masoreten des Westens* I (1927)

At the end of the Codex, which contains 241 leaves each with three columns, the scribe and the Masorete of the Codex, two brothers, give an account of their work.

The scribe's colophon reads: "I, Solomon ha-Levi, son of Buja'a [1]), the pupil of Sa'id, the son of Fargai, also called Balquq, wrote this book of the Torah of Moses, as the good hand of my God is upon me, for our Lord Barhon and for our Lord Salich, the sons of our Lord Maimun ..."

The Masorete writes: "I, Ephraim, son of Rabbi Buja'a, have pointed this Torah, provided it with Masora and completed it, and checked it over as the good hand of my God is upon me, and if there is a fault in it, may God not reckon it to me as a sin. I finished it on Friday, the eighth day of the month Chislev of the year 1241 of the (Seleucid) era, for our Lord Abraham and our Lord Salich, the sons of our Lord Maimun. May this Torah be for them, for us and for all Israel a good sign, a sign of blessing for salvation and for help, for the coming of the Messiah and the building of Jerusalem, and for the gathering of the capitivity of Israel, just as our Creator, the Builder of Jerusalem has assured us, Yahweh will gather the scattered of Israel and raise up a banner for the nations, and gather the scattered of Israel and the slain of Judah from the four corners of the earth (Isa. xi. 12)" [2]).

---

[1]) Solomon ben Buja'a also wrote the Ben Asher Codex in Aleppo (cf. p. 25).

[2]) Text following Kahle, *Masoreten des Westens* I (1927), pp. 58f. The Hebrew text (H. Strack, *Dikduke ha-Te'amim*) was not available to me.

ההר וההר
בער באש ושני
לחת הברית על
שתי ידי וארא
והנה חטאתם
ליהוה אלהיכם
עשיתם לכם
עגל מסכה
סרתם מהר מן
הדרך אשר צוה
יהוה אתכם
ואתפש בשני
הלחת ואשלכם
מעל שתי ידי
ואשברם לעיניכם
ואתנפל לפני
יהוה כראשנה
ארבעים יום
וארבעים לילה

לחם לא אכלתי
ומים לא שתיתי
על כל חטאתכם
אשר חטאתם
לעשות הרע
בעיני יהוה
להכעיסו כי
יגרתי מפני האף
והחמה אשר
קצף יהוה עליכם
להשמיד אתכם
וישמע יהוה
אלי גם בפעם
ההוא ובאהרן
התאנף יהוה
מאד להשמידו
ואתפלל גם בעד
אהרן בעת ההוא
ואת חטאתכם
אשר עשיתם

את העגל
לקחתי ואשרף
אתו באש ואכת
אתו טחון היטב
עד אשר דק
לעפר ואשלך
את עפרו אל
הנחל הירד מן
ההר ובתבערה
ובמסה ובקברת
התאוה מקצפים
הייתם את יהוה
ובשלח יהוה
אתכם מקדש
ברנע לאמר
עלו ורשו את
הארץ אשר
נתתי לכם ותמרו
את פי יהוה
אלהיכם ולא

Plate 20

CODEX LENINGRADENSIS

Cf. p. 26. Illustration (Gen. xxviii. 18-xxix. 22) from a photograph kindly lent by P. Kahle

The following colophon supplies information concerning the age of the manuscript [1]):

"This codex, the whole of the sacred scriptures, was written and provided with pointing and Masora and carefully corrected in the capital of Egypt (Cairo). And it was completed a) in the month Siwan of the year 4770 from the creation of the world.

b) That is the year 1444 from the exile of King Jehoiachin.

c) That is the year (1) 319 of the empire of the Greeks, that is, according to the reckoning of the (Seleucid) era, and from the cessation of prophecy.

d) That is the year 940 from the destruction of the second Temple.

e) That is the year 399 of the rule of the little horn (cf. Dan. viii. 9; Islam is intended). Meboraḥ ben Nathanael, known as Ben Osdad, the priest, acquired it ...".

The dating indicates the following years: a) 1010 A.D.; c) 1008; d) 1009; e) 1008. The date b) falls outside this period and presumably depends upon mistaken evidence. Since the scribe lived in a Mohammedan land, we may trust most the date e) —1008 A.D.

The following postscript refers to Ben Asher:

"Samuel ben Jacob wrote and pointed this codex of the sacred scriptures and provided it with Masora, from the corrected and annotated books which were made by Aaron ben Moshe ben Asher, the teacher. May he rest in the Garden of Eden! And it is corrected, and correctly annotated". The dependence upon Ben Asher manuscripts, which has sometimes been questioned, is confirmed by recent research (cf. BH pp. VIff.).

---

1) The text of the colophon is printed and partly translated by A. Harkavy and H. L. Strack, *Catalog der hebr. Bibelhandschriften der Kaiserlichen Öffentlichen Bibliothek in St. Petersburg* (1875), pp. 265ff.

על ראשה ויקרא את
שם המקום ההוא בית
אל ואולם לוז שם העיר
לראשנה וידר יעקב
נדר לאמר אם יהיה
אלהים עמדי ושמרני
בדרך הזה אשר אנכי
הולך ונתן לי לחם לאכל
ובגד ללבש ושבתי בשלום
אל בית אבי והיה יהוה לי
לאלהים והאבן הזאת
אשר שמתי מצבה יהיה
בית אלהים וכל אשר תתן
לי עשר אעשרנו לך
וישא יעקב רגליו וילך
ארצה בני קדם וירא והנה
באר בשדה והנה שם
שלשה עדרי צאן רבצים
עליה כי מן הבאר ההוא
ישקו העדרים והאבן
גדלה על פי הבאר
ונאספו שמה כל העדרים
וגללו את האבן מעל פי
הבאר והשקו את הצאן
והשיבו את האבן על פי
הבאר למקמה ויאמר
להם יעקב אחי מאין אתם

ויאמרו מחרן אנחנו
ויאמר להם הידעתם את
לבן בן נחור ויאמרו ידענו
ויאמר להם השלום לו
ויאמרו שלום והנה רחל
בתו באה עם הצאן
ויאמר הן עוד היום גדול
לא עת האסף המקנה
השקו הצאן ולכו רעו
ויאמרו לא נוכל עד אשר
יאספו כל העדרים וגללו
את האבן מעל פי הבאר
והשקינו הצאן עודנו מ
מדבר עמם ורחל באה
עם הצאן אשר לאביה
כי רעה היא ויהי כאשר
ראה יעקב את רחל בת
לבן אחי אמו ואת צאן
לבן אחי אמו ויגש יעקב
ויגל את האבן מעל פי
הבאר וישק את צאן לבן
אחי אמו וישק יעקב ל
לרחל וישא את קלו ויבך
ויגד יעקב לרחל כי אחי
אביה הוא וכי בן רבקה
הוא ותרץ ותגד לאביה
ויהי כשמע לבן את שמע

יעקב בן אחתו וירץ
לקראתו ויחבק לו וינשק
לו ויביאהו אל ביתו ויספר
ללבן את כל הדברים האלה
ויאמר לו לבן אך עצמי
ובשרי אתה וישב עמו
חדש ימים ויאמר לבן
ליעקב הכי אחי אתה
ועבדתני חנם הגידה לי
מה משכרתך וללבן שתי
בנות שם הגדלה לאה
ושם הקטנה רחל ועיני
לאה רכות ורחל היתה
יפת תאר ויפת מראה
ויאהב יעקב את רחל
ויאמר אעבדך שבע
שנים ברחל בתך הקטנה
ויאמר לבן טוב תתי אתה
לך מתתי אתה לאיש
אחר שבה עמדי ויעבד
יעקב ברחל שבע שנים
ויהיו בעיניו כימים אחדים
באהבתו אתה ויאמר
יעקב אל לבן הבה את
אשתי כי מלאו ימי ואבואה
אליה ויאסף לבן את כל
אנשי המקום ויעש משתה

Plate 21

A BEN NAPHTALI MANUSCRIPT

Oxford, Bodleian Library

Cf. p. 19. Illustration (Ps. cxii. 2-cxiv. 3) from Kahle, *Masoreten des Westens* II (1930)

The leaf illustrated forms, with five others, the remains of a manuscript of the Psalter which reveals certain peculiarities characteristic of a definite manuscript group. This group, which is clearly differentiated from the Ben Asher manuscripts, is to be connected with Ben Naphtali, as Kahle has shown (cf. *op. cit.* pp. 57*ff.).

In the text illustrated, the following peculiarities as compared with the Ben Asher text may be noted:

1. If א is to be pronounced as a consonant, it has a dot in the middle: בארץ Ps. cxii. 2; אור cxii. 4; איש cxii. 5; יראה cxii. 8; תאות cxii. 10; את cxiii. 1; אם cxiii. 9. If it is not to be pronounced, a line is placed above it: לא cxii. 6, 7, 8.

2. The mappiq in final ה, which indicates its pronunciation as a consonant, is placed under the letter: הללויה cxiii, 1, 9.

3. If a final ו is to be pronounced as a consonant, it has a shewa, placed within the letter: בצריו cxii. 8.

4. ח and ע, at the end of a word, receive a shewa: בטוח cxii. 7; רשע cxii. 10.

5. Furtive pathaḥ is missing where we should expect it: בטוח cxii. 7.

6. The two dots of the composite shewa with ה and ח do not stand next to the vowel sign, but above it: יחרק cxii. 10.

7. The relative particle אשר is not pointed: cxii. 8. Similarly, proper names which occur frequently are either left unpointed or only partially pointed: ישראל cxiv. 2.

The manuscript illustrated was further worked over by a second hand, the additions being substantially the accents of the *textus receptus* (Kahle, *op.cit.* p. 52*).

גבור בארץ יהיה זרעו   דור ישרים יברך
הון ועשר בביתו   וצדקתו עמדת לעד
זרח בחשך אור לישרים   חנון ורחום וצדיק
טוב איש חונן ומלוה   יכלכל דבריו במשפט
כי לעולם לא ימוט   לזכר עולם יהיה צדיק
משמועה רעה לא יירא   נכון לבו בטוח ביהוה
סמוך לבו לא יירא   עד אשר יראה בצריו
פזר נתן לאביונים צדקתו עמדת לעד   קרנו תרום בכבוד
רשע יראה וכעס שניו יחרק ונמס   תאות רשעים תאבד
הללויה

קי״ג

הללו עבדי יהוה   הללו את שם יהוה
יהי שם יהוה מברך   מעתה ועד עולם
ממזרח שמש עד מבואו   מהלל שם יהוה
רם על כל גוים יהוה   על השמים כבודו
מי כיהוה אלהינו   המגביהי לשבת
המשפילי לראות   בשמים ובארץ
מקימי מעפר דל   מאשפות ירים אביון
להושיבי עם נדיבים   עם נדיבי עמו
מושיבי עקרת הבית   אם הבנים שמחה הללויה

קי״ד

בצאת ישראל ממצרים   בית יעקב מעם לעז
היתה יהודה לקדשו   ישראל ממשלותיו
הים ראה וינס   הירדן יסב לאחור

Plate 22

FIRST RABBINIC BIBLE OF FELIX PRATENSIS (1516/17)

Cf. p. 27 n. 3 (Gen. xxi. 32b-xxii. 13). — Illustration by kind permission of the Bodleian Library, Oxford.

Rabbinic Bibles (מקראות גדולות) are the printed copies of the Old Testament, produced from the sixteenth century onwards, in which the Hebrew text, Targum, Masora and Rabbinic commentaries are brought together. The first, as yet without Masora, was published by Felix Pratensis of the Order of Augustinian Hermits in 1516/17 at the Bomberg press in Venice. Felix was the son of a learned rabbi and was thus conversant with Hebrew studies from his youth. After his conversion he engaged in classical studies, and made himself familiar with the scientific methods of classical philology. These he applied to the Hebrew text of the Bible — just as was done at about the same time by the editors of the Complutensian Polyglot (cf. p. 164). By collating many manuscripts, he endeavoured to present a correct text — 'rem equidem perdifficilem nec ob id ab aliis hactenus tentatam' (an extremely difficult matter which has, for this reason, not previously been attempted by others). In contrast to the many faulty manuscripts which were in circulation — in reality they were probably manuscripts from another masoretic school, that of Ben Naphtali — Felix was conscious of having restored to the Hebrew text its 'true and original splendour' (verus et nativus candor). In addition, he was 'the first to show Q^e^re and K^e^tib in a printed Bible, and to introduce into print the *puncta extraordinaria*, the letters which are differently written or placed (*literae majusculae, suspensae, inversae* etc.) following the manuscripts. He also cited as *variae lectiones* small variations in the manuscripts which he used, in regard to vowels, accents and consonants [1]). Since this critically edited first Rabbinic Bible provided in large measure the basis for the second such Bible edited by Jacob ben Chayyim (cf.pp. 27 f.) and the latter was the pattern for many later editions, the work of Felix Pratensis had far-reaching influence.

Further Rabbinic Bibles appeared in Venice (1546/48; 1568, 1617/19); Basle (1618/19, by Johannes Buxtorf the Elder); Amsterdam (1724/25); Warsaw (1860/66, with 32 commentaries [2]).

---

[1]) P. Kahle, *Welt des Orients* (1947), p. 36; cf.; cf. also Kahle in *Tribute to Leo Baeck* (1954), pp. 50ff.; C. D. Ginsburg, *Introduction to the Massoretico-Critical Edition of the Hebrew Bible* (1897), pp. 925ff.

[2]) *Encyclopaedia Judaica* 4 (1929), cols 547f.

צבאו וישבו אל ארץ פלשתים ׃ ויטע אשל בבאר שבע ויקרא שם
בשם יהוה אל עולם ׃ ויגר אברהם בארץ פלשתים ימים רבים ׃
כב ויהי אחר הדברים האלה והאלהים נסה
את אברהם ויאמר אליו אברהם ויאמר הנני ׃ ויאמר קח נא את בנך
את יחידך אשר אהבת את יצחק ולך לך אל ארץ המריה והעלהו
שם לעלה על אחד ההרים אשר אמר אליך ׃ וישכם אברהם בבקר
ויחבש את חמרו ויקח את שני נעריו אתו ואת יצחק בנו ויבקע עצי
עלה ויקם וילך אל המקום אשר אמר לו האלהים ׃ ביום השלישי
וישא אברהם את עיניו וירא את המקום מרחק ׃ ויאמר אברהם אל
נעריו שבו לכם פה עם החמור ואני והנער נלכה עד כה ונשתחוה
ונשובה אליכם ׃ ויקח אברהם את עצי העלה וישם על יצחק בנו
ויקח בידו את האש ואת המאכלת וילכו שניהם יחדו ׃ ויאמר יצחק
אל אברהם אביו ויאמר אבי ויאמר הנני בני ויאמר הנה האש ו
והעצים ואיה השה לעלה ׃ ויאמר אברהם אלהים יראה לו
השה לעלה בני וילכו שניהם יחדו ׃ ויבאו אל המקום אשר
אמר לו האלהים ויבן שם אברהם את המזבח ויערך את העצים
ויעקד את יצחק בנו וישם אתו על המזבח ממעל לעצים ׃
וישלח אברהם את ידו ויקח את המאכלת לשחט את בנו ׃
ויקרא אליו מלאך יהוה מן השמים ויאמר אברהם אברהם ויאמר
הנני ׃ ויאמר אל תשלח ידך אל הנער ואל תעש לו מאומה
כי עתה ידעתי כי ירא אלהים אתה ולא חשכת את בנך את יחידך
ממני ׃ וישא אברהם את עיניו וירא והנה איל אחר נאחז
בסבך בקרניו וילך אברהם ויקח את האיל ויעלהו לעלה תחת

חליה ותבו לארעא דפלשתאי ׃ ונציב אילנא בבאר שבע וצלי תמן
בשמא דיי אלהא דעלמא ׃ ואתותב אברהם בארעא פלשתאי יומין
סגיאין ׃ והוה בתר פתגמיא האלין ויי נסי ית
אברהם ואמר ליה אברהם ואמר הא אנא ׃ ואמר דבר כען ית ברך
ית יחידך די רחימתא ית יצחק ואיזיל לך לארעא פולחנא ואסקיה
קדמי תמן לעלתא על חד מן טוריא די איימר לך ׃ ואקדים אברהם
בצפרא וזריז ית חמריה ודבר ית תרין עולימוהי עמיה וית יצחק
בריה וצלח אעי לעלתא וקם ואזל לאתרא די אמר ליה יי ׃ ביומא
תליתאה וזקף אברהם ית עינוהי וחזא ית אתרא מרחיק ׃ ואמר
אברהם לעולימוהי אוריכו לכון הכא עם חמרא ואנא ועולימא
נתמטי עד כא ונסגוד ונתוב לותכון ׃ ונסיב אברהם ית אעי דעלתא
ושוי על יצחק בריה ונסיב בידיה ית אשתא וית סכינא ואזלו תרויהון
כחדא ׃ ואמר יצחק לאברהם אבוהי ואמר אבא ואמר הא אנא ברי
ואמר הא אשתא ואעיא ואן אמרא לעלתא ׃ ואמר אברהם
קדם יי גלי ליה אמרא לעלתא ברי ואזלו תרויהון כחדא ׃ ואתו
לאתרא די אמר ליה יי ובנא תמן אברהם ית מדבחא וסדר ית
אעיא ועקד ית יצחק בריה ושוי יתיה על מדבחא עיל מן אעיא ׃
ואושיט אברהם ית ידיה ונסיב ית סכינא למיכס ית בריה ׃ וקרא
ליה מלאכא דיי מן שמיא ואמר אברהם אברהם ואמר הא אנא ׃
ואמר לא תושיט ידך בעולימא ולא תעביד ליה מדעם ארי כען
ידעית ארי דחלא דיי את ולא מנעת ית ברך ית יחידך מני ׃
וזקף אברהם ית עינוהי בתר אילין וחזא והא דכר בתר אחיד באילנא
בקרנוהי ואזל אברהם ונסיב ית דיכרא ואסקיה לעלתא חלף

אשל· רב ושמואל חד אמר פרדס היה להביא ממנו פירות לאורחים בסעודה· וחד אמר פונדק לאכסניא ובו כל מיני פירות· ומצינו לשון נטיעה באהלים שנ' ויטע אהלי אפדנו: ויקרא שם וגו'· על ידי אותו אשל הוקרא שמו של הקב"ה אלוה לכל העולם לאחר שאוכלין ושותין אומר להם ברכו למי שאכלתם משלו סבורים אתם שמשלי אכלתם משל מי שאמר והיה העולם אכלתם: ימים רבים· מרובין על של חברון בחברון עשה כה' שנה וכאן כו' שהרי בן שבעים וחמש שנה היה בצאתו מחרן אותה שנה ויבא וישב באלוני ממרא שלא מצינו קודם לכן שנתישב אלא שם שבכל מקומותיו היה כאורח חונה ונוסע והולך שנ' ויעבור אברם ויעתק משם ויהי רעב וירד אבר' מצרי' ובמצרי' לא עשה אלא שלשה חדשי' שהרי שלחו פרעה מיד וילך למסעיו עד ויבא וישב באלוני ממרא אשר בחברון שם ישב עד שנהפכה סדום מיד ויסע משם אברהם מפני בושה של לוט ובא לארץ פלשתים ובן צט' שנה היה שהרי בשלישי למילתו באו אצלו המלאכי' הרי כה' שנה וכאן כתוב ימים רבים מרובים על הראשונים ולא בא הכתוב לסתום אלא לפרש ואם היו מרובים שתי שנים או יותר היה מפרש על כרחך אינם יתרים יותר משנה הרי כו' שנה מיד יצא משם וחזר לחברון' ואותה שנה קדמה לפני עקידתו של יצחק יב' שנים כך בסדר עולם: אחר הדברים האלה· יש מרבותינו אומרי' אחר דבריו של שטן שהיה מקטרג ואומ' מכל סעודה שעשה אברהם לא הקריב לפניך פר אחד או איל אחד אמר לו כלום עשה אלא בשביל בנו אלו הייתי אומר לו זבח אותו לפני לא היה מעכב· ויא' אחר דבריו של ישמעאל שהיה מתפאר על יצחק שמל בן שלש עשרה שנה ולא מיחה אמר לו יצחק באבר אחד אתה מיראני אלו אמר לי הקב"ה זבח עצמך לפני לא הייתי מעכב: הנני· כך היא ענייתם של חסידים לשון ענוה הוא ולשון זימון: קח נא· אין נא אלא לשון בקשה אמר לו בבקשה ממך עמוד לי בזו בנסיון שלא יאמרו הראשונות לא היה בהן ממש: את בנך· אמר לו שני בנים יש לי אמר לו את יחידך אמר לו זה יחיד לאמו וזה יחיד לאמו אמר לו אשר אהבת אמר לו שניהם אני אוהב אמר לו את יצחק ולמה לא גלה לו מתחלה שלא לערבבו פתאום ותזוח דעתו עליו ותטרף וכדי לחבב עליו את המצוה וליתן לו שכר על כל דבור ודבור: ארץ המוריה· ירושלם וכן בדברי הימים לבנות בית ה' בהר המוריה ורבותי' פרשו על שם שמשם הוראה יוצאה לישראל· ואונקלוס תרגמו על שם עבודת הקטורת שיש בו מור נרד ושאר בשמים: והעלהו· לא אמר לו שחטהו לפי שלא היה חפץ הקב"ה לשחטו אלא להעלהו להר לעשותו עולה ומשהעלהו אמר לו הורידהו: אחד ההרים· הקב"ה מתלה הצדיקים ואחר כך מגלה להם וכל זה כדי להרבות שכרן וכן אל הארץ אשר אראך וכן בינוה וקרא עליה את הקריאה: וישכם· נזדרז למצוה: ויחבש· הוא בעצמו ולא צוה לאחד מעבדיו שהאהבה מקלקלת השורה: את שני נעריו· ישמעאל ואליעזר שאין אדם חשוב רשאי לצאת לדרך בלא שני אנשים שאם יצטרך האחד לנקביו ויתרחק יהיה השני עמו: ויבקע· תרגו' וצלח כמו צלחו הירדן לשון בקוע פינדרא בלעז: ביום השלישי· למה אחר מלהראותו מיד כדי שלא יאמרו הממו וערבבו פתאו' וטרף דעתו ואלו היה לו שהות להמלך אל לבו לא היה עושה: וירא את המקום· ראה ענן קשור על ההר: עד כה· כלומר דרך מועט למקום אשר לפנינו· ומדרש אגדה אראה היכן הוא כה שאמר לי המקום כה יהיה זרעך: ונשובה· נתנבא שישובו שניהם: מאכלת· סכין על שם שאוכלת את הבשר כמו וחרבי תאכל בשר ומאכלת על שם שישראל אוכלין בזכותה: וילכו שניהם יחדו· אברהם שהיה יודע שהולך לשחוט את בנו היה הולך ברצון ושמחה כיצחק שלא היה מרגיש בדבר: יראה לו השה· כלומר יראה ויבחר לו השה ואם אין שה לעולה בני ואעפ"י שהבין יצחק שהולך לישחט וילכו שניהם יחדו בלב שוה: ויעקד· ידיו ורגליו מאחוריו הידים והרגלים ביחד הוא עקידה לשון עקודים שהיו קרסוליהם לבנים מקום שעוקדים אותן בו היה ניכר: אל תשלח· לשחוט אמר לו אם כן לחנם באתי לכאן אעשה בו חבלה ואוציא ממנו מעט דם אמר לו אל תעש לו מאומה אל תעש בו מום: כי עתה ידעתי· אמר רבי אבא אמר לו אברהם אפרש לפניך את שיחתי אתמול אמרת לי כי ביצחק יקרא לך זרע וחזרת ואמרת קח נא את בנך עכשיו אתה אומר לי אל תשלח ידך אל הנער· אמר לו הקב"ה לא אחלל בריתי ומוצא שפתי לא אשנה כשאמרתי לך קח לא אמרתי לך שחטהו אלא העלהו אסקתיה אחתיה: כי עתה ידעתי· מעתה יש לי מה להשיב לשטן ולאומות התמהים מה היא חבתי אצלך יש לי פתחון פה עכשיו שרואים כי ירא אלהים אתה: והנה איל· מוכן היה לכך מששת ימי בראשית: אחר· אחרי שאמר לו המלאך אל תשלח ידך ראהו: בסבך· אילן: בקרניו· שהיה רץ אצל אברהם והשטן סובכו ומערבבו באילנות: תחת בנו· מאחר שכתוב ויעלהו לעולה מה תלמוד לומר תחת בנו על כל עבודה שהיה עושה ממנו היה מתפלל ואומר יהי רצון שתהא זו כאלו היא עשויה בבני כאלו בני נשחט כאלו דמו נזרק כאלו בני מופשט כאלו הוא נקטר ונעשה דשן:

ה' יראה

Plate 23

SAMARITAN TRIGLOT

Cf. pp. 31 f. (Illustration (Deut. xxxi.15-19) from Kahle, *Die Handschriften aus der Höhle* (1951)

The illustration shows a leaf obtained by P. Kahle from a valuable triglot in Nablus (Shechem), the so-called Torah Finchasiye, which was written in the year 601 of the Mohammedan era, that is, the year 1204/5 A.D. From right to left, the Hebrew, Aramaic and Arabic texts, all in Samaritan letters, are written in three columns. The script was developed from the Old Hebrew. Kahle comments on it, with reference to the fragments of Leviticus in Old Hebrew script found by de Vaux (cf. Plate 12): "The forms of the letters have naturally developed somewhat further, and certain principles in the method of writing Biblical manuscripts have also evolved in course of time. But apart from this it is amazing to see how constant the Old Hebrew script has remained through the period of 1000 to 1500 years". (Kahle, *op.cit.* pp. 19f.).

The following points in the manuscript may also be noted. The individual words are separated by dots. The first and the last two letters of each line in the Hebrew and Aramaic columns are written exactly under one another. There is also a tendency to write identical letters which occur in adjacent lines directly under one another (cf. for example, lines 7 and 8, 11 and 12). As a rule, Samaritan manuscripts of the Pentateuch contain no vocalisation.

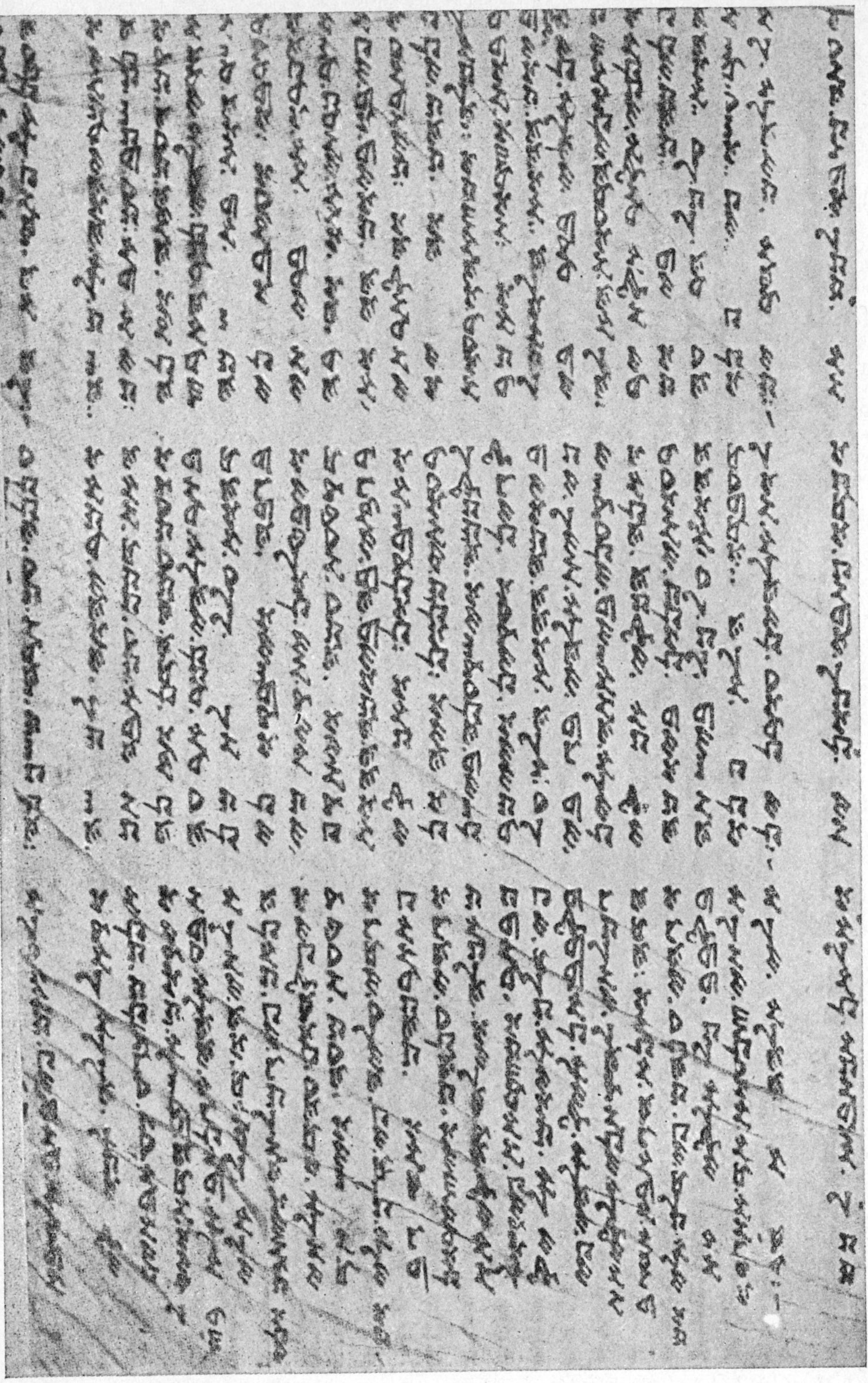

Plate 24

RYLANDS GREEK PAPYRUS (458)

Cf. p. 51. Illustration from a photograph kindly lent by the John Rylands Library, Manchester.

Contents: a) Deut. xxiii.24 (26)-xxiv.3; b) Deut. xxv.1-3; c) Deut. xxvi.12; d) Deut. xxvi.17-19; e) Deut. xxviii.31-33; f) Deut. xxvii.15(?); g) Deut. xxviii.2(?); h) ?

These fragments were discovered in the wrappings of a mummy, obtained by Dr. Rendel Harris in 1917 for the John Rylands Library. They presumably come from the Fayyum, where, as we know, there were two Jewish synagogues. Date: mid-second century B.C. The reverse of the scroll of Deuteronomy, from which the fragments come, was later used for accounts or notes.

Of particular interest is the quite rare system of spacing: "As can be seen from the photograph of fragment (b) the writer regularly leaves a space not only at the end of a verse or sentence, but at the end of a κῶλον or group of words. At the end of a verse ... (fragment (a) line 14 after αυτου in the illustration), a wider space is left and a high point added; otherwise the writer's principle seems to be to leave a fairly large space at the end of a sentence or clause ... (cf. fragment (b)), and a smaller one at the end of a group of words". (C. H. Roberts, *Two biblical Papyri in the John Rylands Library Manchester* (1936), p. 25). Is this division of the text connected with its use in public reading, or is it due to Aramaic influence? Apart from this the papyrus, like all other Greek manuscripts, has no word division.

It is of special significance that the papyrus agrees in some of its readings with late Lucianic manuscripts. "Hinc patet iuniores codices quam antiqua elementa saepe contineant et quam profunda habeat fundamenta Luciani recensio". (A. Vaccari, *Biblica* 17 (1936), p. 504).

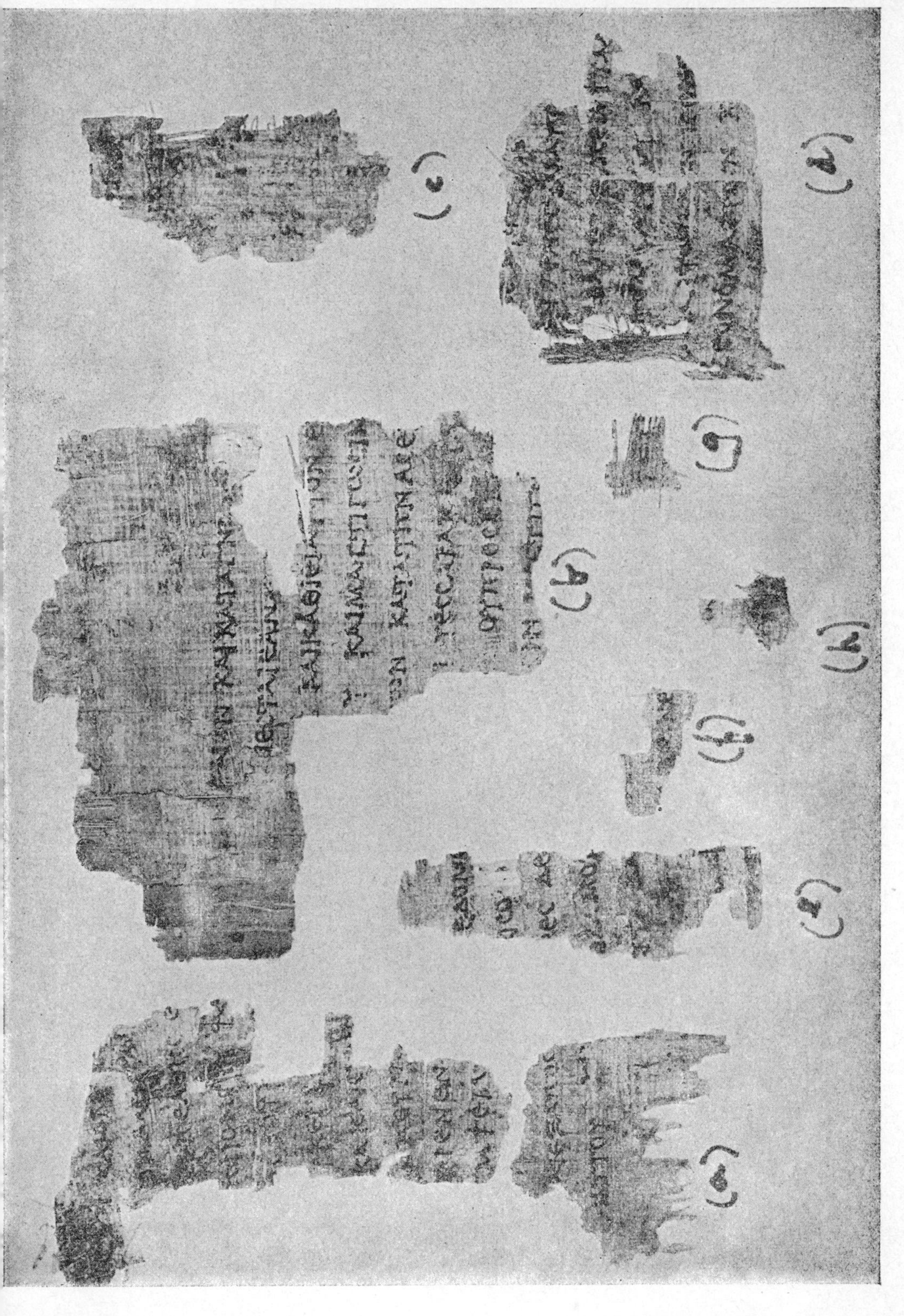

Plate 25

PAPYRUS FOUAD 266

Cf. p. 51. Société Royale de Papyrologie, Kairo; first published by W. G. Waddell, *J.T.S.* 45 (1944), pp. 158ff.

Illustration (Deut. xxxi. 28-xxxii. 6) from Kahle, *Handschriften aus der Höhle* (1951)

This papyrus probably belongs to the first, or perhaps even to the second, century B.C., and is thus, with Rylands Greek Papyrus 458, the oldest witness to the Greek translation of the Old Testament. It was evidently written by a Jew. Of particular interest is the treatment of the divine name Yahweh. With regard to the writing of this name in Greek manuscripts, Jerome reports as follows in the *Prologus Galeatus*: "Nomen Domini tetragrammaton in quibusdam Graecis voluminibus usque hodie antiquis expressum litteris invenimur". (Migne 28, pp. 594f.); and further in *Epistula* 25 *ad Marcellam*: "(Dei nomen est) tetragrammum, quod ἀνεκφώνητον, id est ineffabile, putaverunt et his litteris scribitur: iod, he, vau, he. Quod quidam non intellegentes propter elementorum similitudinem, cum in Graecis libris reppererint, ΠΙΠΙ legere consueverunt". (*Corpus Scriptorum Ecclesiasticorum Latinorum* 54 (1910), p. 219).

Jerome thus knew the custom of writing the name Yahweh in Hebrew letters in Greek manuscripts. The papyrus illustrated here shows the practice in pre-Christian times. In col. ii, lines 7 and 15, in the middle of the Greek text, Yahweh is written in the square script. In fact, the scribe of the Greek text left a space in which another hand inserted the Hebrew letters so small as not to fill the space.

Cf. also the writing of the divine name in the Habakkuk Commentary (Plate 11), and the remarks on this on p. 104.

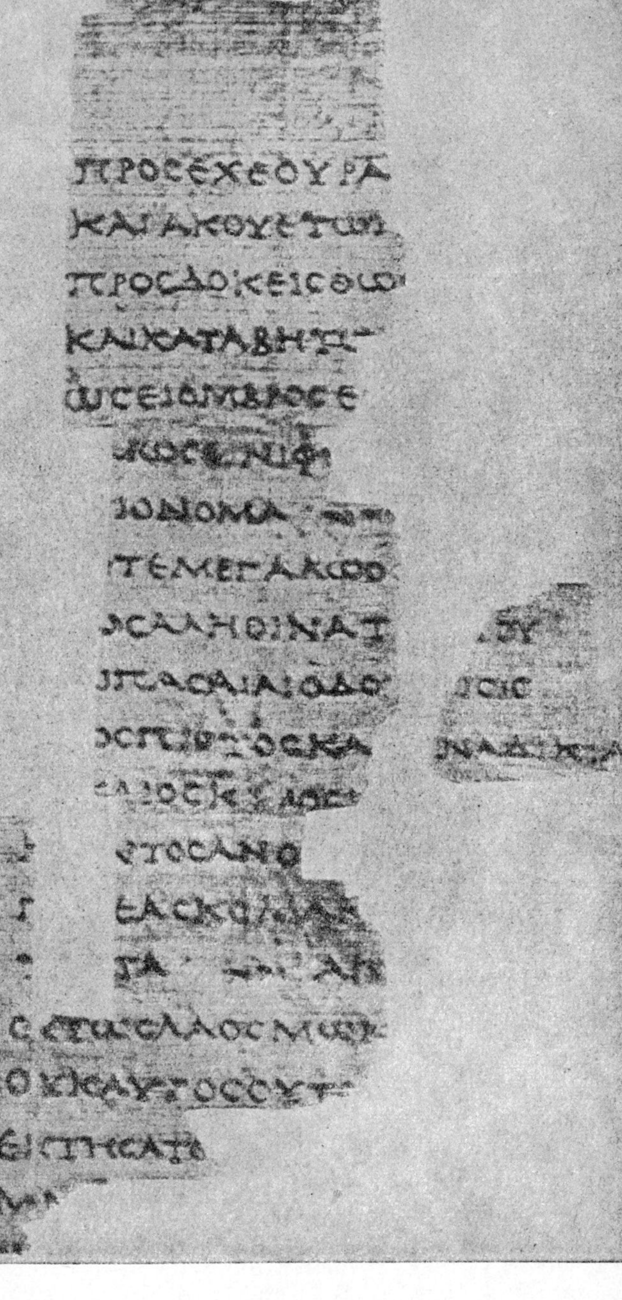
ΠΡΟCΕΧΕΟΥΡΑ
ΚΑΙΑΚΟΥΕΤΩ
ΠΡΟCΔΟΚΕΙCΘΩ
ΚΑΙΚΑΤΑΒΗΤ
ΩCΕΙΟΜΒΡΟCΕ

Plate 26

CHESTER BEATTY PAPYRUS 967

Cf. p. 51. Illustration (Ezek. xvi. 57-xvii. 1) from the edition by F. G. Kenyon mentioned on p. 51 n. 4.

After a detailed examination of the Chester Beatty Papyrus 967 (34 sheets—68 pages of a codex of Ezekiel from the first half of the third century), J. Ziegler came to the following conclusions, reproduced here because of their importance for the problems of 𝔊:

"1. Papyrus 967 supports the oldest, pre-hexaplaric original readings, previously attested only by manuscript B ... Further, these readings in 967 B are normally found in the Old Latin, and frequently in the Coptic. The tradition represented by 967 B La (= 𝔏) Co (𝔎) thus provides the oldest attainable form of the Greek text of Ezekiel.

2. In several places 967 *alone* has preserved the original reading.

3. The chief significance of Pap. 967 is that it shows that already in the period before the Hexapla (even perhaps in the first century A.D.), the LXX of Ezekiel was being corrected from the Hebrew text. The agreements with 𝔐 do in fact often coincide with hexaplaric readings corrected from 𝔐, and also with renderings of the three later Greek translators, Aquila, Symmachus and Theodotion, but are not dependent upon these. This revision was not a thorough one, improvement being introduced only here and there [1]).

4. The vocabulary of Pap. 967 shows that at an early date the Ezekiel text was revised, and since this revision was incorporated in all manuscripts, it was difficult to recognise that it had taken place. In his rendering of the Hebrew original, the translator was much more consistent than formerly appeared to be the case ... Even the rendering of the divine name as κύριος seems to have been consistently carried out. For this reason the theory of the division of the translation between several (three) individuals has become less certain.

5. The occasional agreement of Pap. 967 with readings of the Alexandrian manuscripts (A and its dependent minuscules), of the Lucianic recension (*L*) (BH = 𝔊 Luc) and the Catena Group (*C*), shows that these texts have often used old, pre-hexaplaric sources, and must not therefore be undervalued". (*Z.A.W.* 61 (1945/48), pp. 93f.).

---

[1]) Cf. on this p. 39 n. 3 Kahle, who traces such assimilations back to the pre-Christian era, regards it as certain 'that an Ezekiel text which had been worked over by Jews was the basis for the alterations in this valuable Ezekiel papyrus so far as they represent assimilation to the Hebrew original and to the parallel Jewish translations which Ziegler has noted'. (*T.L.Z.* 79 (1954), col. 89).

[illegible]
ρων συριας και πα[σων]
[τ]ων κυκλω αυτης θυγατε
ρων αλλοφυλων των περιε
χουσων σε κυκλω τας ασεβει
ας σου και τας ανομιας σου συ
κεκομισαι αυτας λεγει κ̅ς̅
και ποιησω εν σοι καθως εποιη
σας ως ητιμωσας ταυτα του
παραβηναι την διαθηκην μου
και μνησθησομαι εγω της δι
αθηκης μου της μετα σου εν
ημεραις νηπιοτητος σου και α
ναστησω σοι διαθηκην αιωνι
ον και μνησθηση την οδον σου
και εξατιμωθηση εν τω ανα
λαβειν με τας αδελφας σου τας
πρεσβυτερας σου συν ταις νε
ωτεραις σου και δωσω αυτας
σοι εις οικοδομην και ουκ εκ
διαθηκης σου και αναστησω
εγω την διαθηκην μου με
τα σου και επιγνωση οτι εγω
κ̅ς̅ ο θ̅ς̅ οπως μνησθης και αι
σχυνθης και μη η σοι ετι ανοι
ξαι το στομα σου απο προσω
που της ατιμιας σου εν τω ε
ξειλασεσθαι με σοι κατα πα[ν]
τα οσα εποιησας λεγει κ̅ς̅ κ[αι]
εγενετο λογος κ̅υ̅ προς με λε

Plate 27

THE BERLIN GENESIS

Cf. p. 52. Illustration (Gen. xxxiv.11-25) from H. A. Sanders and C. Schmidt: *The Minor Prophets in the Freer Collection and the Berlin Fragment of Genesis* (1927).

This Papyrus Codex was obtained by Prof. C. Schmidt in 1906 in Achmim in Upper Egypt, and presented to the Prussian State Library in Berlin. The well-known papyrus expert, Dr. Hugo Ibscher, was able with very great skill to unroll the codex, which was in very bad condition since it had been so long in the ground, and to prepare it for study. Its publication was delayed for various reasons until 1927, and it then appeared together with the related Papyrus Codex of the Minor Prophets in the Freer Collection.

This manuscript is in codex form: 16 double sheets, of which the first is lost, were laid one upon the other and folded to produce a single quire of 32 pages. The script is an early cursive, revealing a variety of stylistic features, but written by one hand. Since the text had to be written on a limited number of pages, the scribe's writing is cramped, especially towards the end (cf. Plate). From the general appearance, and the form of certain letters, the script "may be safely dated toward the end of the third century A.D." (Sanders, *op.cit.* p. 238).

Sanders observed a number of approximations of the text to the Hebrew original which date from the period before Origen. "Origen did not start this form of corruption in the text, though he doubtless increased it". (p. 265).

Plate 28

CODEX SINAITICUS

Cf. pp. 52f. Illustration (I Macc. ix. 12 f.; ix. 20-22. Jer. ix. 2 f.; ix. 9 f. Tobit vi. 5-7; vi. 11 f.) from Milne and Skeat, *Scribes and Correctors of the Codex Sinaiticus* (1938)

The illustration shows specimens of the hands of the three scribes who according to the above-mentioned study, were responsible for the writing of the codex. As was noted above (p. 53), several correctors also worked on the manuscript. Of particular interest in this connection is the note added in the sixth-seventh century at the end of Ezra and Esther. According to this, the codex was compared with a very old manuscript which had itself been corrected by the martyr Pamphilus, and this correction had been made from a copy of the Hexapla corrected by Origen himself.

The main facts concerning the discovery of this valuable manuscript, the last of the great Greek codices to be found, may here be briefly set out. On his first search for material in the East, Constantine von Tischendorf came in 1844 to the monastery of St.Catherine in Sinai. There, when he was in the library, he saw 129 leaves of a very old manuscript in a paper basket, put there for burning by the ignorant monks. 43 leaves — later called the Codex Friderico-Augustanus —were handed over to him, but the monks wished to keep the remainder since its value was now known to them. In 1853 Tischendorf returned to the monastery, to obtain or copy the leaves left behind. This was in vain, for they had been lost by the monks themselves, and could not be found. In 1859, Tischendorf made a further search, this time as envoy of the Russian Czar, the protector of Orthodox Christendom. But again all his efforts seemed to be in vain, until, on the eve of his departure, the steward, whom he had told about his search, showed him a codex in his cell. This not only included the 86 leaves for which he was searching, which had been left behind in 1844, but 112 further leaves of the Old Testament; in addition the whole New Testament was there, and two ancient Church writings which had been lost for centuries, the Letter of Barnabas and the Shepherd of Hermas. After prolonged negotiations, the Codex was brought to the Imperial Library in St.Petersburg, and in 1933 was sold by the Russian Government to the British Museum for the sum of £ 100,000.

ΣΑΛΠΙΓΞΙΝΚΑΙΕΣΑΛ
ΠΙΣΑΝΟΙΠΑΡΑΙΟΥ
ΔΑΚΑΙΑΥΤΟΙΤΑΙΣΣΑΛ
ΠΙΓΞΙΝΚΑΙΕΣΑΛΕΥ
ΘΗΗΓΗΑΠΟΤΗΣΦΩ
ΝΗΣΤΩΝΠΑΡΕΜΒΟ
ΛΩΝΚΑΙΕΓΕΝΕΤΟ
ΟΠΟΛΕΜΟΣΣΥΝΗΜ
ΜΕΝΟΣΑΠΟΠΡΩΙ
ΘΕΝΜΕΧΡΙΕΣΠΕΡΑΣ

ΠΟΛΛΑΣΚΑΙΕΙΠΟΝ
ΠΩΣΕΠΕΣΕΝΔΥΝΑ
ΤΟΣΣΩΖΩΝΤΟΝΙΣΛ
ΚΑΙΤΑΠΕΡΙΣΣΑΤΩΝ
ΛΟΓΩΝΙΟΥΔΑΚΑΙ
ΤΩΝΠΟΛΕΜΩΝΚΑΙ
ΤΩΝΑΝΔΡΑΓΑΘΙΩΝ
ΩΝΕΠΟΙΗΣΕΝΚΑΙ
ΤΗΣΜΕΓΑΛΩΣΥΝΗΣ
ΑΥΤΟΥΟΥΚΑΤΕΓΡΑ

ΣΟΝΨΕΥΔΟΣΚΑΙΟΥ
ΠΙΣΤΙΣΕΝΙΣΧΥΣΕΝ
ΕΠΙΤΗΣΓΗΣΟΤΙΕΚ
ΚΑΚΩΝΕΙΣΚΑΚΑΕ
ΞΗΛΘΟΣΑΝΚΑΙΕ
ΜΕΟΥΚΕΓΝΩΣΑΝ
ΕΚΑΣΤΟΣΑΠΟΤΟΥ
ΠΛΗΣΙΟΝΑΥΤΟΥ
ΦΥΛΑΞΕΣΘΑΙΚΑΙ
ΕΠΑΔΕΛΦΟΙΣΑΥΤΩ

ΤΑΣΤΡΙΒΟΥΣΤΗΣΕ
ΡΗΜΟΥΘΡΗΝΟΝΟ
ΤΙΕΞΕΛΙΠΟΝΠΑΡΑ
ΤΟΜΗΕΙΝΑΙΑΝΟΥΣ
ΟΥΚΗΚΟΥΣΑΝΦΩ
ΝΗΝΥΠΑΡΞΕΩΣ
ΑΠΟΠΕΤΕΙΝΩΝΤΟΥ
ΟΥΡΑΝΟΥΚΑΙΕΩΣ
ΚΤΗΝΩΝΕΞΕΣΤΗ
ΣΑΝΩΧΟΝΤΟΚΑΙ

ΚΑΙΤΟΗΠΑΡΚΑΙΩ
ΠΤΗΣΕΝΤΟΥΙΧΘΥ
ΟΣΚΑΙΕΦΑΓΕΝΚΑΙ
ΑΦΗΚΕΝΕΞΑΥΤΟΥ
ΗΛΙΣΜΕΝΟΝΚΑΙΕ
ΠΟΡΕΥΘΗΣΑΝΑΜ
ΦΟΤΕΡΟΙΚΟΙΝΩΣ
ΕΩΣΗΓΓΙΣΑΝΕΙΣ
ΜΗΔΙΑΝ
ΚΑΙΤΟΤΕΗΡΩΤΗΣΕ
ΤΟΠΑΙΔΑΡΙΟΝΤΟΝ

ΜΑΣΑΥΛΙΣΘΗΝΑΙ
ΚΑΙΟΑΝΘΡΩΠΟΣ
ΣΥΓΓΕΝΗΣΣΟΥΕ
ΣΤΙΝΚΑΙΕΣΤΙΝΑΥ
ΤΩΘΥΓΑΤΗΡΟΝΟ
ΜΑΣΑΡΡΑΚΑΙΥΙΟΣ
ΑΡΣΗΝΟΥΔΕΘΥΓΑΤΗΡ
ΥΠΑΡΧΕΙΑΥΤΩΠΛΗ
ΣΑΡΡΑΣΜΟΝΗΣΚΑΙ
ΣΥΕΓΓΙΣΤΑΑΥΤΗΣ
ΕΙΠΑΡΑΠΑΝΤΑΣ

Plate 29

CODEX COLBERTO-SARRAVIANUS

Cf. p. 53. Illustration from G. M. Perrella,
Introduzione Generale alla Sacra Biblia (1948)

The illustration (Josh. x.12-19) shows the beauty of this manuscript, which has two columns to each page. It belongs probably to the fifth century A.D., though some scholars think it may be fourth century. It has a special place among the uncials because it contains the hexaplaric text with many of the hexaplaric signs. On the page illustrated the following words are marked with obelisk (left-hand column lines 1-5): ηνικα συνεττιψεν αυτους εν γαβαων και συνετρειβησαν απο προσωπου ιη̅λ (= ισραηλ). These words were found by Origin in 𝔊, but are not in the Hebrew text.

Several parts of the text illustrated are supplied with asterisks, indicating that they were not found in 𝔊 by Origen, but were supplied from another Greek translation. If such a passage extends over several lines, the Aristarchian sign is repeated before each line. Cf. for example, verse 15, which is completely omitted from 𝔊 and appears here marked with asterisks (left-hand column at the bottom and right-hand column at the top): και επεστρεψεν ι̅ς̅ (= ιησους) και πας ιη̅λ μετ αυτου εις την παρεμβολην εις γαλγαλαν.

ΗΛ:ΤΗΝΙΚΑΣΥΝΕΤΡΙ
ΨΕΝΑΥΤΟΥΣΕΝΓΑΒΑ
ΩΝ:ΚΑΙΣΥΝΕΤΡΙΒΗ
ΣΑΝΑΠΟΠΡΟΣΩΠΟΥ
ΙΗΛ:ΚΑΙΕΙΠΕΝΙΣΟΗΛΙ
ΟΣΚΑΤΑΓΑΒΑΩΝΣΤΗ
ΤΩΚΑΙΗΣΕΛΗΝΗΚΑ
ΤΑΦΑΡΑΓΓΑΑΪΑΛΩΝ
ΚΑΙΕΣΤΗΟΗΛΙΟΣΚΑΙΗ
ΣΕΛΗΝΗΕΝΣΤΑΣΕΙΣ
ΩΣΗΜΥΝΑΤΟΟΘΣΤΟΥ
ΕΧΘΡΟΥΣΑΥΤΩΝ·ΟΥ
ΧΙΤΟΥΤΟΓΕΓΡΑΜΜΕ
ΝΟΝΕΠΙΒΙΒΛΙΟΥΤΟΥ
ΕΥΘΟΥΣ:ΚΑΙΕΣΤΗΟ
ΗΛΙΟΣΚΑΤΑΜΕΣΟΝΤΟΥ
ΟΥΡΑΝΟΥΟΥΠΡΟΕ
ΠΟΡΕΥΕΤΟΕΙΣΔΥΣΜΑΣ
ΕΙΣΤΕΛΟΣΗΜΕΡΑΣΜΙ
ΑΣ:ΚΑΙΟΥΚΕΓΕΝΕΤΟ
ΗΜΕΡΑΤΟΙΑΥΤΗΟΥΔΕ
ΤΟΠΡΟΤΕΡΟΝΟΥΔΕ
ΤΟΕΣΧΑΤΟΝΩΣΤΕΕ
ΠΑΚΟΥΣΑΙΘΝ·ΦΩ
ΝΗΣ:ΑΝΟΥΟΤΙΚΣΣΥ
ΝΕΠΟΛΕΜΗΣΕΝΤΩ
ΙΗΛ·ΚΑΙΕΠΕΣΤΡΕΨ·
ΙΣΚΑΙΠΑΣΙΗΛΜΕΤΑΥ

·ΤΟΥΕΙΣΤΗΝΠΑΡΕΜΒ
·ΛΗΝΕΙΣΓΑΛΓΑΛΑΝ:
ΚΑΙΕΦΥΓΟΝΟΙΕΒΑΣΙ
ΛΕΙΣΟΥΤΟΙΚΑΙΚΑΤΕ
ΚΡΥΒΗΣΑΝΕΙΣΤΟΣΠΗ
ΛΑΙΟΝΤΟΕΙΣΜΑΚΗΔΑ
ΚΑΙΑΠΗΓΓΕΛΗΤΩΙΥ
ΛΕΓΟΝΤΕΣΕΥΡΗΝΤΑ
ΟΙΕΒΑΣΙΛΕΙΣΚΕΚΡΥ
ΜΕΝΟΙΕΝΤΩΣΠΗ
ΛΑΙΩΤΩΕΝΜΑΚΗΔΑ
ΚΑΙΕΙΠΕΝΙΣΚΥΛΙΣΑΤΕ
ΛΙΘΟΥΣ·ΜΕΓΑΛΟΥΣ:
ΕΠΙΤΟΣΤΟΜΑΤΟΥΣΠΗ
ΛΑΙΟΥΚΑΙΚΑΤΑΣΤΗ
ΣΑΤΕΕΠΑΥΤΟΥΑΝΔΡΑ
ΤΟΥΦΥΛΑΣΣΕΙΝΕΠΑΥ
ΤΟΥΣΥΜΕΙΣΔΕΜΗΕ
ΣΤΗΚΑΤΕΚΑΤΑΔΙΩ
ΚΟΝΤΕΣΟΠΙΣΩΤΩ
ΕΧΘΡΩΝΥΜΩΝΚΑΙ
ΚΑΤΑΛΑΒΕΤΑΙΤΗΝΟΥ
ΡΑΓΙΑΝΑΥΤΩΝ:ΚΑΙΜΗ
ΑΦΗΤΕΑΥΤΟΥΣ:ΕΙΣΕΛ
ΘΕΙΝΕΙΣΤΑΣΠΟΛΕΙΣ
ΑΥΤΩΝΠΑΡΑΔΕΔΩ
ΚΕΝΓΑΡΑΥΤΟΥΣΚΣΟ
ΘΣΗΜΩΝΕΙΣΤΑΣ·

Plate 30

CODEX MARCHALIANUS (vat. gr. 2125)

Cf. p. 53. Illustration from *Specimina Codicum Graecorum Vaticanorum collegerunt P. Franchi de' Cavalieri et I. Lietzmann* (2nd ed. 1929).

The illustration contains Jer. xlii. 11-19 (𝔐 xxxv. 11-19) and clearly reveals the peculiarities of this manuscript. A corrector has added in the margin the hexaplaric readings which assimilate 𝔊 to 𝔐, with their hexaplaric signs. It can be seen that Origen had frequently to complete the Greek text of Jeremiah, since it is considerably shorter than the Hebrew. In the Codex Marchalianus the source of these additions is sometimes indicated. Thus the words εως της ημερας ταυτης οτι ηκουσαν της εντολης του πατρος αυτω̄ come from Aquila (A) and Theodotion (Θ), whereas the phrase missing in 𝔊 in verse 17 has been supplied from Theodotion (Θ).

In his edition of Ezekiel, J. Ziegler has demonstrated two stages of hexaplaric influence upon the Codex Marchalianus: "...the first was already present in the text copied by Q, and the scribe took over into his text the hexaplaric sections without giving any indication of what he had done; the second comes from a redactor who marked with asterisks the hexaplaric sections already present, and added the missing ones in the margin of Q from another source, the same source as was used also by 88 and Syh" (BH = 𝔖h) (*Septuaginta, Ezechiel* (1952), pp. 34 f.). As far as Isaiah and the Twelve Prophets are concerned, the original form of Q is, however, to be classified with the Alexandrian group.

There may also be seen in the illustration the omission of vv. 16-18, caused by homoeoteleuton (the omitted passage has been added in the lower margin), the corrections in the text (lines 14, 19, 24), and the many abbreviations of words which occur frequently. All the readings of the Codex Marchalianus are noted in the apparatus of Swete's edition of the Septuagint, q.v.

ΣΟΜΕΘΑ ΕΙΣ ΙΕΡΟΥΣΑΛΗΜ ΑΠΟ ΠΡΟΣΩ-
ΠΟΥ ΤΩΝ ΧΑΛΔΑΙΩΝ. ΚΑΙ ΑΠΟ ΠΡΟΣΩ-
ΠΟΥ ΤΗΣ ΔΥΝΑΜΕΩΣ ΤΩΝ ΑΣΣΥΡΙΩΝ.
ΚΑΙ ΟΙΚΗΣΑΜΕΝ ΕΚΕΙ: ΚΑΙ ΕΓΕΝΕΤΟ
ΛΟΓΟΣ ΚΥ ΠΡΟΣ ΜΕ ΛΕΓΩΝ ΟΥΤΩΣ ΛΕΓΕΙ
ΚΣ ΠΟΡΕΥΟΥ ΚΑΙ ΕΙΠΟΝ ΑΝΩ ΙΟΥΔΑ.
ΚΑΙ ΤΟΙΣ ΚΑΤΟΙΚΟΥΣΙΝ ΙΛΗΜ ΟΥ ΜΗ
ΛΑΒΗΤΕ ΠΑΙΔΕΙΑΝ. ΑΚΟΥΕΙΝ ΤΟΥΣ ΛΟ-
ΓΟΥΣ ΜΟΥ. ΕΣΤΗΣΑΝ ΡΗΜΑ ΥΙΟΙ ΙΩΝΑ-
ΔΑΒ ΥΙΟΥ ΡΗΧΑΒ, Ο ΕΝΕΤΕΙΛΑΤΟ ΤΟΙΣ ΤΕ-
ΚΝΟΙΣ ΑΥΤΟΥ ΠΡΟΣ ΤΟ ΜΗ ΠΙΕΙΝ ΟΙΝΟΝ.
ΚΑΙ ΟΥΚ ΕΠΙΟΝ. ΚΑΙ ΕΓΩ ΕΛΑΛΗΣΑ ΠΡΟΣ
ΥΜΑΣ ΟΡΘΡΟΥ. ΚΑΙ ΕΛΑΛΗΣΑ ΚΑΙ ΟΥΚ ΗΚΟΥ-
ΣΑΤΕ. ΚΑΙ ΑΠΕΣΤΕΙΛΑ [illegible] ΠΡΟΣ ΥΜΑΣ ΤΟΥΣ
ΔΟΥΛΟΥΣ ΜΟΥ ΤΟΥΣ ΠΡΟΦΗΤΑΣ ΛΕΓΩΝ.
ΑΠΟΣΤΡΑΦΗΤΕ ΕΚΑΣΤΟΣ ΑΠΟ ΤΗΣ ΟΔΟΥ
ΑΥΤΟΥ ΤΗΣ ΠΟΝΗΡΑΣ. ΚΑΙ ΒΕΛΤΙΟΝΑ
ΠΟΙΗΣΑΤΕ ΤΑ ΕΠΙΤΗΔΕΥΜΑΤΑ ΥΜΩΝ.
ΚΑΙ ΟΥ ΠΟΡΕΥΣΕΣΘΕ ΟΠΙΣΩ ΘΕΩΝ ΕΤΕΡΩΝ
ΤΟΥ ΔΟΥΛΕΥΕΙΝ ΑΥΤΟΙΣ. ΚΑΙ ΟΙΚΗΣΕΤΕ
ΕΠΙ ΤΗΣ ΓΗΣ ΗΣ ΕΔΩΚΑ ΥΜΙΝ ΚΑΙ ΤΟΙΣ
ΠΑΤΡΑΣΙΝ ΥΜΩΝ. ΚΑΙ ΟΥΚ ΕΚΛΙΝΑΤΕ
ΤΑ ΩΤΑ ΥΜΩΝ. ΚΑΙ ΟΥΚ ΗΚΟΥΣΑΤΕ.
ΚΑΙ ΕΣΤΗΣΑΝ ΟΙ ΥΙΟΙ ΙΩΝΑΔΑΒ ΥΙΟΥ ΡΗΧΑΒ.
ΤΗΝ ΕΝΤΟΛΗΝ ΤΟΥ ΠΡΣ ΑΥΤΩΝ ΠΟΙΕΙΝ.
ΚΑΘΟΤΙ ΕΝΕΤΕΙΛΑΤΟ ΑΥΤΟΙΣ Ο ΠΗΡ ΑΥ-
ΤΩΝ. ΟΥ ΜΗ ΕΚΛΙΠΗ ΑΝΗΡ ΤΩΝ ΥΙΩΝ
ΙΩΝΑΔΑΒ ΥΙΟΥ ΡΗΧΑΒ ΠΑΡΕΣΤΗΚΩΣ
ΚΑΤΑ ΠΡΟΣΩΠΟΝ ΜΟΥ ΠΑΣΑΣ ΤΑΣ ΗΜΕΡΑΣ.

ΟΙ ΔΕ ΛΑΟΙ ΟΥΤΟΙ ΟΥΚ ΗΚΟΥΣΑΝ ΜΟΥ ΔΙΑ ΤΟΥΤΟ ΟΥΤΩΣ ΕΙΠΕ
ΚΣ ΙΔΟΥ ΕΓΩ ΦΕΡΩ ΕΠΙ ΙΟΥΔΑΝ ΚΑΙ ΕΠΙ ΤΟΥΣ ΚΑΤΟΙ-
ΚΟΥΝΤΑΣ ΙΛΗΜ ΠΑΝΤΑ ΤΑ ΚΑΚΑ Α ΕΛΑΛΗΣΑ ΕΠ ΑΥΤΟΥΣ
ΔΙΑ ΤΟΥΤΟ ΟΥΤΩΣ ΕΙΠΕΝ ΚΣ ΕΠΕΙΔΗ ΗΚΟΥΣΑΝ ΥΙΟΙ ΙΩ-
ΝΑΔΑΒ ΥΙΟΥ ΡΗΧΑΒ ΤΗΝ ΕΝΤΟΛΗΝ ΤΟΥ ΠΑΤΡΟΣ ΑΥΤΩΝ

Plate 31

A MANUSCRIPT OF THE SYROHEXAPLAR FROM THE YEAR 697 A.D.

Cf. p. 40. Illustration (Exod. xxvii.10-15) from E. Tisserant, *Specimina Codicum Orientalium* (1914)

This manuscript (Brit. Mus. Add. 12134) belongs, like the one illustrated in Plate 33, to the collection of hundreds of manuscripts which were brought to the British Museum in 1839 and the following years from the monastery of St.Maria Deipara in the Nitrian Desert of Lower Egypt. From the earliest period of Christian monasticism, there was in the Nitrian Desert a colony of monks which, at the end of the fourth century, numbered several thousand, and which displayed at certain periods a very lively intellectual life. The Syrian monastery of St. Maria Deipara in particular had a fine library, which was considerably enlarged in the tenth century by the efforts of the Abbot, Moses of Nisibis. Later the monasteries declined, and their books remained unused and much neglected, though zealously guarded by the uneducated monks, until in 1839 an Englishman named Tattam, and others after him, were able to obtain hundreds of manuscripts and bring them to England. The immediate result was a considerable increase in Syriac studies.

The manuscript contains the book of Exodus, and was written, according to the colophon, by a certain Lazarus, in the year 1008 of the Seleucid era, that is A.D. 697. It is thus fairly close in time to the translation made by Bishop Paul of Tella (616/7). As the illustration shows, the hexaplaric signs are preserved in the text (obelos lines 7, 13, 14f., 20; asterisk line 12). The translations of Aquila, Symmachus and Theodotion are noted in the margin. The longer marginal note opposite lines 2ff. provides an explanation of ψαλιδος (Syriac *psalidis*). και ψαλιδος is written in red in the upper margin.

86

ΚΑΙΨΑΛΙΔΟC

ܘܦܣܠܝܕܘܣ ܕܠܗܘܢ ܕܣܐܡܐ܀ — ܐܬ. ܕܩܘ̈ܩܣܐ܀
ܗܟܢܐ ܠܡܦܢܝܬܐ ܗܝ ܕܠܘܬ ܓܪܒܝܐ.
ܘܐܣ̈ܬܠܘܗܝ ܕܡܐܐ ܐܡ̈ܝܢ ܐܘܪܟܐ.
ܘܥܡܘ̈ܕܐ ܕܠܗܘܢ ܥܣܪܝܢ. ܘܒܣ̈ܝܣܗ
ܕܠܗܘܢ ܥܣܪܝܢ ܕܢܚܫܐ.
ܘܩܘܩ̈ܣܐ ܕܠܗܘܢ. ܘܦܣܠܝܕܘܣ
ܕܐܣܛܘܢܐ ܀ ܘܚܦ̈ܝܢ ܡܚܦܝܢ
ܒܣܐܡܐ. ܝ. ܘܦܬܝܘܬܗ̇ ܕܕܪܬܐ
ܕܠܘܬ ܝܡܐ. ܘܐܣ̈ܬܠܘܗܝ ܕܚܡܫܝܢ
ܐܡ̈ܝܢ. ܥܡܘ̈ܕܐ ܕܠܗܘܢ ܥܣܪܐ.
ܘܒܣ̈ܝܣܗ ܕܠܗܘܢ ܥܣܪܐ. ܀
ܘܦܬܝܘܬܗ̇ ܕܕܪܬܐ ܗ̇ ܕܡܕܢܚܐ ܕܠܘܬ
ܡܕܢܚܐ. ܘܐܣ̈ܬܠܘܗܝ ܕܚܡܫܝܢ ܐܡ̈ܝܢ.
ܥܡܘ̈ܕܐ ܕܠܗܘܢ ܥܣܪܐ.
ܘܒܣ̈ܝܣܗ ܕܠܗܘܢ ܥܣܪܐ܀
ܘܕܚܡܫܥܣܪܐ ܐܡ̈ܝܢ ܪܘܡܐ
ܕܐܣ̈ܬܠܘܗܝ ܠܡܦܢܝܬܐ ܚܕܐ. ܥܡܘ̈ܕܐ
ܕܠܗܘܢ ܬܠܬܐ. ܘܒܣ̈ܝܣܗ ܕܠܗܘܢ
ܬܠܬܐ. ܘܠܡܦܢܝܬܐ ܗܝ ܬܪܝܢܝܬܐ.
ܕܚܡܫܥܣܪܐ ܐܡ̈ܝܢ ܀ ܪܘܡܐ
ܕܐܣ̈ܬܠܘܗܝ. ܥܡܘ̈ܕܐ ܕܠܗܘܢ
ܬܠܬܐ. ܘܒܣ̈ܝܣܗ ܕܠܗܘܢ ܬܠܬܐ܀

ܦܣܠܝܕܘܣ ܠܒܪ̈ܬܐ
ܐܝܬܝܗܝܢ ܕܣܐܡܐ.
ܐܘ ܕܦܘܪܩܐ ܐܘ
ܕܩܘ̈ܩܣܐ ܡܣܪ̈ܟܐ.
ܗܢܝܢ ܕܬܘܠܐ ܘܠܟܢ
ܠܥܝܕ ܒܥܡܘ̈ܕܐ܀

ܐ. ܬ. ܠܡܦܢܝܬܐ܀
ܗ. ܠܡܣܒܠ ܦܪܕܐ.

ܐ. ܗ. ܬ. ܕܟܬܦܐ
ܚܕܐ܀

ܐ. ܗ̄. ܬ. ܘܠܟܬܦܐ
ܬܪܝܢܝܬܐ܀

Plate 32

MANUSCRIPT OF A CATENA (NINTH CENTURY A.D.)

Cf. p. 43. n. 1. Illustration (Job. vi.5) from *Specimina Codicum Graecorum Vaticanorum collegerunt P. Franchi de' Cavalieri et I. Lietzmann* (2nd ed. 1929)

"By a catena is understood a collection which, by contrast with the more general term florilegium, gathers together merely exegetical comments by various authors as links in a long chain, in order to explain a Biblical book. By means of it the reader is enabled in a short space of time to know what are, for any particular passage, the views of the most important exegetes of the Church, and so to formulate his own opinion." [1]) The catenas are of significance for the patristic scholar as well as for the textual critic; for the former, because of the fragments they preserve of otherwise lost works of patristic literature; for the latter, because of the material they offer for the history of the text. Rahlfs has established that there was a special catena-recension of the Septuagint (cf. p. 43).

On the basis of their external appearance, a distinction may be drawn between 'marginal catenas' and 'text catenas'. "The most elegant, and perhaps also the oldest form of the catena commentary is the 'marginal catena'. In a space carefully measured out beforehand in the middle of the page, the scribe wrote the sacred text, and then, in the wide margin, much exceeding in size the space allotted to the text itself, he wrote the explanations in narrower lines" [2]). (Cf. Plate). "The second main form of the catena arose when the explanations corresponding to particular verses of the sacred text were placed after the verses themselves, so that the catena also was written within the whole space available for writing in the book" [3]).

The titles (lemmata) of the individual fragments are picked out in red in the manuscript illustrated. (cf. for example Διδύμου, καὶ μετ' ὀλίγα) [4]).

---

[1]) H. Lietzmann, *Catenen. Mitteilungen über ihre Geschichte und handschriftliche Überlieferung* (1897), p. 1.

[2]) *op.cit.* p. 9.

[3]) *op.cit.* p. 11.

[4]) G. Karo and H. Lietzmann published a catalogue: Catenarum Graecarum Catalogus, *Nachrichten der Gesellschaft der Wissenschaften zu Göttingen*, Phil.-hist. Klasse (1902); cf. p. 322 there.

ΔΙΔΥΜ

ΟΛΥΜΠΙΟΔΩΡ

ΤΙ ΓΑΡ ΜΗ ΔΙΑ
ΚΕΝΗΣ ΚΕΚΡΑ
ΞΕΤΑΙ ΟΝΟΣ Α
ΓΡΙΟΣ· ΑΛΛ' Η
ΤΑ ΣΙΤΑ ΖΗ
ΤΩΝ·
ΕΙ ΔΕ ΚΑΙ ΡΗΞΕΙ
ΦΩΝΗΝ ΒΟΥΣ
ΕΠΙ ΦΑΤΝΗΣ
ΕΧΩΝ ΤΑ ΒΡΩ
ΜΑΤΑ·

ΑΛΛΩΣ

ΔΙΔΥΜΟΥ

ΚΑΙ ΜΕΤ' ΟΛΙΓΑ

ΠΟΛΥ

Plate 33

A PESHITTA MANUSCRIPT FROM THE YEAR 464 A.D.

Cf. pp. 59 ff. Illustration (Exod. xiii. 8-17) from *The Palaeographical Society, Facsimiles of Manuscripts and Inscriptions* (Oriental Series), edited by W. Wright (1875-83).

This west-Syriac manuscript on parchment (Brit. Mus. Add. 14425) is one of the manuscripts which came from the Nitrian Desert (cf. p. 144) and contains the books of Gen., Exod., Num. and Deut. in the old Estrangela script. The first two books were written in Amid (= Diyarbekr) in the year 775 of the Seleucid era, that is 464 A.D., by a certain John. The other two books come from another scribe, probably from the same period. This is the oldest existing Biblical manuscript containing a note giving its exact date. It is of approximately the same age as the Greek Codex Alexandrinus.

Plate 34

THE CONSTANCE FRAGMENTS OF THE OLD LATIN PROPHETS

Cf. p. 63. Illustration (Ezek. xx. 43-47 𝔚) by kind consent of P. A. Dold.

The illustration shows fragments of a beautiful Old Latin manuscript of the Prophets, which was found by P. A. Dold at the back of Codex 191 of the Court Library of Fürstenberg in Donaueschingen. The manuscript of the Prophets, which was probably written in the fifth century in Northern Italy, came into the Cathedral Library of Constance, and in about 1450 was there cut up and used to bind various parchment manuscripts. 26 of these manuscripts, containing in their binding fragments of the old manuscript, were discovered in Fulda, Darmstadt, Stuttgart, Donaueschingen, and in the Benedictine monastery of St. Paul in Kärnten. These texts have great importance in view of the scarcity of Old Latin texts, since, before these were discovered, the only available texts of the Prophets earlier than Jerome in Bible manuscripts were the fragments of the Würzburg Palimpsest (cf. p. 64). Further Old Latin texts of the Prophets from St. Gall (Ezek., Dan., the Twelve) were published by P. A. Dold in the appendix to the book mentioned on p. 63.

Note the glosses in the margin by a later hand (sixth century), in which Greek readings and other material were included.

MINULTIS
UESTRIS
DIAUESTRA
QUIBUSEGO
NABAMIN
EIS ETCED
FACIES U
INOMNIB
MALITIIS UESTRIS
ETCOGNOSCE
TIS QUIA EGO SUM
DMS DUM F
ERO UOBIS
NOMEN MEUM
NON
TUR SECUN
UIAS UESTRAS
MALAS ET

Plate 35

CODEX LUGDUNENSIS

Cf. pp. 63 f. Illustration (Gen. xxvii.46-xxviii.11) from a photograph kindly lent by P. A. Dold.

The Codex Lugdunensis, with Old Latin text, belongs to the manuscript evidence for the Vetus Latina which has become known since Sabatier. It has had a chequered history. Originally it belonged to the Chapter library of the Canons, Counts of Lyons, and came later into the town library of Lyons. At some stage it was divided into two, and the second part (now Ms. 1964) was removed from Lyons, but was recovered in 1895 and returned to Lyons. From the first part (now Ms. 403) Libri stole 79 leaves and sold them in 1847 to Lord Ashburnham, whose son generously returned them to the library in 1880 when their contents were recognised.

According to Robert, the manuscript was written by three different scribes. It "was used for liturgical reading; for this reason it has various marginal notes by different hands and from different periods, though probably all these originated in Lyons. Two whole readings are inserted: I Kings xxi for the Traditio symboli, and I Pet. ii for the Cathedra Petri; the text of these is the Vulgate. Similarly the many corrections made to particular passages by later hands (to some extent in Tironian notes) [1]) are mainly assimilations to the Vulgate". (*Vetus Latina, Genesis*, ed. by P. B. Fischer (1951), p. 6). This assimilation is of importance for the history of the Vetus Latina, which was eventually supplanted by the Vulgate.

---

[1]) A form of Latin shorthand.

DIXITAUTEMREBECCA
ADISACDESTINAUIANI
MOMEOPROPTERFI
LIASFILIORUMCHET
SIACCEPERITIACOB
UXOREMAFILIABUS
TERRAEHUIUSUTQUID
MIHIUIUERE
UOCAUITAUTEMISAAC
IACOBADSEETBENE
DIXITEUMETPRAECE
PITEIDICENSNON
ACCIPIESUXOREM
AFILIABUSCHANNA
NEORUMSEDSURGE
ETUADEINMESOPO
TAMIAMINDOMU
BATHUELISPATRIS
MATRISTUAEETACCI
PEINDETIBIUXORE
EXFILIAB LABEPATRIS
MATRISTUAEETAC
CIPETIBIINDEUXORE
DSAUTEMMEUSBE
NEDICATTEETAUGEAT
TEETREPLEATTEET

ERISINECCLESIISGEN
TIUMETDETTIBIBE
NEDICTIONEMPATRIS
MEIABRAHAEETSE
MINITUOPOSTTE
HEREDITARETERRA
HABITATIONISTUAE
QUAMDEDITDSAB
RAHAE
ETDIMISITISACIACOB
ETABIITINMESOPO
TAMIAMADLABAN
FILIUMBATHUELIS
SYRIFRATREMREBEC
CAEMATRISIACOB
ETESAU
UIDITAUTEMESAUQUIA
BENEDIXITISACIACOB
ETQUIAABIITINMESO
POTAMIAMSYRIAE
ACCIPERESIBIINDE
UXOREMINEOQUOD
BENEDIXERITEUM
ETPRAECEPERITEI
DICENSNONACCIPIES
UXOREMAFILIABUS

CHANNANEORUMET
QUODAUDIERITIACOB
PATREMSUUMETMA
TREMSUAMETABIE
RITINMESOPOTAMIA
ETTUNCPOSTQUAM
UIDITESAUQUIAMA
LIGNAESUNTFILIAE
CHANNANEORUM
ANTEISACPATREM
SUUMABIITADISMA
HELETACCEPITMAHEL
FILIAMISMAELFILII
ABRAHAESOROREM
NABEOTHADMULIE
RESSUASSIBIUXOREM
L ETEXIITIACOBAPUTEO
IURAMENTIUTIRET
INCHARRANETPER
UENITINQUENDAM
LOCUMETMANSITIBI
OCCIDERATENIMSOL
ACCEPITLAPIDEM
EXLAPIDIBUSLOCIILLIUS
ETPOSUITADCAPUT
SUUMETDORMIUIT

Plate 36

PALIMPSEST OF THE VULGATE FROM THE FIFTH CENTURY A.D.

Cf. pp. 64 ff. Illustration (Judg. v.15-22) from a photograph kindly lent by P. A. Dold with the consent of the Herzog August Library at Wolfenbüttel

Among the books at one time treasured by the monastery of Bobbio in Northern Italy, there were two manuscripts of Isidore from the eighth century A.D., of which one found its way into the Vatican Library and the other into the Herzog August Library at Wolfenbüttel. These manuscripts were written on leaves of parchment taken from older codices cleaned of their writing for re-use. Some of these were from an uncial of the Bible of the fifth century, and some from a half-uncial of the sixth century. The old manuscripts, which follow the translation of Jerome, were deciphered by P. A. Dold with the aid of a method of photographing palimpsests developed in the Abbey of Beuron, and then published [1]).

The illustration shows one page of the old uncial, "one of the finest Bible manuscripts, or more strictly, manuscripts of part of the Bible, from the earliest period". (Dold). There have survived the larger part of the book of Judges and 13 verses of Ruth. It is possible that the manuscript only contained these two books. The place of origin is almost certainly Italy. A comparison of this, the oldest known text of Jerome, with the official Vulgate (= Vg) (BH = 𝔅) and the Codex Amiatinus (= A), gives the following result: "Of about 600 passages compared, this manuscript deviates about 200 times from the Vg with A, and about 180 times from A with the Vg; in addition it deviates a further 220 times from both A and Vg, and offers its own readings, admittedly usually only slightly different' [2]).

This uncial and the half-uncial mentioned (Job. i.1-xv.24) are of very great importance for the restoration of the oldest form of Jerome's text. "In these two manuscripts, of such great age, we have gained most valuable links between the lost original of Jerome and the Codex Amiatinus, previously the oldest known Vulgate text. As appears from the whole style of their writing, we have in both these manuscripts copies which have been written with incomparable care and devotion, guaranteeing therefore good and reliable readings" [3]).

---

[1]) Zwei Bobbienser Palimpseste mit frühestem Vulgatatext, herausgegeben und bearbeitet von P. Alban Dold, *Texte und Arbeiten herausgegeben durch die Erzabtei Beuron* 1, 19/20 (1931).

[2]) Dold, *op.cit*, p. IL.

[3]) *op.cit.* p. LVII.

Plate 37

CODEX AMIATINUS

Cf. p. 66 n. 4. Illustration (Ps. xxii (𝔅 xxi). 25-xxv (xxiv). 5) from a photograph kindly lent by the Biblioteca Medicea-Laurenziana.

This well-known and highly valued codex of the Vulgate, which is named after the Abbey of Monte Amiata, to which it once belonged, comes from England. Ceolfrid, Abbot of the monasteries at Jarrow and Wearmouth in Northumberland, which were under direct control of the Holy See, had it written in order to present it to the Pope on his last journey to Rome. Ceolfrid died on the way, in Langres (716 A.D.), but some of his companions brought the codex to Rome. It is the only one that survives of three codices written for Ceolfrid in one of his monasteries between 690 and 716, all of which contained the *nova translatio,* that is, the translation of Jerome [1]). The text of Amiatinus depends upon an original which came from Italy, but "the Anglo-Saxon copyists could not write out a foreign text without giving it what we may call the 'local colour' of the text of their own land". (S. Berger, *Histoire de la Vulgate pendant les premiers siècles du moyen âge* (1893), p. 38). This accounts for the relationship between this text and Anglo-Saxon manuscripts, in spite of its mainly Italian character. Amiatinus is not, in any case, a pure Vulgate manuscript, particularly in the Wisdom books.

The Codex Amiatinus contains prefaces which go back, directly or indirectly, to the Latin 'Codex grandior' of Cassiodorus, which had come to England either in the original or in a copy [2]). But does the *text* of Amiatinus also reveal contacts with Cassiodorus' recension of Jerome's translation? (cf. p. 66) The earlier view was that such contacts could be demonstrated. This has been denied by H. Quentin, but H. John Chapman has produced a detailed refutation of his position, (*Revue bénédictine* 38-40 (1926-28).). "There can really be no definite proof for or against the connection with the school of Cassiodorus; but the older view seems on the whole to be the sounder". (F. Stummer, *Einleitung in die lateinische Bibel* (1928), p. 131).

---

[1]) A few leaves of one of the two lost codices have been discovered since 1909 — they had in part been used as 'wrappers for estate papers' — and are now in the British Museum.

[2]) According to H. Blum, *Zentralblatt für Bibliothekswesen* (1950), pp. 52ff., the Codex grandior was acquired by Ceolfrid in Rome in 674.

qm non dispexit neque contempsit
modestiam pauperis
et non abscondit faciem suam a me
et cum clamarem ad eum exaudivit me
apud te laus mea in ecclesia multa
vota mea reddam in conspectu
timentium eum.
Comedent mites et saturabuntur
laudabunt dñm quaerentes eum
vivet cor vestrum in sempiternum
recordabuntur et convertentur
ad dñm omnes fines terrae
et adorabunt coram eo universae
cogitationes gentium
quia dñi est regnum et domina
bitur gentibus
comederunt et adoraverunt
omnes pingues terrae
ante faciem eius curvabunt genu
universi qui discendunt in pulverem
et anima eius ipsi vivet
et semen serviet ei
narrabunt dño in generatione
venient et adorabunt iustitiam eius
populo qui nascitur quas fecit
psalmus david vox ecclesiae
post baptismum
22 Dns pascit me nihil mihi deerit
in pascuis herbarum adclinavit me
super aquas refectionis
enutrivit me
animam meam refecit
duxit me super semitas iustitiae
propter nomen suum
sed et si ambulavero in valle mortis
non timebo mala qm tu mecum es
virga tua et baculus tuus ipsa
consolabuntur me
pones coram me mensam ad
adversus hostes meos
in pinguasti oleo caput meum
calix meus inebrians
sed et benignitas et misericor
dia subsequitur me

omnibus diebus vitae meae
et habitabo in domo dñi
in longitudinem dierum
psalmus prima sabbati
confirmatio populi credentis
portae quas dicit principum vel
inferni vox xpi diligentibus se
23 Dñi est terra et plenitudo eius
orbis et habitatores eius
qui ipse super maria fundavit eum
et super flumina stabilivit illum
quis ascendet in montem dñi
et quis stabit in loco sco eius
innocens manib et mundo corde
qui non exaltavit frustra
animam suam
et non iuravit dolose
accipiet benedictionem a dño
et misericordiam a dõ salutari suo
haec est generatio quaerentium eum
quaerentium faciem dei iacob semper
levate portae capita vestra
et elevamini ianuae sempiternae
et ingredietur rex gloriae
quis est iste rex gloriae
dns fortis et potens dns
fortis in proelio
levate portae capita vestra
et erigite ianuae sempiternae
et ingredietur rex gloriae
quis est iste rex gloriae
dns exercituum ipse est rex gloriae
psalmus david canticum
24 Ad te dñe animam meam levabo
ds meus in te confisus sum
ne confundar
ne laetentur inimici mei
sed universi qui sperant in te
non confundantur
confundantur qui iniqua gerunt
frustra
vias tuas dñe ostende mihi
semitas tuas doce me
deduc me in veritate tua

Plate 38

A COPTIC PAPYRUS CODEX

Cf. pp. 67 f. Illustration (Deut. xxxiv. 11, 12; Jonah i. 1-4) from E. Wallis Budge, *Coptic Biblical Texts in the Dialect of Upper Egypt* (1912).

In 1911 the British Museum obtained this papyrus codex found in Upper Egypt, which contains large parts of Deuteronomy, the whole book of Jonah, and the larger part of the Acts of the Apostles. It is to be dated in the fourth century A.D., and is thus of very great age.

The illustration shows the end of the book of Deuteronomy: the title is written in large letters at the end of the book. There follows a blessing in Greek on scribe and reader, and then the beginning of the book of Jonah.

ϩⲙ̄ϩⲁⲗⲁⲧⲏⲣ ... ϥⲕⲁϩⲙ̄
ⲛⲟϭⲛ̄ϣⲡⲏⲣⲉⲁ ... ⲓϫⲉⲧ
ϫⲟⲟⲣⲉⲛⲧⲁⲙⲱⲩⲥⲏⲥ ⲁⲁⲩ ⲙ̄
ⲡⲉⲙ̄ⲧⲟ ⲉⲃⲟⲗ ⲙ̄ⲡⲓⲥⲣⲁⲏⲗ
ⲧⲏⲣϥ

ⲠⲈⲨⲦⲈ
ⲢⲞⲚⲞⲘⲒⲞⲚ:

ⲈⲒⲢⲎⲚⲎ ⲦⲰ ⲄⲢⲀⲮⲀⲚⲦⲒ
ⲔⲀⲒ ⲦⲰ
ⲀⲚⲀⲄⲒⲚⲰⲤⲔⲞⲚⲦⲒ

ⲓⲱⲛⲁⲥ

ⲡϣⲁϫⲉ ⲙ̄ⲡϫⲟⲉⲓⲥ ⲁϥϣⲱⲡⲉ ϣⲁ
ⲓⲱⲛⲁⲥ ⲡϣⲏⲣⲉ ⲙ̄ⲁⲙⲁⲑⲓ ⲉϥϫⲱ
ⲙ̄ⲙⲟⲥ ϫⲉ ⲧⲱⲟⲩⲛ ⲛ̄ⲅⲃⲱⲕ ⲉϩⲣⲁⲓ̈
ⲉⲧⲛⲓⲛⲉⲩⲏ ⲧⲛⲟϭ ⲙ̄ⲡⲟⲗⲉⲓⲥ ⲛ̄ⲅ
ⲕⲏⲣⲩⲥⲥⲉ ⲉϩⲣⲁⲓ̈ ⲛ̄ϩⲏⲧⲥ̄ ϫⲉ ⲁⲡⲉⲩⲟ
ⲉⲓϣ ⲛ̄ⲧⲉⲥⲕⲁⲕⲓⲁ ⲉⲓ ⲉϩⲣⲁⲓ̈ ⲙ̄ⲡⲁⲙ
ⲧⲟ ⲉⲃⲟⲗ· ⲁⲩⲱ ⲁϥⲧⲱⲟⲩⲛ ⲛ̄ϭⲓ
ⲓⲱⲛⲁⲥ ⲉⲡⲱⲧ ⲉⲑⲁⲣϣⲉⲓⲥ ⲛ̄ⲛⲁϩ
ⲣⲛ̄ ⲡϩⲟ ⲙ̄ⲡϫⲟⲉⲓⲥ· ⲁⲩⲱ ⲁϥⲃⲱⲕ
ⲉϩⲣⲁⲓ̈ ⲉⲓⲟⲡⲡⲏ· ⲁϥϭⲛ̄ ⲟⲩϫⲟⲉⲓ ⲉϥⲛⲁ
ⲥϭⲏⲣ ⲉⲑⲁⲣϣⲉⲓⲥ ⲁϥϯ ⲧⲉϥϩⲏⲙⲉ ⲁϥ
ⲧⲁⲗⲉ ⲉⲣⲟϥ ⲉⲥϭⲏⲣ ⲛ̄ⲙ̄ⲙⲁⲩ ⲉⲑⲁⲣϣⲉⲓⲥ
ⲛ̄ⲛⲁϩⲣⲛ̄ ⲡϩⲟ ⲙ̄ⲡϫⲟⲉⲓⲥ· ⲁⲩⲱ ⲁⲡϫⲟ
ⲉⲓⲥ ⲁϥⲧⲟⲩⲛⲉⲥ ⲟⲩⲛⲟϭ ⲛ̄ⲧⲏⲩ
ⲉϩⲣⲁⲓ̈ ⲉⲑⲁⲗⲁⲥⲥⲁ· ⲁⲩⲛⲟϭ ⲛ̄

Plate 39

AN ETHIOPIC MANUSCRIPT

Cf. p. 68. Illustration (Susanna 1-5) from O. Löfgren, *Die äthiopische Übersetzung des Propheten Daniel* (1927)

The manuscript from which the illustration is taken contains the books of Job and Daniel. Löfgren describes it thus: "From the palaeographical point of view this manuscript is of great interest. Its general appearance, as well as many small details, point to its great age. The large, angular script, about 6 mm. high, which differs only slightly from the form of the letters used in inscriptions; the simple decoration, limited to rows of dots, and the St. Anthony's cross or similar marginal design; and the arrangement in two columns—all place S (i.e. this manuscript) among the comparatively small group of ancient Ethiopic manuscripts, which were gradually supplanted about the middle of the fifteenth century by a new type with a more beautiful style of writing and richer ornamentation". (*op.cit.* p. XXII). It was probably written between 1300 and 1400. "Since this manuscript is written with care throughout, and is free from any considerable corrections or interpolations, we have in it a valuable witness to the text circulating about 1300, probably not yet revised". (*op.cit.* p. XXV).

Whereas this manuscript has thus preserved the original Ethiopic translation, traces of various processes of revision can be seen in the later manuscripts. To some extent they point to revision from the Syro-Arabic side, which began in about the fourteenth century; others offer a text revised from the Hebrew in the fifteenth/sixteenth centuries. Naturally, for the purposes of textual work on the Septuagint, only those manuscripts are of importance which preserve the original, old Ethiopic text of this daughter translation of the Septuagint.

✝ ዘዳንኤል፡ ነ
፩ ቢይ።
ወሀሎ፡ ሊሖጁ፡
ብእሲ፡ ዘይነ
ብር፡ ባቢሎን፡
ወስሙ፡ ኢዮአ
ቄም፡ ወአውሰ
በ፡ ዘእሲተ፡ እ
ንተ፡ ስማ፡ ሶስና፡
ወለተ፡ ኬልቅ
ዩ፡ ወሠናይት፡
ጥቀ፡ ወትፈርሆ
እግዚእ፡ ብሔ
ር። ወአዝማዲ
ሃኒ፡ ጻድቃን፡
ወመሀርዋ፡ ለ
ወለቶሙ፡ አሪ
ተ፡ ሙሴ፡ ወኢዮ
ዋቄም፡ ብዑል፡
ጥቀ፡ ወቦ፡ ዐጸ

ደ፡ አኅማልጎሬ፡
ቤቱ።
ወይመጽኡ፡ ኀ
ቤሁ፡ አይሁድ፡
እስመ፡ ውእቱ፡
ይኬብር፡ እምኵ
ሎሙ።
ወአስተርአዩ፡
ክልኤቱ፡ ረባና
ት፡ መድልዋንበ
ውእቱ፡ ዓመት፡
እለ፡ በእንቲአሆ
ሙ፡ ነገረ፡ እግ
ዚእ፡ ብሔር፡
ከሙ፡ እምባቢ
ሎን፡ ወፅአት፡
ኃጢአት፡ እም
ረባናት፡ መደል
ዋን፡ እለ፡ ይብኵ፡
ንዎ ቅበሙለ

Plate 40

AN ARABIC MANUSCRIPT

Cf. p. 69. Illustration (Job. xxii.12-xxiii.2) from *The Palaeographical Society, Facsimiles of Manuscripts and Inscriptions* (Oriental Series), ed. by W. Wright (1875-1883)

The variety of the Arabic translations of Job, of which a page of the oldest is here illustrated, may be regarded as typical of the Arabic Bible translations as a whole. "Among the various translations of Job, at least four in number, one belongs to the oldest group of documents of Christian Arabic Literature. The manuscript, which contains fair sized fragments of it, Brit. Mus. arab. 1475, was written in the first half of the ninth century, and probably came from the monastery of Sabas. The translation itself depends upon a Syro-hexaplaric original.

We know the originator of another translation of Job, namely Pethion (Fatyun ibn Aiyub), who was probably active as a translator in Bagdad in the middle of the ninth century; he also translated Ben Sira and the Prophets. Pethion's text of Job, divided into fifteen chapters, claims to have been made from the Hebrew, according to the evidence in the London manuscript, but in reality it was made from the Syriac. Other translations of Job also go back to the Peshitta or to the Coptic". (G. Graf, Geschichte der christlichen arabischen Literature, Vol. 1: Die Übersetzungen, *Studi e Testi* 118 (1944), p. 126).

13

العلي ما حكمه والذين يفتلون بالقوه في لهم وانت قلت
من اين تدري في الهوي وضننت ان الضباب حولك
وسوا الفضا وان السحاب كل سر اعمالك لان لا ترى
وعلى لم اطراف الارض من بريه وسالكي العقبه
من حيث الذي يمشي فيه الصالحين ولم يدري
بانك توحد بلا وقت من الذي يحمل الانهار على
الجبال كذلك يهلك المتجبرين الذين يقولو
ما الذي يصنع بنا الرب واستخلف علينا الهلاك
كل الذين ملوا بيوتهم من الخير وهو امرو المنه
فهو بعيده من الرب والصالحين ينظرون
اليهم ويضحكوا ومن كان غير مذنب يشمت
بهم بان يسرع هلاك قوامهم وبركتهم تاكل
النار فاطرح من فمك ما لا ينبغا واحفظ قول
الرب على قلبك لانك رجعت وخضعت بين يدي
الرب فابعد من صدرك الاوجاع وتجلسك
على صخره قويه وتحوطك اوديه الحيه والعسجد
ضانيك الكل ويخلصك من العدو وينصرك
بنيا سليه فضه مسبوكه وتقوم بين يدي الرب
مستبشر وتنظر الى السما فوقك دائبه واذا
كلفت اليه يسمعك ويعطيك وتبذر له الانذار
ويرد عليك طعام الصلاح ولتكون الضو الذي
للعمر في طرقك بانك اتضعت بنفسك بين يديه
وتطرح عند العوه وينظر هو عبيد بين يديه
وهو يسلمك وهو يسلم الزكي ويرد عليك مواهبه

اجاب ايوب وقال

انا اعلم بان توبيخي بين يدي هو صادق ثقيله

Plate 41

THE COMPLUTENSIAN POLYGLOT

Illustration (Gen. xxi.28-xxii.3) by kind permission of the Bodleian Library, Oxford, from the copy there

The Polyglots, which printed in parallel columns the original text and translations of the Bible for the purpose of convenient comparison, provided a valuable aid to text-critical work. The oldest, called Complutensian from the place where it appeared (Complutum = Alcala de Henares), was edited in 1514-17 by Francisco Ximenez, Archbishop of Toledo and founder of the University of Alcala. (It was published only in 1522, because of the delay of the papal authorisation). For the work on the Old Testament, Jewish converts were brought in, for they alone at that time had the necessary training. They included the famous Alfonso de Zamora, who, since 1512, had been Professor of Oriental Languages in Alcala.

The Hebrew text of the Complutensian Polyglot reveals some interesting variants from the normal. Of the accents of the Tiberian system, only the Athnaḥ appears, but this is here used not simply for the main division of the verse, with the result that it may appear twice in a single verse (cf. for example, Gen. xxii.3). It is, moreover, not placed with the accented syllable, but after the word. Maqqeph is entirely lacking. The Ḥatephs appear only rarely, the appropriate vowel being used without shewa in most cases. Cf. in the illustration עַצֵי, אַשֶׁר, אֶלֹהִים etc. These peculiarities are not due to the caprice of the editors, as one might imagine. The editors depended rather as they claim upon the usage in ancient manuscripts. Since the peculiarities mentioned are characteristic of the simpleBabylonian pointing (cf. p. 18), P. Kahle has rightly concluded that'the editors of the Polyglot had at their disposal manuscripts of that type[1]), and that the study of these texts which they regarded as 'vetus-tissima exemplaria', as coming from the 'veteres Hebraei', had influenced them. They evidently had tried to imitate them in the edition of the Hebrew text of the Polyglot'. [2]) These manuscripts have now disappeared, presumably having been destroyed. On the Greek text of the Complutensian Polyglot cf. p. 54.

Of the later Polyglots, the most comprehensive is the 'London Polyglot', edited by Brian Walton in 1654-57.

---

[1]) as well as Ben Asher Mss.

[2]) P. Kahle, *Homenaje a Millas-Vallicrosa*, (Barcelona, 1954), I pp. 749f.

Trāsla.Grē.lxx.cū interp.latina.	Trāsla.B.Hiero.	Ter.Heb. Gen. Ca.xxi.	Priuatiua heb.

et statuit abraā septē agnas ouiū
καὶ ἔστησεν ἀβραὰμ ἑπτὰ ἀμνάδας προβάτων
solas. et dixit abimelech abraam. quid
μόνας. καὶ εἶπεν ἀβιμέλεχ τῷ ἀβραάμ. τί εἰ-
sunt septē agne ouiū harū: quas
σιν αἱ ἑπτὰ ἀμνάδες τῶν προβάτων τούτων, ἃς
statuisti solas. et dixit quia septē agnas
ἔστησας μόνας. καὶ εἶπεν ὅτι τὰς ἑπτὰ ἀμνά-
accipies a me: vt sint mihi in testimoniū:
δας λήψῃ παρ᾽ ἐμοῦ, ἵνα ὦσί μοι εἰς μαρτύριον,
quia ego fodi puteū hunc. ppter hoc vo-
ὅτι ἐγὼ ὤρυξα τὸ φρέαρ τοῦτο. διὰ τοῦτο ἐπω-
cauit nomē loci illius: puteū iu-
νόμασε τὸ ὄνομα τοῦ τόπου ἐκείνου, φρέαρ ὁρ-
ramenti. quia illic iurauerūt ambo: et posuerūt
κισμοῦ. ὅτι ἐκεῖ ὤμοσαν ἀμφότεροι, καὶ ἔθηκαν
fedus sup puteū iuramēti. surrexit aūt abi
διαθήκην ἐπὶ τὸ φρέαρ τοῦ ὁρκισμοῦ. ἀνέστη δὲ ἀβι-
melech et ochozad pronubus eius et phi
μέλεχ καὶ ὀχοζὰθ ὁ νυμφαγωγὸς αὐτοῦ καὶ ὁ φι-
chol princeps exercitus eius: et re
χὼλ ὁ ἀρχιστράτηγος τῆς δυνάμεως αὐτοῦ, καὶ ἀ-
uersi sunt in terrā philistijm. et plan-
πέστρεψαν εἰς τὴν γῆν τῶν φυλιστιείμ. καὶ ἐφύ-
tauit abraam agrū sup puteū iu-
τευσεν ἀβραὰμ ἄρουραν ἐπὶ τῷ φρέατι τοῦ ὁρ-
ramēti. et inuocauit ibi nomē dñi: deus
κου. καὶ ἐπεκαλέσατο ἐκεῖ τὸ ὄνομα κυρίου, θεὸς
eternus. habitauit aūt abraā in terra phi-
αἰώνιος. παρῴκησε δὲ ἀβραὰμ ἐν τῇ γῇ τῶν φυ-
listiim dies multos.
λιστιείμ ἡμέρας πολλάς.

Ca. 22.

A Et factū ē post verba hec: deus
καὶ ἐγένετο μετὰ τὰ ῥήματα ταῦτα, ὁ θεὸς
tentauit abraā. et dixit ei: abraam
Judith 8.c. Heb.11 d. ἐπείρασε τὸν ἀβραάμ. καὶ εἶπεν αὐτῷ, ἀβραὰμ
abraā. et dixit. ecce ego. et dixit: accipe fi-
ἀβραάμ. καὶ εἶπεν, ἰδοὺ ἐγώ. καὶ εἶπεν, λάβε τὸν υἱ-
liū tuū dilectū: quē dilexisti isaac: et
όν σου τὸν ἀγαπητόν, ὃν ἠγάπησας τὸν ἰσαάκ, καὶ
vade in terrā excelsā. et offer eū
πορεύθητι εἰς τὴν γῆν τὴν ὑψηλήν. καὶ ἀνένεγκε αὐ-
ibi in holocaustū sup vnū montiū: quos
τὸν ἐκεῖ εἰς ὁλοκάρπωσιν ἐφ᾽ ἓν τῶν ὀρέων, ὧν ἄν
tibi dixero. surgēs aūt abraā mane strauit
σοι εἴπω. ἀναστὰς δὲ ἀβραὰμ τὸ πρωῒ ἐπέσαξεν
asinū suū. assumpsit aūt secū duos pue-
τὴν ὄνον αὐτοῦ. παρέλαβε δὲ μεθ᾽ ἑαυτοῦ δύο παῖ-
ros: et isaac filiū suū. et scindēs ligna in
δας, καὶ ἰσαὰκ τὸν υἱὸν αὐτοῦ. καὶ σχίσας ξύλα εἰς
holocaustū: surgens abijt. et venerūt in
ὁλοκάρπωσιν, ἀναστὰς ἐπορεύθη. καὶ ἦλθον εἰς
locū quē dixit ei deus: die
τὸν τόπον ὃν εἶπεν αὐτῷ ὁ θεός, τῇ ἡμέρᾳ

Et statuit abraam septem agnas gregis seorsū. Cui dixit abimelech. Quid sibi volunt septem agne iste: quas stare fecisti seorsum? At ille. Septem inquit agnas accipies de manu mea: vt sint mihi in testimoniū: quōniam ego fodi puteū istū. Idcirco vocatus ē locus ille bersabee: quia ibi vterq; iurauit. & inierunt fedus p puteo iuramēti. Surrexit aūt abimelech & phicol princeps exercitus eius: reuersiq; sūt ī terrā palestiorū. Abraā vero plātauit nemus in bersabee: & inuocauit ibi nomen dñi dei eterni: & fuit colonus terre palestiorū diebus multis.

Ca.22.

Que postquā gesta sunt: tentauit deus abraam: & dixit ad eū. Abraam abraam. At ille rñdit. adsū. ait illi. Tolle filiū tuū vnigenitum quem diligis isaac: & vade in terrā visionis: atq; ibi offeres eū in holocaustum sup vnū montiū: quem monstrauero tibi. Igitur abraā de nocte consurgens strauit asinū suum ducens secum duos iuuenes & isaac filiū suum. Cumq; concidisset ligna in holocaustum: abiit ad locum quem preceperat ei deus. Die autem

ויצב אברהם את שבע כבשת
הצאן לבדהן: ויאמר אבימלך אל — צבד
אברהם מה הנה שבע כבשת
האלה אשר הצבת לבדנה: — יצג
ויאמר כי את שבע כבשת תקח
מידי בעבור תהיה לי לעדה כי — עד היה
חפרתי את הבאר הזאת: על כן
קרא למקום ההוא באר שבע כי — קום
שם נשבעו שניהם: ויכרתו — שבע
ברית בבאר שבע ויקם אבימלך — קום
ופיכל שר צבאו וישבו אל ארץ — שור שוב
פלשתים: ויטע אשל בבאר — נטע
שבע ויקרא שם בשם יהוה אל — קרא
עולם: ויגר אברהם בארץ — עלם גור
פלשתים ימים רבים: — יום רבה

Cap.xxii.

ויהי אחר הדברים האלה — היה
והאלהים נסה את אברהם
ויאמר אליו אברהם ויאמר הנני: — אמר
ויאמר קח נא את בנך את יחידך — לקח יחד
אשר אהבת את יצחק ולך לך אל — ילך
ארץ המריה והעלהו שם לעלה — עלה
על אחד ההרים אשר אמר — הרר
אליך: וישכם אברהם בבקר — שכם
ויחבש את חמרו ויקח את שני — חבש שנה
נעריו אתו ואת יצחק בנו ויבקע — בקע
עצי עלה ויקם וילך אל המקום — קום קום
אשר אמר לו האלהים: ביום

Transla.Chal.

ואקים אברהם ית שבע חורפאן דען בלחודיהון: ואמר אבימלך לאברהם מה
אינין שבע חורפאן האלין דאקימתא בלחודיהון: ואמר ארי ית שבע חורפאן תיסב
מן ידי בדיל דתהא לי לסהיד ארי חפרית ית בירא הדין: על כן קרא לאתרא
ההוא באר שבע ארי תמן קיימו תרויהון: וגזרו קיים בבאר שבע וקם אבימלך
ופיכל רב חיליה ותבו לארע פלשתאי: ונצב נצבא בבאר שבע וצלי תמן בשמא
דיי אלה עלמא: ואתותב אברהם בארע פלשתאי יומין סגיאין:

Ca.xxij.

והוה בתר פתגמיא האילין ויי נסי ית אברהם ואמר ליה אברהם ואמר הא אנא:
ואמר דבר כען ית ברך ית יחידך דרחימתא ית יצחק ואיזיל לך לארע פולחנא
ואסקיהי קדמי תמן לעלתא על חד מן טוריא דאימר לך: ואקדים אברהם בצפרא
וזריז ית חמריה ודבר ית תרין עולימוהי עמיה וית יצחק בריה וצלח אעי דעלתא
וקם ואזל לאתרא דאמר ליה יי: ביומא

Interp.chal.

Et statuit abraham septē agnas ouium seorsum. Dixitq; abimelech ad abraham. Que sunt iste septem agne quas statuisti seorsum. Et ait. Quoniam septem agnas accipies de manu mea: vt sit mihi in testimonium quoniā fodi puteum istum. Propterea vocauit locum illū bersabee: quia ibi iurauerūt ambo: et inierunt pactū in bersabee. Surrexitq; abimelech et phicol princeps exercitus eius: et reuersi sunt in terram philistinorum. Et plantauit plantationem in bersabee: et orauit ibi in nomine domini dei eterni. Et peregrinatus est abraham in terra philistinorum diebus multis.

Cap. 22.

Et factū est post verba hec: et deus tentauit abraham: et dixit ei. Abraham. Et ait: ecce ego. Et dixit. Tolle nunc filium tuū vnicum tuū quem diligis isaac: et vade in terram diuini cultus: et offer illum coram me ibi in holocaustum super vnū montium quē dixero tibi. Et surrexit abraham mane et strauit asinum suum: et tulit duos pueros suos secum: et isaac filium suum: et concidit ligna in holocaustum: et surrexit et abijt in locum quē dixerat ei deus. Die autem

Priuatiua chal.

קום חד
אל נסב
היה
קום קום
רבב תוב צלא
יתב
אל נסה
אזל
נסק עלה קדם
אתא
קום

LIST OF PLATES

LIST OF SIGLA DISCUSSED

Mp = Masora parva 21
MSS = Hebrew manuscripts according to the editions of Kennicott, de Rossi and Ginsburg 28—30
Occ = Western Masoretes 11
Ochla = Ochla weOchla, ed. Frensdorff. 22
Or = Eastern Masoretes 11
Q = Qere 14
Q^{Or} = Qere of the Eastern Masoretes 11
Q^{Occ} = Qere of the Western Masoretes 11
ɯ = Samaritan Pentateuch 31f.
ɯ^{T} = Samaritan Targum 59
Σ = Symmachus 38
𝔖 (𝔖^{W}) = Peshitta according to the London Polyglot (Pentateuch according to Barnes' edition) 61
𝔖^{A} = Codex Ambrosianus of the Peshitta 60
𝔖^{Aphr} = Aphraates Syriac Bible quotations 60
𝔖^{h} = Syrohexaplar 40, 144. Pl. 31
𝔖^{L} = Lee's edition of the Peshitta 61
𝔖^{U} = Urmia edition of the Peshitta 61
Sah = Sahidic translation 67f.
Sor = Soraei (Masoretes of Sura) 11
𝔗 = Targum 56 ff.
𝔗^{O} = Targum Onkelos 58
𝔗^{B} = Targum of the Second Rabbinic Bible 27f., 59
𝔗^{J} = Targum Pseudo-Jonathan 58
𝔗^{JII} = Targum Jerusalem II 58
𝔗^{L} = Lagarde's edition of the Targum 59
𝔗^{M} = Merx, *Chrestomathia targumica* 59
𝔗^{P} = Palestinian Targum 57
𝔗^{Pr} = Praetorius' edition of the Targum (Josh., Judg.) 59
𝔗^{W} = Targum of the London Polyglot 59
𝔙 = Vulgate 64 ff.
𝔙^{A} = Codex Amiatinus of the Vulgate 66, 156. Pl. 37
Var^{B} = Variants according to Baer's edition 29
Var$^{E\ 1.2.3}$ = Variants of the three Erfurt Codices 26
V(ar)^{F} = Variants from the first collection of Firkowitsch 22
V(ar)^{G} = Variants according to Ginsburg's edition 30
V(ar)J = Variants from Yemenite manuscripts 30
V(ar)^{Ka} = Variants from Babylonian manuscripts, collected by Kahle 18
V(ar)^{Ken} = Variants according to Kennicott's edition 28 f.
V(ar)^{M} = Variants according to Michaelis' edition 28
V(ar)^{O} = Variants according to the scholastic Odo 30
V(ar)^{P} = Variants according to the Petersburg Codex of the Prophets 26
V(ar)^{pal} = Variants according to the fragments with Palestinian pointing, edited by Kahle 18
V(ar)^{S} = Variants according to Strack, *Grammatik des Biblisch-Aramäischen* 30f.
V(ar)^{W} = Variants according to Wickes 31

---

c ast = marked with an asterisk 39
c ob = marked with an obelos 39
conj = conjecture (suggested correct reading) 81
dittogr = dittography 73
gl. = gloss 75
haplogr = haplography 72
Hex, hex = Hexapla 39 f.
homoeotel = homoioteleuton 73
Orig = Origen 39 f
Seb = Sebir 13f.
Sev = Codex Severi 27
Tiq soph = Tiqqun Sopherim 14f.

BIBLIOGRAPHY

SELECTED LIST OF BOOKS [1]

General Works: *Einleitung in das AT* by C. Steuernagel (1912), by J. Goettsberger (1928), by O. Eissfeldt (2nd ed. 1956), by A. Weiser (2nd ed. 1949); *Introduction to the OT* by R. H. Pfeiffer (2nd ed. 1948), by A. Bentzen (1948/49, 2nd ed. 1952); M. Noth, *Die Welt des AT* (2nd ed. 1953).—A. Geiger, *Urschrift und Übersetzungen der Bibel in ihrer Abhängigkeit von der inneren Entwickelung des Judenthums* (1857; new edition with foreword by Kahle, 1928).—F. G. Kenyon, *Our Bible and the ancient Manuscripts* (4th ed. 1948).—B. J. Roberts, *The OT Text and Versions* (1951; with 29 pages of Bibliography).—H. Wheeler Robinson ed., *The Bible in its Ancient and English Versions* (2nd ed. 1954); I. M. Price (ed. by W. A. Irwin and A. P. Wikgren), *The Ancestry of our English Bible* (2nd ed. 1949); F. F. Bruce, *The Books and the Parchments* (1950); F. C. Burkitt, Art. Text and Versions in *Encyclopaedia Biblica*; S. R. Driver, Introduction to *Notes on the Hebrew Text of the Books of Samuel* (2nd ed. 1913).—D. Winton Thomas, The Textual Criticism of the Old Testament, in *The Old Testament and Modern Study*, ed. H. H. Rowley (1951), pp. 238ff., and especially the literature listed on pp. 259ff.

On I.A.: G. R. Driver, *Semitic Writing* (Schweich Lectures 1944; rev. ed. 1954).—D. Diringer, *The Alphabet* (1948).—A. Bea, Die Entstehung des Alphabets; eine kritische Übersicht, *Studi e Testi* 126 (1946), pp. 1ff.—L. Blau, *Studien zum althebräischen Buchwesen* (1902).—W. Schubart, *Das Buch bei den Griechen und Römern* (2nd ed. 1921).—id., *Einführung in die Papyruskunde* (1918).—C. Wendel, *Die griechisch-römische Buchbeschreibung verglichen mit der des Vorderen Orients* (1949).

On I.B.: C. D. Ginsburg, *Introduction to the Massoretico-Critical Edition of the Hebrew Bible* (1897).—P. Kahle, *Der masoretische Text des AT nach der Überlieferung der babylonischen Juden* (1902).—id., *Masoreten des Ostens* (1913).—id., Untersuchungen zur Geschichte des Pentateuchtextes, *Theol. Stud. u. Krit.* 88 (1915), pp. 399ff. — id., §§ 6-9 in Bauer-Leander, *Historische Grammatik der hebr. Sprache* (1922). — id., Die Punktation der Masoreten, *Martifestschrift* (1925), pp. 167ff. — id., *Masoreten des Westens* I (1927), II (1930). — id., *Die Handschriften aus der Höhle* (1951). — id., The Hebrew Ben Asher Bible Manuscripts, *Vet.Test.* I (1951), pp. 161ff. — V. Aptowitzer, *Das Schriftwort in der rabbinischen Literatur* (Sitz.-Ber. Ak. Wiss. Wien, Phil. hist. Kl. 153, 6 (1906); 160, 7 (1908); Jahresbericht der Isr.-theol. Lehranstalt Wien 18 (1911); 22 (1915)). — E. Ehrentreu, *Untersuchungen über die Masora,*

[1] Reference should also be made to the literature mentioned in the text and notes, since, for reasons of space, it is not in general included again here.

Beiträge zur semit. Philologie und Linguistik 6 (1925). — L. Lipschütz, *Ben Ascher — Ben Naftali. Der Bibeltext der tiberischen Masoreten*, Bonner Orient. Studien 25 (1937). — G. Gerleman, *Synoptic Studies in the OT*, Lund Univ. Arskrift N.F. I, 44 (1948). — J. L. Teicher, The Ben Asher Bible Manuscripts, *J.J.S.* ii (1951), pp. 17ff. — On the Dead Sea (Qumran) Scrolls, cf. the lists of literature in W. Baumgartner, *Th. Rundschau* 17 (1948/49); 19 (1951), and the reports continued by O. Eissfeldt, P. Kahle and others in *T.L.Z.* (1949ff.). Cf. also the bibliography in H. H. Rowley, *The Zadokite Fragments and the Dead Sea Scrolls* (1952), and *The Biblical Archaeologist*. M. Burrows, *The Dead Sea Scrolls* (1955).

On I.C.: W. Gesenius, *De Pentateuchi Samaritani origine, indole et auctoritate commentatio philologico-critica* (1815). — A. Geiger, *Urschrift und Übersetzungen der Bibel* (1857, new ed. 1928). — P. Kahle, Aus der Geschichte der ältesten hebr. Bibelhandschrift, *Baudissinfestschrift* (1918), pp. 247ff.

On II.B. H. B. Swete, *An Introduction to the OT in Greek* (2nd ed. 1914). — O. Pretzl, Septuagintaprobleme im Buche der Richter, *Biblica* 7 (1926). — A. Sperber, Probleme e. Edition der Septuaginta, *Kahlefestschrift* (1935), pp. 39ff. — Rehm, *Textkritische Untersuchungen zu den Parallelstellen der Sam.-Königsbücher und der Chronik*, Alt. Abh. (1937). — A. Allgeier, *Die Chester-Beatty-Papyri zum Pentateuch*, Stud. z. Gesch. u. Kultur d. Altertums XXI, 2 (1938). — O. Stegmüller, *Berliner Septuagintafragmente*, Berliner Klassikertexte 8 (1939). — I. L. Seeligmann, Problemen en Perspectieven in het moderne Septuaginta-Onderzoek, *Jaarbericht van het vooraziatisch-egyptisch Gezelschap Ex Oriente Lux* II, 6-8 (1939-42), pp. 359ff., 763ff. (A comprehensive survey of the problems and the literature). — id., *The Septuagint Version of Isaiah* (1948). — G. Gerleman, *Studies in the Septuagint*. 1. The Book of Job (1946); 2. Chronicles (1946). — G. Mercati, Il problema della colonna II dell'Esaplo, *Biblica* 28 (1947). — P. Katz, *Philo's Bible. The aberrant Text of Bible Quotations in some Philonic Writings and its place in the Textual History of the Greek Bible* (1950). — I. Soisalon-Soininen, *Die Textformen der Septuaginta-Übersetzung des Richterbuches*, Annales Acad. Scient. Fennicae 72 (1951). — R. H. Ottley, *The Book of Isaiah according to the Septuagint* B. J. Roberts, *The OT Text and Versions* (1951). — J. W. Wevers, (1904, 1906). — H. M. Orlinsky, works mentioned in bibliography in Septuaginta-Forschungen, *Th. R.* (1954), pp. 85ff., 171ff., with a comprehensive bibliography.

On II.C.: S. Wohl, *Das Palästinische Pentateuch-Targum. Untersuchungen zu den Geniza-Fragmenten und ihrem Verhältnis zu den übrigen Targumen und der Peschitta*, Diss. (Bonn 1935). — C. Peters, Vom palästinensischen Targum und seiner Geschichte, *Pal. Hefte d.Dt. Vereins vom*

Hl. Lande 24-27 (1940), pp. 9ff. — J. F. Stenning, *The Targum of Isaiah* (1949). — L. Goldberg, *Das Samaritanische Pentateuchtargum. Eine Untersuchung seiner handschriftl. Quellen*, Bonner Orient. Studien 11 (1935).

On II.D.: L. Haefeli, *Die Peschitta des AT mit Rücksicht auf ihre textkritische Bearbeitung und Herausgabe* (1927). — A. Baumstark, Peschitta und palästinisches Targum, *Bibl. Zeitschr.* (1931). — id., Neue orientalische Probleme biblischer Textgeschichte, *Z.D.M.G.* (1935), pp. 89ff. — C. Peters, Peschitta und Targumim des Pentateuchs, *Le Muséon* (1935), pp. 1ff. — id., Peschitta-Psalter und Psalmentargum, *Le Muséon* (1939), pp. 275ff. — H. Schneider, Wenig beachtete Rezensionen der Peschitta, *Z.A.W.* N.F. 21 (1949/50), pp. 168ff.

On III.A.: A. Allgeier, *Die altlateinischen Psalterien* (1928). — H. Schneider, *Die altlateinischen biblischen Cantica*, Texte und Arbeiten, published by the Erzabtei Beuron, 29/30 (1938). — J. Schildenberger, *Die altlateinischen Texte des Proverbienbuches*, Texte und Arbeiten, 32/33 (1941).

On III.B.: F. Stummer, Die neue römische Ausgabe der Vulgata zur Genesis, *Z.A.W.* N.F. 4 (1927), pp. 141ff. — id., Spuren jüdischer und christlicher Einflüsse auf die Übersetzung der Grossen Propheten durch Hieronymus, *J.A.O.S.* 8 (1928), pp. 35ff. — id., Hauptprobleme der Erforschung der alttest. Vulgata, B.Z.A.W. 66 (1936), pp. 233ff. — id., Griechisch-römische Bildung und christl. Theologie in der Vulgata des Hieronymus, *Z.A.W.* N.F. 17 (1940/41), pp. 251ff. — id., Beiträge zur Exegese der Vulgata, *Z.A.W.* N.F. 21 (1949/50), pp. 152ff. — H. Lietzmann, Die neue römische Vulgata, *T.L.Z.* 65 (1940), cols. 225ff.

On III.C.: E. A. W. Budge, *Coptic Biblical Texts in the Dialect of Upper Egypt* (1912). — A. Vaschalde, Ce qui a été publié des versions coptes de la Bible textes sahidiques, *Revue bibl.* (1919-22); also published separately. — F. H. Hallock, The Coptic OT, *A.J.S.L.* (1933), pp. 325ff.

On III.D.: E. Littmann, Geschichte der äthiop. Litteratur, *Litt. des Ostens* VII, 2 (1907), pp. 223ff. — J. Harden, *An Introduction to Ethiopic Christian Literature* (1926), — J. Guidi, *Storia della letteratura etiopica* (1932). — H. C. Gleave, *The Ethiopic Version of the Song of Songs* (1951).

On III.E.: F. N. Finck, Geschichte der armenischen Litteratur, *Litt. des Ostens* VII, 2 (1907), pp. 75ff.

On III.F.: P. Kahle, *Die arabischen Bibelübersetzungen* (1904). — G. Graf, Geschichte der christl. arabischen Lit. I, *Studi e Testi* 118 (1944), pp. 85ff.

On IV: H. Kantorowicz, *Einführung in die Textkritik. Systematische Darstellung der textkritischen Grundsätze für Philologen und*

Juristen (1921). — P. Maas, *Textkritik, Einl. in die Altertumswissenschaft* I, 2 (1927). H. S. Nyberg, Das textkritische Problem des AT am Hoseabuche demonstriert, *Z.A.W.* N.F. 11 (1934), pp. 241ff. — id., *Studien zum Hoseabuche*, Uppsala Univ. Arsskrift (1935). — J. Begrich, Zur Frage der alttestamentlichen Textkritik, *Orient. Lit. Zeit.* XLII (1939), cols. 473ff. — D. Winton Thomas, *The Recovery of the Ancient Hebrew Language* (1939). — J. Coppens, La Critique du texte Hébreu de l'Ancien Testament, *Biblica* 25 (1944); also published separately.